SACRAMENTO PUBLIC LIBRARY

D0426046

CENTRAL LIBRARY
828 "I" STREET
SACRAMENTO, CA 95814

DEC - 1999

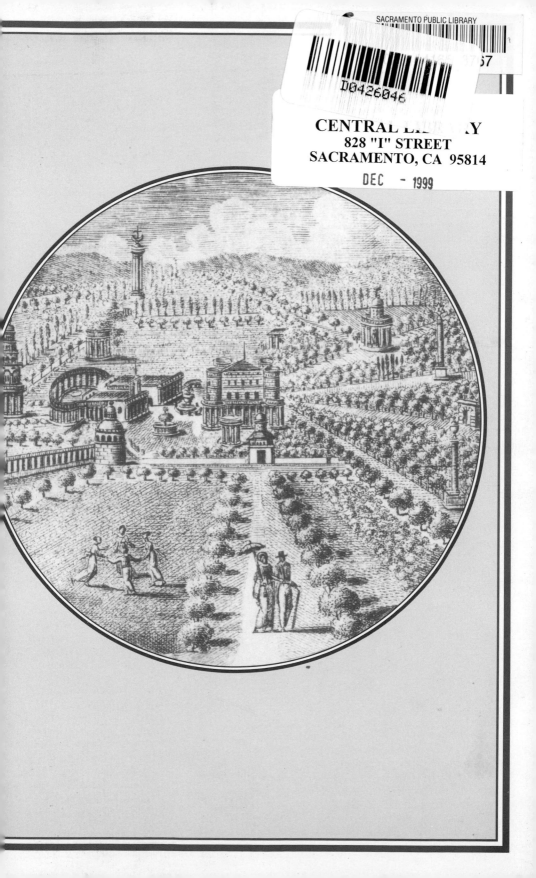

ALSO BY JOHN RICHARDSON

Manet

Georges Braque

Braque

A Life of Picasso, Volume I, 1881–1906

A Life of Picasso, Volume II, 1907–1917

THE
SORCERER'S
APPRENTICE

THE
SORCERER'S
APPRENTICE

PICASSO,
PROVENCE, AND
DOUGLAS COOPER

JOHN
RICHARDSON

ALFRED A. KNOPF NEW YORK 1999

THIS IS A BORZOI BOOK
PUBLISHED BY ALFRED A. KNOPF

Copyright © 1999 by John Richardson Fine Arts Ltd.

All rights reserved under International and Pan-American
Copyright Conventions. Published in the United States by Alfred A. Knopf,
a division of Random House, Inc., New York, and simultaneously in Canada
by Random House of Canada Limited, Toronto. Distributed by
Random House, Inc., New York.

www.randomhouse.com

Knopf, Borzoi Books, and the colophon are registered trademarks
of Random House, Inc.

Library of Congress Cataloging-in-Publication Data
Richardson, John, [date]
The sorcerer's apprentice : Picasso, Provence, and Douglas Cooper /
by John Richardson. — 1st ed.
p.   cm.
Includes bibliographical references and index.
ISBN 0-375-40033-8
1. Richardson, John, [date].   2. Art historians—United States—Biography.
3. Cooper, Douglas, 1911–1984.   4. Art, Modern—20th century—France—
Provence.   5. Picasso, Pablo, 1881–1973.
I. Title.
N7483.R52A3   1999
709'.2 — dc21
[B]   99-27200
CIP

Manufactured in the United States of America

First Edition

FOR MY FRIEND RICHARD WOLLHEIM

CONTENTS

CONTENTS

ACKNOWLEDGMENTS

In the course of writing this memoir, I have relied on notes that I made whenever I spent any time with Picasso or Braque, as well as on letters I sent my mother and Stuart Preston.

I would also like to express my gratitude to the following: Suzanne Barnier, Sid and Mercedes Bass, Heinz Berggruen, Bill Blass, Marc Blondeau, Peter Brandt, Thekla Clark, Lucien Clergue, Roderick Coupe, James Douglas, David Douglas Duncan, John Eastman, Gloria Etting, Everett Fahy, Maxime de la Falaise, Lucian Freud, John Golding, Kosei Hara, Priscilla Higham, Mark Holborn, Robin Hurlstone, Elsbeth Juda, Dorothy Kosinski, Wayne Lawson, Rui Lopes, James Lord, Marilyn McCully, Camilla McGrath, Sonny Mehta, Bernard Minoret, Karen Mugler, Claude Picasso, Stuart Preston, Michael Raeburn, Annette de la Renta, Fredric and Hilde Ridenour, John and Rosamund Russell, Sarah Saint-George, Charles Scheips, Jr., Robert Silvers, Jean Vallier, André Villers, Shelley Wanger, Andrew Wylie, Richard Wollheim.

THE
SORCERER'S
APPRENTICE

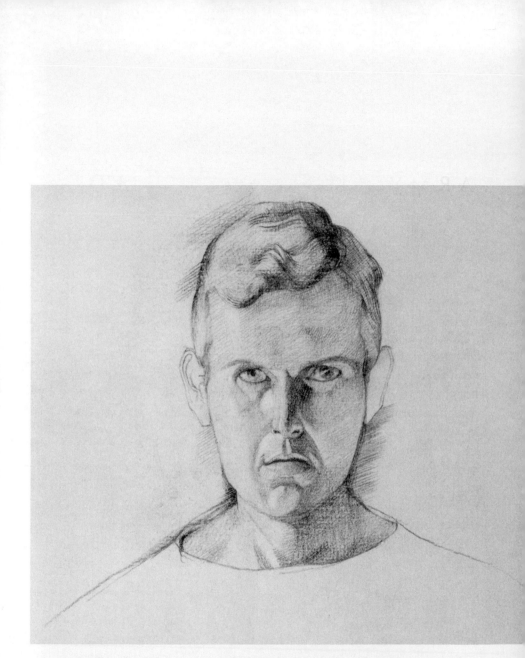

Geoffrey Bennison, Portrait of John Richardson, *pencil, ca. 1942*

ARMY AND NAVY CHILD

My earliest, indeed happiest, memories are bound up with the Army and Navy Stores—not a shop selling surplus camouflage gear but a once celebrated London department store, which my father had helped to found and continued, as vice chairman, to run very efficiently until his death. As a four-year-old, I longed for Thursdays to come round. My father would return from his weekly board meeting with the toy department's finest electric train or toy motorcar or, best of all, a building set—anything to gratify the son and heir he was so proud of having produced at the age of seventy. I also enjoyed going to the imposing Victoria Street store, where my father had set up the best food halls and wine and cigar departments of any store in London and, much to my delight, a zoo department, where I got to play with the monkeys. The staff treated me like a little prince and hung a framed photograph of me in one of the elevators. Even my mother turned out to have an Army and Navy provenance. Not that she was very forthcoming about it; however, she filled me in on my father's role in the great enterprise she always referred to as "the Stores."

My father had been the youngest of a group of twelve subalterns who had pooled their resources and, around 1870, formed a cooperative society for the wholesale purchase of provisions for their mess as well as for their personal requirements. Yorkshire hams and jars of Stilton, cases of claret and port and Madeira (for elevenses with the requisite slice of seed cake) would follow my father to Africa in the 1870s and 1880s, where he battled Ashantis and Kaffirs and Zulus and helped his friend Kitchener defeat the Khalifa at Omdurman. In the South African War, he became Quartermaster-General and was popular with the troops for a revolutionary innovation, refrigerated meat. After being decorated by Queen Victoria and knighted by Edward VII, he retired and devoted his logistical skills to transforming the cooperative society of his youth into a phenomenally successful department store. At its height—between 1890 and 1940—the Army and Navy Stores was more than a mere emporium: it was a key cog in the machinery of the Empire.

Besides the flagship store in London, which supplied the British establishment with everything it could possibly want, the Stores had outlets in the principal army and navy bases Aldershot, Portsmouth, and Plymouth for the convenience of people in the services. But the two greatest jewels in the Stores' crown were the enormous branches in Calcutta and Bombay, which functioned as travel agents, bankers, caterers, undertakers, and insurance brokers, as well as purveyors of the pith helmets, thunder-boxes, plum puddings, and all the other myriad things listed in the Army and Navy's catalogue, which ran to more than a thousand pages. This catalogue was the bible of the British Raj. Kipling's Mrs. Vansuythen and Mrs. Hauksbee would have been unable to function without it. The loss of the Empire after World War II would eventually deprive the Army and Navy Stores of its imperial luster. Bomb damage made matters worse. To repair the building, the Stores employed a construction company that turned out to be a subsidiary of their principal rival, Harrods. This strategy allegedly enabled Harrods to take over the Stores and reduce it to the downmarket establishment it remains today.

When he was almost seventy, my dashing, surprisingly liberal father caused a stir by falling in love with one of the Stores' employees, an attractive thirty-five-year-old woman of much warmth and humor called Patty Crocker, whose job was to retouch photographic portraits. Thanks to her training as a miniaturist, she was able to whittle inches off the waists of stout matrons in court dress and add a lifelike sparkle to the expressions of loved ones lost in the recent war. Horrified at first by her boss's advances, the fetching retoucher soon capitulated and married the elderly though still seductive vice chairman in 1923. They were idyllically happy, especially when I was born to them in 1924. A daughter arrived the following year, and another son four years later. In July 1929, my father died of a stroke at the age of seventy-five, brought on, I sus-

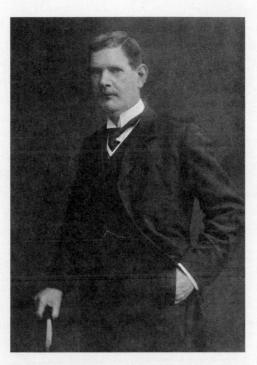

Sir Wodehouse Richardson, ca. 1920

pect, by all this autumnal fathering. I was five at the time. His death hit me very hard—all the harder because my mother told me that he had gone off to South Africa to visit old battlefields. Death would have been easier to accept than this fictitious desertion. Seventy years later, I still miss him. Unfortunately, my father had focused his organizational skills on the Stores rather than on his own fortunes. He had saved relatively little and allowed our once thriving family business—a private bank that managed the finances of an ever diminishing number of Indian princes— to fall into the hands of a racist relative. The sale of my father's large, ugly villa at the top of a hill near the Crystal Palace—a perfect venue for one of Sherlock Holmes's cases—generated enough money for my mother to buy a small house in South Kensington and educate us children, but not enough to give us much of a start in life.

Shortly after my father's death, my mother made another ill-advised but well-intentioned decision. She packed me off to a horrendous boarding school, for no better reason than that my cousin Maurice had been a pupil there twenty years before. Unbeknownst to my mother, Maurice—a fervent left-wing journalist of anarchic wit— had loathed the place and was in the process of writing a polemical attack on private education in the form of a roman à clef about it. And then, unbeknownst to me, the book was published, and I became the catalyst of the masters' indignation. Classes would be kept in "because of Richardson," and I would be left dangling by the wrists from a hook in the ceiling, my shrieks disregarded by those in authority. For an entire term I was "sent to Coventry," which meant that the other boys were not allowed to speak to me. Appeals to my loving, uncomprehending mother were met with injunctions to "be a little man—cousin Maurice *loved* the place." Unable to stand the bullying any longer, I took advantage of what I had precociously perceived as my mother's weakest spot. I told her—quite untruthfully—that after her previous visit to the school, the headmaster's wife was overheard to say that Lady Richardson was not her idea of a lady. I was instantly removed to a more serious school, where, after ice-cold baths at dawn, pupils were given Latin dictionaries and expected to translate ten lines of Milton into hexameters and pentameters.

My family's anomalous circumstances were the more puzzling for being unmentionable. My father's formidable spinster sisters—Aunts Ella, Alice, and Maude—lived in a big house at Blackheath, a beautiful, unspoiled area of south London, where my grandfather (born in 1814) had owned land that is still called "Richardson's fields." They played a lot of croquet, said "ain't" and dropped their g's—"we're goin' for a turn on the heath"—like fashionable people a hundred years earlier. My mother's sisters, Auntie Louie and Auntie Vi, lived very differently in a snug little semi-detached house in depressing Streatham, where they treated us to scrumptious high teas of bread-and-dripping, bubble-and-squeak, and toad-in-the-hole in their funky kitchen. Why then did my mother and her sisters have such a stash of linen embroidered with coroneted *R*'s? I was a nosy child and soon discovered that the *R* stood for Rosebery or Rothschild. I fantasized that I was illegitimate—maybe Jewish. When asked about these things, my mother blushed. I was sixteen before she divulged the fact that my grandmother had been lady's maid to Hannah Rothschild, who had married Lord Rosebery. Was she light-fingered? I asked. No, the Roseberys had been open-handed: after

Hannah Rosebery died, my grandmother had been allowed to take whatever mementos she wanted from her bedroom. Other members of my mother's family had been gamekeepers or butlers at Mentmore or one or other of the Rothschild estates in the Thames Valley. One of them had even claimed to have heard Lord Rosebery utter his famous after-dinner dismissal of his Rothschild relations, "Children of Israel, back to your tents!" Far from being dismayed by my mother's revelation, I was rather proud. To have worked for such exigent employers, my maternal relations must have been very good at whatever it was they did. Over the years my upstairs-downstairs background has proved, if anything, an advantage. I like to think it has enabled me to see things simultaneously from very different angles, like a cubist painter, and arrive at sharper, more ironical perceptions.

At thirteen I went to Stowe, the youngest and least traditional of England's public schools. The magnificence of the buildings—Stowe is one of the largest and stateliest of English houses—made up for the degradation endemic to all boys' schools of the period. Everyday exposure to Vanbrugh's and Adam's façades and Capability Brown's landscaping engendered a taste for eighteenth-century architecture, which developed into a passion and provided the following pages with a subplot. A special veneration for the grottoes and temples that dotted the park resulted from their being the scenes of my first sexual experiences. One of these escapades ended ignominiously. A friend and I were caught on a rug in a distant folly by the Hunt Club: the club's pack of hounds had mistakenly followed our scent. There was a lot of ribald ragging, but the urbane, supposedly gay headmaster, who must have heard about it, failed to take punitive action.

Stowe's greatest advantage, for me at least, was its progressive art school. This was run by an enterprising Canadian couple, Robin and Dodo Watt. I will always be grateful to them for introducing us to avant-garde art magazines like *XXe Siècle, Verve,* and *Minotaure,* which enabled me, from the age of thirteen to fifteen, to understand and keep up with what the masters of the School of Paris were doing. Besides triggering an obsession with Picasso, these magazines encouraged me to dabble in modern art. The results were atrocious: dumb daubs embellished with seed packets, snapshots, and railway tickets. "Schwitters," I would murmur fatuously.

Back in London, I spent my pocket money on the latest Parisian publications at Zwemmer's wonderful bookshop on the Charing Cross Road. Picasso's greatest print, *Minotauromachie,* had just appeared. It cost fifty pounds. In the hope that my mother would advance the rest of my year's allowance, I reserved a copy. She not only refused to do so, she called up nice Mr. Zwemmer and told him she had a good mind to put the police onto him for trying to swindle little boys out of their pocket money. A signed copy of *Minotauromachie* recently fetched $1.5 million, the highest price ever paid for a print.

The outbreak of war in 1939 stranded me and my family on holiday at Dinard in Brittany. Tourists were panicking and forming mile-long queues for the ferry. My mother turned to me for help. Why not stay on in France and enjoy ourselves? I said, and then economize by settling in nearby Jersey (in those days the Channel Isles were famously inexpensive). A school for my sister was found in Saint Helier. Meanwhile I went in search of a tutor and ended up with the father of the painter Graham Sutherland, a railway official who had run away with a neighbor's wife and ended up, like many another black sheep, on this louche island. Besides studying with Mr. Sutherland, I had my first glimpse into the heady world of Proust, thanks to being taken up by a charming Parisian couple—a handsome concert pianist, Prince George Chavchavadze, and his wife, the *richissime* Elizabeth de Breteuil, whose two daughters attended the same school as my sister. The Chavchavadzes regarded the Jersey manor house they had rented as a rustic wartime refuge. To me it seemed the epitome of luxe. In Paris after the war, I would go back for another taste of Chavchavadze life—a great mistake.

My mother had been assured by the local governor's wife that the Germans would never invade Jersey. One night, however, the sky to the south turned orange as Saint-Malo went up in flames. Disregard the governor's wife, I told my mother, and rent a truck so that we can get our belongings—above all, my art books—onto the Southampton boat. We were lucky. Subsequent boats restricted people to one small bag. The closest we came to danger was when a German plane on the way back from bombing Portsmouth treated us to a brief burst of machine-gun fire. We still had to go through customs.

To escape the bombing, my mother took my brother and sister off to a farm in the country. I stayed on by myself in London but eventually enrolled at the Slade School, a faculty of the University of London that had been "evacuated" for the duration of the war to Oxford. I was a month short of seventeen and thrilled to be an art student. It did not take me long to realize that I would never be much good—better write about painting than actually do it. Fifty-three years later, I would take some pride in returning to Oxford for a year as Slade Professor of Art History, the first Slade student to do so.

Besides making friends with two art students, Geoffrey Bennison and James Bailey, whose lives would continue to be intricately involved in mine, I embarked on a romance with an attractive, fattish girl called Diana, who fulfilled my adolescent dream of pneumatic bliss. We thought we were madly in love with each other; in fact we were in love with love. Diana like to fantasize. One day we were Heathcliff and Catherine; next day Rodolfo and Mimi; we were never ourselves. While staying with her parents in the depths of Devonshire, we announced we were going to get married. Her charming, sensible father took the matter lightly, but her socially ambitious mother was horrified; and so, with the help of Diana's ancient aunt, we decided to elope. It was ever so romantic—trysts on Dartmoor at midnight—but it was also a disaster. We were too young and too poor and too silly even to think of marriage. There was a further problem: Diana's Catholicism. She insisted that I convert to her faith, which I was only too happy to do. Unfortunately, she also insisted on remaining a virgin. In the face of her inflexibility on this point, I had an unsatisfactory fling on the side with another girl and then opted for the inevitable alternative. When she realized the situation, Diana returned to her family. In the hope of better luck next time, her mother packed her off to a fashionable quack to be slimmed down. In no time she became a living skeleton, and then glandular problems developed, and she died a year or two later.

Meanwhile I had been called up. As the son of a distinguished soldier, I felt obliged to apply for a commission in a "good regiment." The Irish Guards accepted me, but a week later I was struck down by rheumatic fever and invalided out of the army before I even had time to put on a uniform. I felt guilty. I also felt relieved; the regiment would suffer appalling casualties in the Italian campaign. I spent the rest of the war in London with my mother and two siblings. During the day I worked as an industrial designer. At night I was on call as an air-raid warden or fire-fighter, but was usually to be found in basement nightclubs, dancing away as the bombs rained down. I enjoyed the blitz; it brought out good nature in even the nastiest people.

After the war, Geoffrey Bennison, James Bailey, and I were chosen to design a section of a large exhibition at the Victoria and Albert Museum, optimistically called "Britain Can Make It." There were all too many props, which Britain could not or did not make. I had to go to Paris in search of them. On one of those trips I paid a call on the Chav-chavadzes. George turned out to be delighted to see me; he needed an assistant. I couldn't resist his offer. It would surely be more interest-ing than designing plastic teacups.

If George had practiced harder, he might have played better and been able to extend his repertoire beyond the Schumann and Grieg con-certos. It was his dashing Georgian looks and princely panache rather than his pianism, however, that had won him the hand of Elizabeth de Breteuil, owner of a Renaissance villa outside Florence, a floor of the Palazzo Polignac in Venice, and a magnificent *hôtel particulier* on the rue de Bellechasse, which her American fortune enabled her to run more lavishly than any other Parisian hostess. And that was where I would spend the next few months in black-market splendor beyond the wildest dreams of someone who, for the last five years, had been living off Spam and powdered eggs. In lieu of wages, George gave me a bed in a library adjoining his bedroom, and my keep. There was very little to do. George already had a French secretary and valet, an English agent, and a Mexican bodyguard called Puma. My job, it turned out, was to sleep with the boss. I declined to do so, less out of physical distaste—he was nothing if not handsome—than indignation at his *droit-du-seigneurial* assumption that I had no right to turn down a princely pass. Also, I had become fond of his wife. When Elizabeth left for America, I found myself at George's mercy, even more of a prisoner than Proust's Alber-tine, and at the same time a player in a Proustian game whose rules were way beyond my juvenile comprehension. Too late, I discovered what a liability virtue could be. Having used up all my traveler's checks, I had no access to cash, and couldn't leave. However, after Puma playfully threw a knife at me, just missing my ear ("You disobey Prince, next time you get knife in eye"), I managed to borrow enough money for a ticket home. To recover, I went for a week or two to Cornwall. "For God's sake, stay there," my mother wrote. "There's a Mexican squatting on the front doorstep. He says he needs to see you. What *have* you been up to?"

When things had quieted down, I returned to London, and went to celebrate New Year's Eve with my old friend Viva King in her house on Thurloe Square. Viva was the wife of an eccentric British Museum curator—mauve in the face from too much sherry—who felt that his institution should be closed to the public and that the treasures in his charge should be available only to scholars. Viva had become famous for her Sunday parties, which attracted such literary luminaries as Norman Douglas, Ivy Compton-Burnett, and Angus Wilson. Her taste for artistic young men had earned her a certain notoriety: "a friend of Mrs. King" was a genteel euphemism for "homosexual." On this particular evening, Viva lived up to her reputation. She was co-hosting the party with someone she claimed to dislike: "a sinister bugger," she said, but he had promised to pay for the booze, if she would "round up the boys" and do the sandwiches. The man's name was Douglas Cooper. I knew very little about him except that he was reputed to have the finest collection of modern art in England, to be "mad, bad, and dangerous to know," and, worse, Australian. I had spotted him immediately: a fattish figure in his late thirties, bulging self-importantly out of an RAF uniform. He looked put out, as well he might: he had just caught the French boy he had brought to the party up to no good with one of Viva's protégés on the stairs. Toward the end of the evening, I spotted Douglas Cooper bearing down on me in a meaningful way. I fled to my mother's house, which was just around the corner.

On the way home, I passed a youngish man with a luminous face, who was often to be seen prancing about the neighborhood—evidently a painter. As usual, he was lugging canvases in or out of the house opposite ours. His paintings, of which I had only the briefest, most tantalizing glimpse, intrigued me. They looked as if they might be by a mysterious artist whose work I knew only from a single, unforgettable reproduction of a *Crucifixion,* painted fifteen years earlier—an orgasmic gush of white paint—in Herbert Read's *Art Now,* an artist called Francis Bacon. Nobody seemed to be familiar with him or his work. Finally I found someone who knew him, the painter Michael Wishart. My instincts had been correct. The youngish man was indeed Francis Bacon, and the house opposite ours belonged to his cousin, a Miss Watson, who owned virtually all that was left of the several hundred paintings Francis had destroyed. Forget about her, Michael said, come and meet Francis.

Francis lived across from South Kensington Station in a vast, gloomy studio that had belonged to the Pre-Raphaelite painter Millais. There was a wonderful, ominous, ninetyish decadence to it. Dorian Gray's portrait could have been painted there. Michael had told me all about the illicit roulette parties that Francis, who was an accomplished croupier, liked to organize. He had also told me about the rough trade and the drinking and the fishnet stockings. What he had not mentioned was Francis's sightless old nanny, Jessie Lightfoot, who sat knitting in a rocking chair, mumbling away about the wickedness of the Duchess of Windsor: "They better bring back the gibbet for her." At night, the kitchen table doubled as her bed. Nanny Lightfoot, I suddenly realized, must have given Francis the idea for the central panel of his early masterpiece, *Three Studies for Figures at the Base of a Crucifixion*. She must have taught him the same game that many old-time nannies (mine included) taught their charges: how to turn a fist into a face. Make a fist, stick the tip of your thumb between the knuckles of your first and second fingers and the black ends of two matches either side of the second and third ones, drape a handkerchief over the fist, and it turns into a head like the one in the Bacon. I thought it wiser to keep this discovery to myself.

On a later visit I found Francis ensconced in front of a mirror, seemingly making up his face. In fact he was rehearsing those heavily loaded brushstrokes that would give his portraits, above all his self-portraits, their sumptuous gyroscopic spin. Francis would let his beard grow for a few days until it resembled the unprimed, paper-bag-colored back of the canvas, which he characteristically preferred to the smooth, white front. He would then cake pads with different shades of Max Factor's pancake makeup and apply them, this way and that, across his stubble in great swoops, which simulated the way the furry nap he liked to work on "took" paint. It was as if the surface of his face were the page of a sketchbook. This tied in with Francis's habit of mixing his paint on his hand or his fine, fleshy forearm instead of on a palette—a habit that would result in turpentine poisoning and an eventual switch to acrylic. It

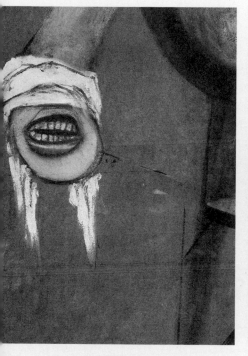 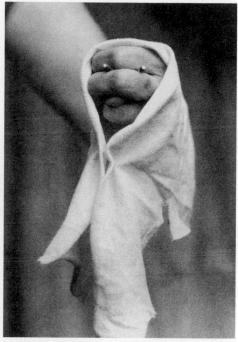

is Bacon, detail of central panel of Three
ies for Figures at the Base of a
:ifixion, *1944*

An English nanny's game: turning a fist into a
face

also tied in with the violence that he challenged his lovers to inflict on his infinitely receptive body, hence the pain and degradation of his imagery. At his best, Francis imbued paint with such palpable physicality that it seems to slobber, shudder, and scream. At his worst, he allowed melodrama, contrivance, and cheap thrills to become ends in themselves.

Everything about Francis was surprising: his strangely skewed intelligence, his instinctive courtesy and charm, no less than his baroque bitchery and kinky exhibitionism. If people were shocked, so much the better. That was the impact he intended his behavior as well as his work to have. I remember Francis going into gruesome detail about a recent experience with a Belgian traveling salesman, how excited he had been to find a little marcasite watch nestling in the hairs on the man's wrist.

The mention of Douglas Cooper detonated a vituperative blast. Eschewing the masculine pronoun as was his way, Francis admitted to having "known that treacherous woman. She's even more loathsome than she looks." Apparently an elderly cousin of Cooper's had answered one of Francis's advertisements in the personals column of the London *Times,* which solicited a job as a "gentleman's companion." After being vetted by Nanny Lightfoot, the elderly cousin had paid Francis for his services and found him part-time work as a telephone operator in a London club; he had also invoked Cooper's help in promoting Francis as a designer of furniture and interiors (curtains of white surgical rubber were his trademark), also as a budding painter. Before the relationship with his cousin foundered, Cooper had commissioned a desk from Francis, a massive Bauhausy piece painted battleship gray. He had also arranged for his paintings to be shown at the Mayor Gallery, of which he was part owner, and persuaded Herbert Read, the foremost British modernist of the day, to reproduce the *Crucifixion*—which had made such an impression on me and so many others of my generation—in his book. Sixty years later, I can only imagine that the reason we were so struck by this work was that few if any of us had seen the deeply disturbing *Crucifixion* that Picasso had painted three years earlier, and that had all too evidently inspired Bacon's ectoplasmic version.

Cooper's behavior struck me as anything but treacherous. After all, he had been one of the first people to take Francis up. However, it turned out that he had been one of the first to drop him. "We were not exactly each other's cup of tea," Francis said, but obviously the trouble went much deeper than that. I would later find out that Cooper was convinced that Francis had blackmailed his aged cousin. ("Did you?" Lucian Freud asked him. Francis thought for a bit and then said, "Did I blackmail him? I don't *think* I did.") The more famous Francis became, the more eager Cooper was to denigrate him. The two of them gave each other an ever wider berth. "Does Cooper really have such a good eye for modern art?" I asked Francis. "She's only got one, so it better be good," he said. And the famous collection? "Too Museum of Modern Arty for my taste, but there are some wonderful things. Take a look at your own risk. She'll try to lure you into bed, and then she'll turn on you. She always does." Francis's predictions had a way of coming true.

Douglas Cooper would not recross my path for another two years. Meanwhile I had given up any thought of being a painter, and was doing my best to become a book reviewer like my clever cousin, Maurice, a pillar of the London *Observer*. In this resolve I was lucky to have been taken up by a writer called Cuthbert Worsley, theater critic and assistant literary editor of the most enlightened of Britain's weekly journals, the *New Statesman*. Cuthbert had once been a schoolmaster, and still looked and behaved like one. He had taken me as well as my prose in hand, starting me off with short, unsigned reviews, which he made me rewrite again and again until the seams no longer showed. "Use your ears," he would say. "Listen to yourself. Stop shunting back and forth like a drunken engine driver." In return I did what I could to mitigate Cuthbert's depression, which manifested itself in deluges of tears. The tears stemmed from an unfounded conviction that to save himself from drowning, he had caused an adolescent brother's death. The attention he devoted to his young writers seems to have been a strategy to exorcise this obsession.

Tall, skinny, and small of head, Cuthbert resembled a Giacometti figure in his looks as well as his corroded spirit. The salt in his tears might as well have been lye, to judge by the rawness of his face. It was impossible not to feel pity for him, but pity made for guilt and guilt made for resentment, and I began to fear that my efforts to rescue Cuthbert from his swamp of despair might end with him dragging me into it—a fear that my ever-increasing obligation to him made more and more likely. He not only arranged for me to review art and fiction under my own name, but to cover ballet, anagrammatically, under the name of Richard Johnson. As a result, we spent all the more time together. At least three evenings a week, Cuthbert would take me to the theater or I would take him to the ballet. More often than not, the evening would end in floods of tears too Niagaran to staunch.

To cheer myself up, I would sneak off with friends my own age. Sometimes we would cruise the Soho pubs, especially the Golden Lion, or the French Pub, where we would watch Francis Bacon on the prowl. Sometimes we would go to the Gargoyle Club, whose mirrored dance floor had seen up the knickers of most of the girls I knew, not to mention their mothers', but it was too full of raffish upper-class drunks for my taste. In quest of hotter music, we would go to the darker, loucher Caribbean Club, where we would find more stimulating company— Lucian Freud or Michael Wishart or some wild girls we had known at the Slade—and boogie the night away. I picked up my first and last whore at the Caribbean. Carmencita, she was called. As I hoped to be a father, I thought this experience would straighten me out. No such luck. Carmencita had a terrible cold and, instead of being exhilaratingly whorish, was depressingly genteel. After it was all over, she told me there was "a little pink taowel at the bottom of the bed."

And then one fateful day, in the spring of 1949, Cuthbert said he was taking me to a party given by John Lehmann, the editor of a little magazine called *New Writing*, in honor of the publication of Paul Bowles's painfully good book, *The Sheltering Sky*. I was delighted. American writers had a way of heading straight for Paris and missing out on London. Scenting free drink, Grub Street arrived en masse, and the wine ran out even faster than usual. Lehmann was famously parsimonious, and used postwar shortages as a cover for his economies. Unless they had brought hip flasks, thirsty guests had to fall back on assorted bottles of invalid port, cooking sherry, or a nausea-inducing "cup." Bowles had arrived from Tangier with a supply of hashish fudge, something few of us had tried.

As the mixture of drinks, not to mention the fudge, began to take effect, I realized I was being stalked by a stout pink man in a loud checked suit. At first I did not recognize him out of uniform. "You may not remember me," he said in his aggressively accented voice. "We met at the house of that *Poufmutter*, Mrs. King. My name is Douglas Cooper." This time I was too full of curiosity to flee. I blurted out that I wanted to see his pictures. "Right now, my dear, if you can tear yourself away from these hideous mediocrities," he replied. Despite (or maybe because of) Francis's warnings, I agreed to do so. Then, remembering that Cuthbert expected me to dine with him, I hurried over to ask him whether he minded. "Of course I don't," he said. As if to confirm that this was not true, he allowed a tear to trickle slowly out from under his glasses. People noticed, nudged each other, and pointed. "Poor old Cuthbert," somebody said as I left the room. Parked outside was Douglas's car (at least he said it was his): an ancient Rolls-Royce two-seater with a jump seat at the back. It was painted bright yellow and black like a wasp—a villain's car if ever I saw one. I climbed up into it, and after some tallyho blasts on an antiquated horn, we sped away—and then abruptly stopped, a mere two or three hundred yards away. Home, Douglas announced, disconcertingly. That this would soon be my home never occurred to me.

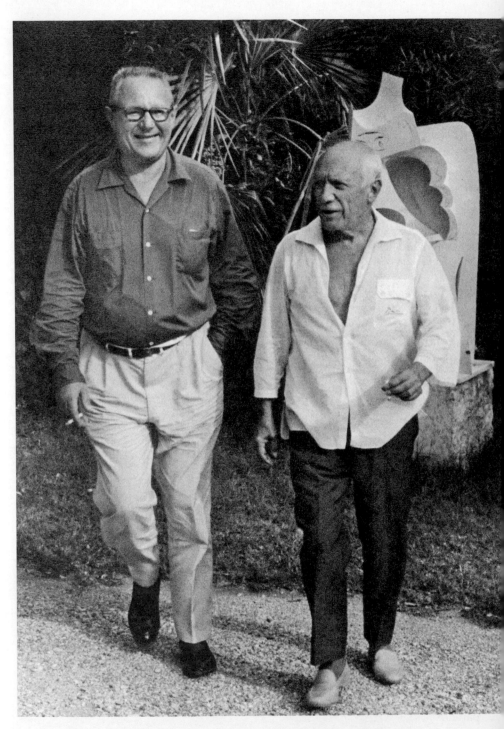

Douglas Cooper and Picasso at La Californie, Picasso's villa at Cannes, 1961

DOUGLAS COOPER

There was one point about himself that Douglas Cooper always made very, very clear: he was *not* Australian. True, his antecedents—who were traders, not convicts—had sailed away to Sydney early in the 1800s and had made an enormous fortune by the middle of the century. The Coopers ended up owning much of the soon-to-be prosperous Woollahra section of Sydney; they were also the biggest shippers of gold in Australia. Douglas's great-grandfather became a member of Parliament and Speaker of the House of New South Wales in 1856 and was made a baronet in 1863 (Sir Daniel Cooper of Woollahra). From then on he spent as much time in England as he did in Australia, eventually settling permanently in London, where he died. His son and grandson followed his example. To Douglas's eternal rage, the Cooper family sold their Australian holdings sometime in the 1920s. Given his and his father's lifelong possession of British passports and his mother's Dorset lineage, Douglas understandably resented his country-men's tendency to endow him with an erroneous—i.e., Australian—provenance. ("My parents visited Australia on their honeymoon," he said, "so I may have been conceived there, but that's the closest I ever got.") A further irritant: his money was wrongly assumed to derive from Cooper's sheep dip, hence the jokes about Australian sheep bleating "Bra-a-a-que." A very minor matter, one might have thought. Unfortunately, resentment made for paranoia; paranoia made for Anglophobia; and Anglophobia made for the outlandish accents, outré clothes, and preposterous manner that Douglas cultivated. There was also a hint of paradox to his behavior. Douglas's idées fixes only made sense if they were turned upside down, or seen in the light of willful provocation or

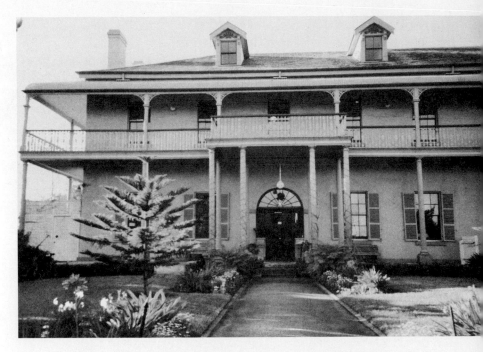

Juniper Hall, 1995, Woollahra, Sydney; one of the properties of DC's great-grandfather Sir Daniel Cooper of Woollahra

perversity. Anglophobia was the only form of patriotism that Douglas could permit himself.

The vehemence that was to have such a corrosive effect on Douglas's character was a legacy from his father, "Artie" Cooper, a bowler-hatted major who radiated disapproval. In the father's case, vehemence was compounded by stupidity; and in the son's case, it was mitigated, some of the time, by intelligence. "My father did absolutely nothing with his life," Douglas told me, "except live off his considerable fortune, vent his temper on anyone who disagreed with him, and atone by indulging in a lot of Masonic mumbo-jumbo." To his shame, Douglas, who set great store by men's looks, had inherited his father's scary little avian eyes. In most other respects he looked like his homely, much-put-upon mother, who was as cozy and plump as a cottage loaf.

Mabel Cooper came of a long line of backwoods baronets that God had all of a sudden decided to terminate. In the space of two years

(1941–42), the Smith-Marriotts' handsome Dorset seat, the Down House, had been commandeered by the army and burned to the ground; and then the last two baronets—Mabel's dissolute, horsy, bachelor brothers (one of them aptly named after his Wyldbore antecedents)—died within a year of each other. So did their spinster sister, Dorothea. Almost everything went in death duties. To the family's dismay, Dorothea turned out to have left her mischievous nephew the beautiful neglected arboretum at the core of the Down House estate in the hope, Douglas could only imagine, that he would do something dreadful and nondendrological with it—something that would upset the other Coopers. For once, Douglas behaved impeccably—maybe he felt he was being set up—and chose to sign over the arboretum to the other heirs. He had not always been so easy on his parents. To get back at them for trying to steer him into one boring profession after another—diplomacy, accountancy, the law—when he wanted only to study art history, Douglas had played cruel tricks on them. Shortly before the war, he had telephoned his mother in an assumed voice, claiming to be a detective-inspector. "I regret to inform you that your son has committed suicide. We will have to ask you to identify the body."

Douglas had two younger brothers. The elder, Geoffrey, was the object of his intense loathing for having made off with the wine he had left in storage when he was away at the wars. Douglas sued and won, and thereafter claimed that the only way of communicating with his "crooked sibling" was by writ. He liked his younger brother, Bobby, well enough, although he had once dangled him as a baby over the stairwell of the Coopers' large Eaton Place house, and had to be talked out of dropping him onto the stone floor fifty feet below by his beloved nanny: "You'll have to clean up the mess, master Douglas." After being badly wounded during the war, Bobby had endeared himself to Douglas by marrying Princess Teri of Albania, a daughter of the former King Zog's eldest sister, Princess Adili. Asked by his mother about Muslim wedding customs, Douglas told her to "take up the carpets and hang them out of the windows; it will cheer up Eaton Place no end." When Douglas took me to visit his brother, who farmed the Down House estate, he could not resist making trouble. Suspecting that Princess Adili was kept hidden, he went in search of her and, according to him, found her stirring away at a cauldron—"a noxious goat-tail stew, my dear." After scolding Bobby for banishing his royal mother-in-law to the kitchen, he insisted we take our leave—"before they ask us to stay for dinner."

Although his parents were excessively philistine (a bad Bouguereau was a prized possession), there was a family precedent for Douglas's involvement in the arts. A bachelor uncle, Gerald Cooper, had been a musicologist and spent most of his fortune collecting Purcell manuscripts and memorabilia. On his death, Gerald left this archive to his friend Edward Dent, the leading expert in the field, to distribute as he thought fit, an act that scandalized the Coopers. The archive was very valuable, and, worse, it transpired that Gerald, like Dent, had been gay. Douglas owed more than he liked to admit to his uncle, who had taken him, when he was twelve or thirteen—that is to say, in the mid-1920s—on a trip that would have a formative effect on his taste: to Monte Carlo, where the Diaghilev company was performing. Memories of the ballets Douglas saw on this occasion came in useful fifty years later, when he wrote his book *Picasso Theatre*. Gerald Cooper was also a patron of contemporary music, and he saw to it that his nephew developed an ear for Stravinsky, Webern, and Bartók as well as the classics. When Douglas went to Repton—a school he loathed, especially a master (subsequently Archbishop of Canterbury) whom he accused of converting him to atheism—he was well placed to enjoy the concerts that his uncle organized in nearby Derby.

Nicholas Lawford, the British diplomat, who ended up sharing a house on Long Island with the fashion photographer Horst, and who had known Douglas at Repton as well as Cambridge, remembered him as "a Botticelli angel" who was much more sophisticated than the other boys. It was not until Douglas went up to Cambridge in 1929 that he became a rebel, an aesthete, and an exhibitionist who sported an Elizabethan cane dangling with pompons. "Very flamboyant he was," Nicholas said. "I believe I once chased him round the court with a hunting crop." At Cambridge he was known to many as "Cousin Douglas," because so many of his contemporaries—Pennys, Bankses, Wyldbore-Smiths, Wingfield-Digbys—were cousins of his mother's. In later years Douglas chose to lose touch with these cousins—"much too British, my dear"—or was it the cousins who chose to lose touch with him? After a year or so, Douglas removed himself from Cambridge. He seems not to have been sent down but to have left of his own volition to study art his-

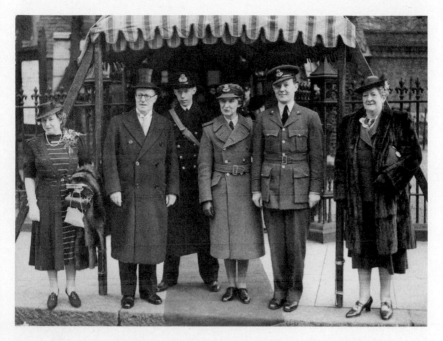

In London, 1941: DC's father (in top hat) next to Bobby Cooper; DC and his mother at far right

tory, which was not as yet possible at Cambridge. There was, however, a rumor that a landlady had got him into trouble for draping the reproduction of a Raphael madonna above his bed in his black silk pajamas.

At the age of twenty-one, Douglas had come into a trust fund of £100,000 (the equivalent then of about $500,000). Today this would not generate the price of a Picasso drawing, but by the standards of 1932, Douglas was rich. Money meant that he could flout his father and devote himself to art history (at the Sorbonne and Marburg-in-Hessen) and— no less horrifying to his family—the pursuit of cubist works of art and good-looking young men.

Douglas began his professional career with an experimental stint as an art dealer. It was not a success. He had bought a share in a gallery belonging to an acquaintance, Freddy Mayor—a most genial man, but hardly the right partner for an uncompromising modernist.

Freddy was short, stout, and rubicund. He was a racing man and a ladies' man, and he greatly enjoyed getting drunk with the chaps. He liked modern art well enough, although, to believe Douglas, he could not tell the difference between a Braque and a Bruno Hatt (the spoof abstractionist foisted by Evelyn Waugh's friends on London's art world). Freddy catered to his own ilk—sporting bons vivants who fancied a spot of fauve color on their walls—and felt ready to risk a bet on Matisse, as if he were a promising outsider in the Grand National.

Douglas had a more serious agenda. With the help of such avant-garde Parisian dealers as D. H. Kahnweiler and Pierre Loeb, he hoped to put on small shows of current work by Picasso, Léger, Miró, and Klee, but there were few takers. Freddy played it safe and did better. Mutual dislike and distrust doomed the partnership from the start. Douglas made the break as painful as he could. He withdrew his backing at a time when the bookies had left his partner more than usually short of funds. In lieu of cash, he ended up with much of the stock, including a lot of Mirós.

With some justice, Douglas blamed his failure as a dealer on what he called "ghastly English philistinism," as epitomized by the Tate Gallery (the only museum in London mandated to acquire contemporary art). He and only he, Douglas felt, was qualified to make acquisitions for the modern part of the Tate. He was probably right. With him on the staff, this fuddy-duddy institution would have given New York's Museum of Modern Art a run for its money. And so Douglas applied for a job there—unsuccessfully. The Tate was administered by the Treasury, the staff were civil servants, and they had no intention of employing anyone as intransigent as Douglas. Nevertheless, he continued to harbor illusions: "Somebody had to stop those feeble hacks at the Tate buying all that genteel British rubbish."

Douglas thought there might be a change for the better in 1938, when the then director, J. B. Manson, made a drunken fool of himself and had to be fired. His replacement, John Rothenstein, turned out to be just as disastrous. Manson may have been a clown, but Rothenstein was a toady, a smug chauvinist with a distaste for modern art. If eventually he came around to adulating Francis Bacon, it was out of expedience, but the conversion did not enhance his record or his credibility. I had reason to share Douglas's dislike of the Rothenstein family. As an art student, I had suffered from the dismal teaching of John's father, Sir William Rothenstein, and his inept uncle, Albert Rutherston (head of Oxford's Ruskin School, where the Slade School of Art took refuge during the war). We students were not bothered by Rutherston's ineptitude so much as his insistence that we work from a nude model, said to be his mistress. She was pretty enough, but seemingly afflicted with Saint Vitus' dance. "The moving target," we called her. When her wiggling became intolerable, some of us in the life class would hum a song from a wartime revue: "I'm a nude on the dole / struck off the roll / because I couldn't keep still. . . ."

Douglas's rage at the lack of response on the part of Rothenstein and the Tate trustees to fauvism, cubism, and surrealism, the fundamental cause of what would come to be called "the Tate Affair," was a catalyst for his own collection—a collection that would show up the Tate's modernist holdings as shamefully inadequate. He set aside a third of his inheritance and by the time World War II broke out had acquired some 137 cubist works, a number of them masterpieces. He was lucky in that he had very few rivals in the field, and prices for cubist works had remained amazingly low. Of the four artists in Douglas's cubist pantheon, only one, Juan Gris, had died. The other three—Picasso, Braque, and Léger—were very much alive and very hard at work. Léger was especially delighted to have an enthusiastic new patron—one, moreover, who wanted to write about his work. He and Douglas remained friends for life. Braque, too, was pleased to find a collector intent on charting his cubist development, phase by phase, year by year. At first Douglas made little headway with Picasso. The artist already had a young British collector in his entourage, Roland Penrose, scion of a rich Quaker family, who had recently joined the Surrealists. Penrose had met Picasso through Paul Eluard, the artist's poet laureate. Eluard proceeded to sell Penrose the numerous works that Picasso had contributed to the poet's support. Just as Eluard had made his wife, Nusch, available to Picasso, Penrose offered up his future wife, Lee Miller, the American photographer, to the artist, when they all spent the summer of 1938 together in the same hotel at Mougins. In view of Douglas's competitiveness, Roland did not encourage Picasso to include him in his predominantly Surrealist circle.

Fifteen years later, the dynamics would change. By going to live in

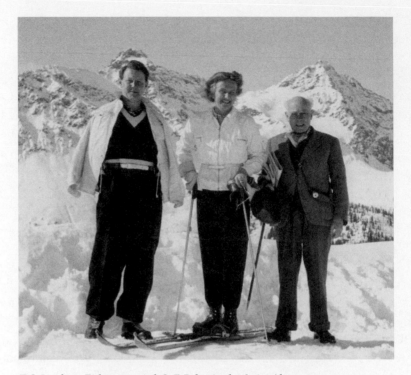

DC, Ingeborg Eichmann, and G. F. Reber in the Swiss Alps, 1937

the south of France, Douglas saw rather more of Picasso than Roland did. This would make for epic resentments, which the artist enjoyed fanning. The two Englishmen were very competitive about each other's collections. Douglas dismissed Roland's as "ready-made." "I don't call it collecting," he used to say, "if you combine Picasso's handouts to his Surrealist friends with a collection bought lock, stock, and barrel from a Belgian." True, Roland had acquired René Gaffé's collection *en bloc;* however, Douglas had done a similar thing, only on a much bigger scale.

Most of the finest paintings that Douglas amassed between 1932 and 1939 came from a single source: a shadowy German called G. F. Reber. Reber lived lavishly, if somewhat precariously, in a château outside Lausanne filled with by far the largest collection of cubist and post-cubist art in private hands. Douglas did not like to admit that it was

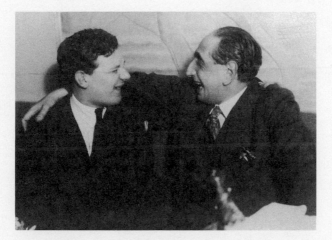

DC with the brilliant Berlin art dealer Alfred Flechtheim,
Paris, 1937

Reber's example he had followed when he limited his acquisitions to works by the four great cubists. In other respects their approach to collecting was very different. Whereas Reber was an art investor, a stockpiler of modern masterpieces, Douglas was an art historian out to chart in depth the work of the four creators of cubism, subject by subject, medium by medium, year by year. And what he wanted from his collection was not financial advantage but recognition—or better still, fame.

Today Reber is forgotten, but in the 1920s and early 1930s he was one of the biggest players in the field of modern art. Born to an impoverished Protestant minister in the Ruhr, he had made enough money out of an early venture in textiles to indulge his passion for post-impressionist painting. Marriage to a rich, cultivated wife enabled him to splurge even more. By the age of thirty, in 1910, he had assembled a superb group of twenty-seven Cézannes, as well as works by van Gogh, Gauguin, Courbet, Degas, Renoir, and Manet. Besides collecting art, Reber was fascinated by magic and mysticism. That he was also a leading Freemason might explain the Communist Spartacists' attempt to arrest or kidnap him when they broke into his house in 1919. In fear for his life, Reber fled Germany for Switzerland, where he eventually

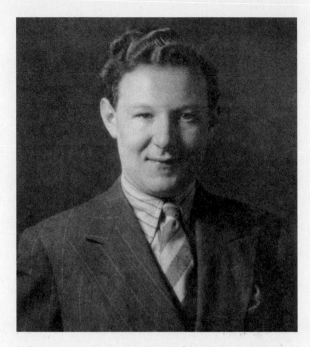

DC at age twenty-seven, in New York, 1938

settled in some splendor in the Château de Béthusy at Lausanne. In the early 1920s Reber modernized his collection. Out went the impressionists and post-impressionists (with the exception of Cézanne's *Boy in a Red Waistcoat*), and in came the great Picassos (some sixty of them), sixteen Braques, eleven Légers, and eighty-nine Juan Grises. It was by far the largest and finest ensemble of its kind. Douglas would skim much of the cream off it.

Douglas and Reber came into each other's lives around 1932, at an opportune time for both of them. Heavy losses on the Paris Bourse in 1929 had transformed the man who had been the most adventurous art investor of the 1920s into a panic-stricken unloader. And so a young collector who had the means as well as the courage to live up to his modernist convictions was very welcome. For his part, Douglas would take full advantage of the fact that Reber was broke—so broke that he had had to use many of his remaining paintings as collateral for loans. The greatest Picasso that Douglas ever acquired, the 1907 *Nudes in the Forest*

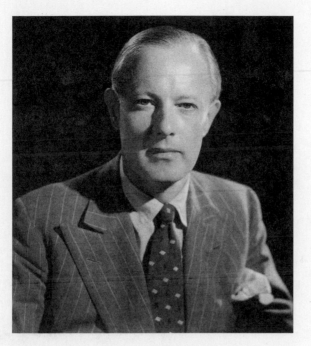

The Hon. Sholto MacKenzie (later Lord Amulree)

(now one of the glories of the Musée Picasso), had to be redeemed from the municipal pawnshop in Geneva for £10,000.

Reber hoped to extract a further favor from Douglas. Some years earlier his daughter, Gisela, had brought home a school friend—a bright, attractive girl from the Sudetenland, Ingeborg Eichmann. Ingeborg was well off—her family manufactured the paper on which Czech banknotes were printed—and, like Douglas, she aspired to study and collect modern art. Reber made her his mistress and, over the years, sold her a number of fine modern paintings. The centerpiece of her collection was Picasso's cubist masterpiece, the 1913 *Seated Woman* (which would fetch $21 million in the 1997 Victor Ganz sale). Since Ingeborg and Douglas liked each other well enough and shared a passion for cubism, Reber tried to manipulate them into marriage. It would be a union of kindred spirits, which would engender paintings rather than babies. More to the point, a British passport would save Ingeborg from the curse of being born in a part of the world that involved successive changes of nationality. (The Sudetenland was Austrian until 1918, Czech until 1938, German until 1945.) True, marriage might have made Douglas appear less homosexual—still a stigma in the 1930s—but that is not necessarily what he would have wanted. Far from concealing his orientation, he consciously or not flaunted it. Like Francis Bacon he was not above using vitriolic camp as a weapon. And then, fond as he was of Ingeborg, Douglas was physically terrified of women—all the more reason not to saddle himself with a bride for the greater convenience of an art investor who could not afford to leave his wife.

In 1938, Douglas and Ingeborg left for the United States, where they made a prolonged tour of American museums and private collections. While they were on the other side of the Atlantic, Chamberlain and Daladier allowed Hitler to annex Czechoslovakia. Ingeborg was not Jewish, but she had no intention of living under the Nazis. And since Douglas was not prepared to marry her, she became stateless in her own country. Ingeborg was not one to bear a grudge. She realized that marriage, even if in name only, would have left Douglas feeling threatened. Despite his misogyny, he could be very fond, even jealous, of his women friends, but woe betide them if they made undue demands or tried to move in on him. Ingeborg never did, and remained a friend for life.

Sometime in the early 1930s, Douglas had embarked on a lifelong relationship with a handsome Scotsman some ten years older than himself. To most people he was known as Sholto MacKenzie. Douglas found this too much of a mouthful and called him Basil. Basil called him Dougal, as would many of his friends. Basil's father had been one of four sons of a Lowland Scottish farmer. The eldest remained a farmer; the second son invented the cardiogram; the third became a minister; and the fourth, Basil's father, a liberal politician and lawyer, was raised to the peerage. Basil inherited the title in 1942, whereupon Douglas would usually refer to him as "our Lord." Basil might have followed his father into the law, but he suffered from a terrible stammer, and so he became a doctor like his very distinguished uncle James. On the side he was an amateur historian; he also devoted much of his time to being Douglas's gofer. For his part, Douglas was totally reliant on Basil's gyroscopic steadiness. He would write him at considerable length once or twice a week, over a period of close on fifty years. Alas, this correspondence, which was returned to Douglas after Basil's death, seems to have disappeared.

Unlike Douglas, Basil was a man of exemplary virtue: dutiful, thoughtful, a good companion. Far from remonstrating with Douglas for his outrageous behavior, this gentle, repressed Scot would end up living vicariously through it. Paradoxically, he would get a far bigger kick out of "bad" Douglas—the flamboyant fiend who was the scourge of the art world—than out of "good" Douglas, the conscientious art historian who was good with students and impressionable art lovers provided no one challenged him. I suspect that Douglas's rage served as a catalyst for the rage that this exemplary Scotsman had suppressed so rigidly that it boiled up only in the form of his seismic stammer. In an effort to mouth words beginning with *b* ("bugger" was apt to be a problem), Basil would turn pink and shake until the monocle popped out of his eye socket.

Basil and Douglas were indefatigable sightseers. Whenever Basil could escape his multifarious duties, they would go off on architectural tours—Romanesque churches, Palladian villas, Crusader castles. In the summer of 1938, they were motoring back from the south of France with a young stockbroker in tow, when Douglas fell asleep at the wheel and crashed into a tree on the Route Nationale 7. His companions were unscathed, but Douglas's face was smashed up. He regained consciousness in a hospital at Moulins, just in time to prevent the nuns from removing one of his eyes. Instead he had himself driven to Zürich and delivered into the hands of the famous Dr. Voigt. This philanthropic man overcharged the rich so that he could afford to undercharge the poor. However, when the mood was on him, Voigt turned into a sadistic maniac: out the eye must come, and no nonsense about anesthetics. Douglas would never forget the horror of the doctor's morning visits, when he would gleefully plunge a hypodermic needle directly into his damaged pupil. A corneal graft did not restore his sight, but left the eye looking more or less normal. Anyone who peered deep into Douglas's sharp little eyes would be disconcerted to discover that the pupil of the sightless one was shaped like an inverted keyhole—a disturbingly

Magritte-like effect. The accident left Douglas prey to appalling headaches and nervous depressions, which his wartime experiences would do much to exacerbate.

Douglas was twenty-eight when World War II broke out. Delighted that his injury exempted him from serving in the British army, he left London for Paris and joined a small, fashionable ambulance unit organized by the waspish, Charlus-like art patron Count Etienne de Beaumont. Etienne had commissioned works from Picasso and Braque and Satie. He had also been the inspiration of Raymond Radiguet's novel *Le Bal du Comte Orgel*. The very grand costume balls the Beaumonts gave in their very grand *hôtel particulier* (both Proust and Picasso had been guests at the 1921 ball) were prompted as much by chic and spite as hospitality. To keep their guests guessing, the Beaumonts made a point of *not* inviting two or three especially vulnerable friends. An excellent principle, Douglas said. "One should always keep one's friends and loved ones on their toes."

For Douglas—as for Jean Cocteau, twenty-five years before—Etienne was something of a *beau idéal.* He saw himself playing the same sort of role in Etienne's ambulance unit that Cocteau had played in it in World War I, when he had been put in charge of the portable showers and, to the rage of a jealous sergeant, had fallen in love with a Moroccan sharpshooter. If Etienne had not intervened, the poet might have been murdered. And then there had been trouble in 1915, when Etienne and Cocteau had set off for the Western Front and stopped for the night at the first available hotel. Before dinner they had gone upstairs to slip out of their Poiret-designed uniforms into something less martial: silk pajamas, one black, one pink, and jangling ankle bracelets. Unfortunately their hotel turned out to be the headquarters of the British High Command, and when they made their entry into the dining room, Lord Haig's staff made their homophobia felt.

Twenty-five years later, Douglas was a bit more circumspect. In the winter before the German breakthrough, Etienne used his ambulances as mobile libraries to deliver books and magazines to the Maginot Line, and also for casual pickups. In the course of his duties, Douglas fell for a "faun-like" soldier who had slithered through the mud to grab a library book from him. The mud, Douglas said, made the encounter all the more romantic. The two of them remained in touch. After the war, the "faun" came to stay in London, dumped Douglas for someone younger and handsomer at a party at Viva King's, and gave him the watch that Douglas had just given him.

When battle was finally joined in June 1940, Douglas entrusted two recently purchased Picasso pastels to the concierge at the Ritz (who, amazingly, returned them to him, only slightly foxed, four years later) and went into action. He turned out to be an extremely cool and effective *ambulancier*. Disaster evoked his courage and steeliness. Despite strafing by German planes and panic-stricken refugees blocking all roads to the south, Douglas and his co-driver, C. Denis Freeman, brought their quota of wounded safely to Bordeaux, where a British destroyer waited to take them to Plymouth. Their book about these experiences, *The Road to Bordeaux*, portrayed the mass stampede so vividly that the Ministry of Information used excerpts for an anti-panic leaflet.

For accomplishing this mission, the French awarded Douglas the *médaille militaire*. The British packed him, as well as Freeman, off to Liverpool, where they were detained. Because he had no papers, wore an odd French uniform, and behaved in an autocratic way, Douglas was assumed to be an impostor or a spy. A day or two passed before a friend discovered where he was, established his identity, and got him released. Although he treated his detainment as a laughing matter, Douglas never forgave the "ghastly English" for it. They would pay for it, he always said, and pay for it they did. This was another justification for leaving none of his paintings to a British institution.

If Douglas was still determined to "do his bit," this was not so much for crown and country as to defeat the fascist foe. Many of his art-historian friends had gone to work as spy-catchers or code-breakers at Bletchley Park. Douglas's linguistic skills would have qualified him for this work, but those in charge may have felt that he was too volatile for a hush-hush organization. In the end Basil prevailed upon his father to get Douglas a commission in air force intelligence. Poking around in the wreckage of shot-down German planes and investigating the burned bodies of the pilots was his first assignment. For someone as fastidious and high-strung as Douglas, this was acutely nauseating. He would never get over "the macabre barbecue smell of newly charred flesh." Douglas was good at pulling strings, however, and soon had himself transferred to the infinitely more congenial task of interrogating prisoners of war.

Douglas's "evil queen" ferocity, penetrating intelligence, and refusal to take no for an answer, as well as his ability to storm, rant, and browbeat in Hochdeutsch, dialect, or argot, were just the qualifications that his new job required. As soon as the Allies began to push the Germans back into Libya, the RAF packed him off to Cairo to grill high-ranking officers. Torquemada could hardly have done better. By alternating threats with cajolery—softening-up dinners at Shepherd's Hotel—he managed to manipulate many a susceptible prisoner into blurting out where in the desert Rommel had hidden his matériel. On overhearing Douglas's high-pitched interrogation of some wretched Hun, an Air Vice Marshal on a tour of inspection expressed surprise: was the RAF using women interrogators? Douglas also did some spy-chasing, and had fun monitoring the activities of a pro-German belly dancer in a houseboat on the Nile.

Cairo during the North African campaign was much to Douglas's taste. There were ancient monuments to be visited and approved or written off. (On the whole, he preferred Islamic and Coptic art to dynastic Egyptian—"all those clones in profile".) Also, social life was extremely convivial and, as usual in wartime, dissolute. Old friends in the forces were always turning up on leave. And then, he got on well with the Cairenes—everyone from archeologists to a gay old cousin of the king who lived in a seedy Second Empire palace "which hadn't received a lick of paint since the opening of *Aida.*" He also loved Alexandria, not least the Cavafyish hustlers. Alexandrines, he said, were far more pampered and decadent than Cairenes. One effete bachelor would give parties at which guests were assigned to first- or second-class salons, according to their looks, wealth, or social position, and titillated with glimpses of the host's yellow diamond collection. Another Alexandrine dandy would not wear the shoes that Lobb had made for him until he had tested them by bowling them the length of his ballroom; shoes that failed to end up toe-first went back to the maker. Douglas was fascinated but appalled by the beau monde, as was a prewar friend of his and Francis Bacon's, Patrick White, the Australian novelist and future Nobel laureate. White, who was also in air force intelligence, had recently embarked on a lifelong relationship with Manoly Lascaris, a cultivated and charming Alexandrine Greek whose impoverished family could trace its origins back to Byzantium. Douglas was envious. Why couldn't *he* find someone like that?

And then, all of a sudden, Douglas's career as an interrogator came to an end. Exactly what happened is unclear. Thanks to hints dropped by Douglas in a rare confessional mood and scraps of corroboration from Basil, I believe I have been able to reconstruct what happened. An attractive German officer—senior in rank but young in years—came up before Douglas for interrogation. He was thought to know the where-abouts of tanks or planes or ammunition dumps. In the course of grilling the prisoner—playing on his anti-Nazi or, possibly, homosexual feelings as well as doing him favors—Douglas fell for the man. Whether or not this enhanced his interrogatory powers, he managed to break him. After spilling the precious beans, the officer hung himself. Douglas had a ner-vous collapse, which inflicted further damage on a psyche already trau-matized by the loss of sight in one eye and incapacitating headaches.

Instead of sending him back to a desk job in London, the RAF transferred Douglas to the most relentlessly bombarded base in the Mediterranean, the island of Malta. There he and two lusty local sponge fishermen were assigned to a submarine. Their job was to explore the seabed around Sicily and the toe of Italy, where the allies proposed to invade. Because Douglas was mildly claustrophobic, he did not enjoy being pinned to the Mediterranean floor by depth charges for days at a time. He felt like a turbot at the mercy of a trawler, he said, and, "oh, the smell—a mixture of BO, farts, and fear." Back on the besieged island, life was even worse: the bombs rained down and rations were minimal. Douglas survived on black-market chickens and eggs, bought at vast expense from an archbishop.

As the war drew to an end, Douglas managed to have himself reas-signed to the Monuments and Fine Arts branch of the Control Commis-sion for Germany, the body that the Allies had set up to rescue and protect works of art and buildings from war damage, looting, vandalism, and the elements. His familiarity with European collectors, scholars, and dealers, as well as shippers, framers, and restorers, enabled Douglas to become one of the Commission's most effective agents—as assiduous as Vautrin, according to a colleague, in his pursuit of Nazi looters. A principal target of Douglas's sleuthing was the Swiss-born Herr Montag, one of Hitler's art advisers, who had assembled a "private" collection of mostly looted works for the Führer. Douglas ran his quarry to earth in a mountain village near Innsbruck, where he had him arrested. However, Montag invoked a higher authority and got himself released. Douglas promptly had him rearrested; forty-eight hours later he was free again. The higher authority turned out to be Winston Churchill. Churchill had been taught to paint by "dear old Montag," and refused to believe that he could have done anything reprehensible. "Thanks to the Prime Minister's interference," Douglas said, "we never managed to keep this criminal behind bars."

Another of Douglas's Nazi quarries, Walter Andreas Hofer, was someone he knew all about from the past. Hofer had once been Reber's assistant, and had married Reber's secretary's sister. Later he had set up as a dealer and, after assiduously licking Goering's boots, was appointed his art adviser. It was Hofer and his partners in crime, Karl Haberstock (Hitler's art dealer) and Hans Wendland, who set up the nefarious "Swiss system" in partnership with the Swiss auctioneer Theodor Fischer of Lucerne, organizer of the Nazis' infamous sale of "degenerate" art in 1939. The "Swiss system" enabled Hofer and Fischer and above all Goering to make huge profits. Swiss francs, generated by the sale of modern paintings looted from Jewish collections, financed the Reichsmarschall's acquisition of ever more Cranachs and Dürers for his Valhalla-like hunting lodge. Hector Feliciano, whose excellent book on Nazi art thefts, *The Lost Museum,* makes good use of Douglas's memoranda, has identified some twenty-eight major deals involving hundreds of paintings as the outcome of the "Swiss system." There was another aspect to these transactions: outside Switzerland, Swiss francs were extremely scarce, and impressionist and post-impressionist paintings, which the Nazis despised and the Swiss loved, became an alternate form of hard currency. Picassos and Matisses were as negotiable as Swiss francs.

To Douglas's embarrassment, Reber—desperate, as always, for money—turned out to have acted, briefly, as Hofer's agent in Italy and thus to have had dealings with Goering. For some reason, Hofer turned against Reber and, with Goering's help, had him investigated by the Gestapo, stripped of his German citizenship, and declared persona non grata by the Swiss authorities. As a result, Reber had to remain in Florence, frantically appeasing the Reichsmarschall with occasional offerings from what was left of his collection. He was not allowed back into Switzerland until 1947.

As an art sleuth, Douglas was especially proud of having commandeered the so-called Schenker Papers—records kept by the Paris branch of the principal German art shippers—which enabled him to track down virtually all the art that had been transported, legally or illegally, to Germany. These records were even more useful for recording payments, provenances, and destinations. Besides establishing that some of the most prestigious Parisian dealers in old masters and antique furniture presided like vultures over the liquidation of their former clients' collections and their former colleagues' stock, the Schenker Archive revealed the extent of the role played by German museums, notably the Folkwang Museum in Essen, in the looting of Jewish collections. Among much else, it also helped to establish the responsibility of Hitler's so-called art experts—not least Eva Braun's dim-witted girlfriend, Maria Dietrich—for shipping hundreds of paintings to the Führer's museum at Linz. It was up to Douglas and his colleagues on the Fine Arts Commission to trace these pillaged works, and they did an extremely effective job.

Douglas was also very proud of uncovering the wartime activities of the powerful Jewish dealer Georges Wildenstein. He alleged that after the German invasion, Wildenstein had made a deal, as he often had before, with Hitler's representative Haberstock, involving some major old masters; and that he then left for the United States, but not before Aryanizing his Paris gallery by putting it in the name of his head salesman, Roger Dequoy, so that it could continue to function under the Occupation. For the rest of the war Wildenstein helped to direct the affairs of Dequoy et Compagnie from the safety of New York, allegedly taking advantage of the situation created by the Nazi suppression of Jewish dealers and collectors. After the war Wildenstein and Dequoy were never nailed, and Wildenstein's heirs consistently deny the allegations. However, according to Douglas some members of the French Fine Art Commission took the rumors so seriously that Georges Wildenstein never realized his dream of becoming a *membre de l'Académie*. In subsequent dealings with the Wildensteins, Douglas emerged as anything but a hero. In 1965 he wrote a blistering review of Georges Wildenstein's supposedly definitive Gauguin *catalogue raisonné*, dismissing several works with a Wildenstein provenance as fakes or misattributions. The dealer sued him. After a great show of bravado, Douglas caved in and, to the utter amazement of interested observers, eventually agreed to an out-of-court settlement "on friendly terms." The wily dealers knew just how to play on their opponent's vanity, his enjoyment of being treated as a VIP. Why didn't *he* revise their Gauguin catalogue, Wildenstein flatteringly suggested. Douglas was thrilled to accept, and devoted most of his last years to this project. "Georges Wildenstein is dead," he would say rather lamely, "and they make such a fuss of me." Although the revised catalogue was virtually finished by the time he died in 1984, there has been no talk of its publication. Scholars who had applauded Douglas's attacks on the dealer were saddened that, after all the huffing and puffing, he should sell out and, worse, try to inveigle one or two of them into following his self-serving example.

His pursuit of Nazi loot and looters took Douglas frequently to Switzerland. Although the commission had no authority there, and Swiss law was—indeed, still is—much too favorable to people who buy works of art knowing full well they have been looted or stolen, Douglas did not hesitate to manipulate or embarrass the Nibelungen of Zürich into returning their ill-gotten gains. A major offender was the German-born Emil Bührle, a onetime student of art history who had married an armaments heiress and made an incalculable fortune during the war selling his Oerlikon cannons to the Wehrmacht as well as to the Allies. Although Bührle had benefited from Goering and Hofer's "Swiss system" of barter, he was not disposed to make restitution to the rightful owners without a fight—a fight that this sinister war profiteer ultimately lost.

Under the terms of the German peace agreement, the Allies had the power to seize all German assets in Switzerland. Easier decreed than done. Douglas found the Swiss banks extremely uncooperative, and there were seldom any paper trails to follow, as there had been in Paris. Then again, many of the German assets in Switzerland did not belong to the Nazis but to the Nazis' victims, a fact that did not necessarily exempt them from seizure. At one moment Paul Klee's family was in danger of losing his very valuable estate to the Allies. When he died in Bern in 1940, this German-Swiss artist, whom the Nazis had stigmatized as *entartete* (decadent) was still in possession of a German passport. The Allies would thus have had the right to seize the vast accumulation of work he had left to his widow, Lily, and his son, Felix, a soldier in the German army who had ended up in a Russian prisoner-of-war camp.

In the course of his sleuthing visits to Switzerland, Douglas had renewed his friendship with Lily Klee and had dined with her in Bern the night before she died. He had also become very friendly with Rolf Bürgi, a powerful Bernese insurance man who had amassed the world's largest and finest private collection of the artist's work. Hundreds of Klees covered the walls of Schlössli Belp, the Bürgis' snug little castle outside Bern, where Douglas liked to stay. Inevitably this new friendship involved a conflict of interest: Bürgi headed the group of Klee fanciers who had rescued the artist's estate from Allied sequestration by arranging a "sale" that made it Swiss property. The more important works were deeded to a Klee *Stiftung* (foundation) at the Bern Museum. The rest became the property of a *Gesellschaft* (corporation) under the administration of Bürgi and his friends. They would have the right to settle prices and sell whatever they chose. Part of the proceeds were supposedly set aside for Felix Klee. Douglas did not question this arrangement. Bürgi had arranged for the *Gesellschaft* to sell him a number of very fine Klees very reasonably.

Back in London, in 1947, Douglas moved in with Basil, hung as much of the collection as the walls of Basil's newly purchased Egerton Terrace house would hold, and embarked on a career of connoisseurship punctuated by controversy. The articles on nineteenth- and twentieth-century art that poured from his pen were superb—trenchant, innovative, eye-opening—especially when he was writing about the dead rather than the living, for instance, the art criticism of Delacroix or Baudelaire or Félix Fénéon. But if for some reason or another the subject raised his infinitely sensitive hackles, Douglas could be petty and spiteful. Alan Pryce-Jones, editor of the *Times Literary Supplement,* and an old friend, welcomed Douglas's controversial contributions; they enlivened many an otherwise dullish issue. Unfortunately Douglas used the anonymity of the journal as cover from which to snipe on friend and foe alike, castigating them in interminable *sottisiers* for misplaced accents and typos rather than more heinous shortcomings. Douglas's other organ of choice was the *Burlington Magazine,* whose pages were famous for giving rise to dusty but deadly art-historical disputes. Douglas bought a block of shares in the *Burlington* for their nuisance value.

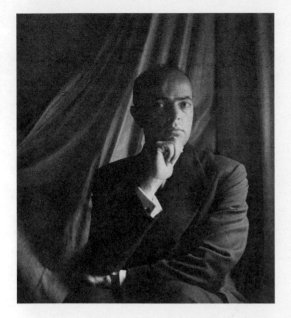

Stuart Preston, New York Times *art critic, ca. 1950*

The shares did not give him much control over the contents, but they enabled him to make the life of the editor, Benedict Nicolson—son of Harold Nicolson and Vita Sackville-West, and supposedly a friend—an intermittent misery. "Somebody has to put some starch in that rag doll," he said. "One laughs," Douglas said of Ben on another fraught occasion, "but opens the jaws of the trap a little wider and snap—that head will soon be in the basket."

The resentment that his articles stirred up exacerbated Douglas's Anglophobia. What had started as an aggressive pose became second nature and eventually got the better of him. One can hardly blame the English for retaliating. No sooner had he settled in with Basil than Douglas took to traveling monthly to Paris—"the only place for an intellectual to live," he said. He claimed to feel more at home with the left-wing intelligentsia, which revolved around Picasso and Sartre, than he did with "those awful prissy Bloomsberries" back in London.

Douglas also decided to give New York a try. He had not been there for almost ten years and was anxious to spy out the art world and also to gather ammunition for an attack on the School of New York. Abstractionism, which Douglas saw as "cubism's misbegotten child," was having a resurgence in America. Abstraction died with Mondrian, he said; we cannot have it coming back to life. He also wanted to see how the Museum of Modern Art—and, more particularly, its director, his old friend and sometime enemy Alfred Barr—had transformed the way twentieth-century art was perceived: exhibited, collected, promoted, studied, and, not least, bought and sold. Douglas was in the market for additions to his collection, also for a lover (Basil had long since become emeritus). He renewed old contacts and made a whole raft of new ones, among them Bill Lieberman (then curator of drawings at MoMA), who became a close friend and acted as his cicerone, and Stuart Preston (then art critic on the *New York Times*), who would act as Douglas's New York eyes and ears.

So stimulating did Douglas find New York that he was very tempted—particularly by one of his new friends—to settle there, collection and all. If he did not do so, it was probably because of ego. For all his Anglophobia, London enabled Douglas to behave like a very large toad in a relatively small pool. In New York that would have been impossible. The pool was much bigger and already full of toads, some of them every bit as formidable as himself. Another consideration: Douglas might have been inveigled into settling on the other side of the Atlantic, if he had not at this juncture met me.

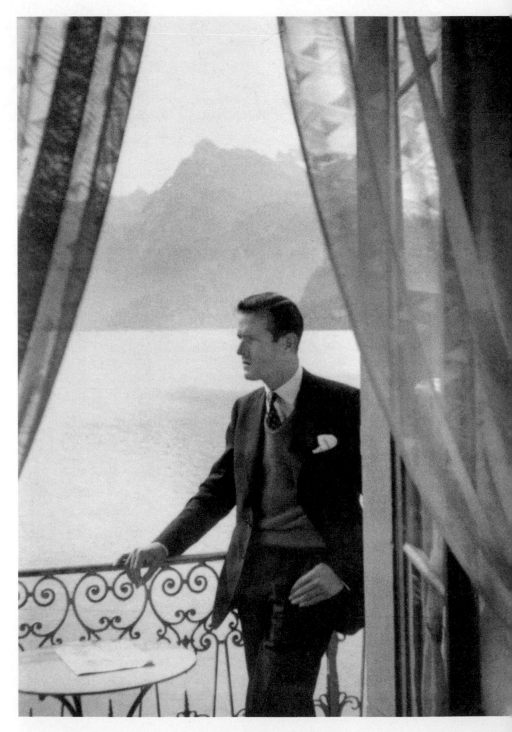

JR at Lake Lucerne, 1950

FIRST NIGHT

Our destination after the Lehmann party turned out to be a charmingly situated house in Egerton Terrace, a quiet cul de sac off the Brompton Road. "Our Lord," as Douglas called Basil Amulree, owner of the Rolls as well as the house, had recently become Liberal Whip in the House of Lords, and was away on Parliamentary business. The genteel decor—cream paint, beige moquette, and forgettable furniture—did less than justice to the cubist masterpieces cramming the walls. However, the sheer quality and profusion had more of an impact on me than any previous exposure to modern art. Delighted that I shared his taste for cubism, Douglas described how he had built up his collection, sometimes spending years in pursuit of a specific item, so as to give the fullest possible account of the movement as represented by its two inventors, Picasso and Braque, and its other two major exponents, Léger and Juan Gris. There were also a dozen or so Klees and a few fine small Mirós.

Douglas liked nothing better than showing off his collection. He turned into a genial sorcerer, immensely informative and enthusiastic and occasionally very, very funny. What he enjoyed even more than showing his paintings to fellow experts and connoisseurs was opening receptive young minds to the glories of the movement he regarded, with some justice, as the principal begetter of modernism. Hitherto I had found the work of Fernand Léger crass and simplistic, but on the strength of Douglas's magnificent series of *Contrastes de Formes*, which lined the stairs, I had a change of heart. Douglas enjoyed converting people to Léger. That very evening he found a promising neophyte in me, and I a potential mentor in him.

At one point I accepted the offer of one of "Our Lord's" cigars. To Douglas's embarrassment, the box was empty. Instead he got me drunk on framboise. And then came the inevitable pass. Out of courtesy and curiosity, I lurched upstairs after him. I was twenty-five (thirteen years younger than Douglas) and, in those days, extremely insecure and out to please.

Alcohol overcame my initial revulsion. A kiss from me, I fantasized, would transform this toad into a prince, or at least a Rubens Bacchus. However, Douglas turned out to be as rubbery as a Dalí biomorph. No wonder he was mad at the world. This realization triggered a rush of compassion, which enabled me to acquit myself on this ominous night. It was not until I read Stefan Zweig's sentimental but unforgettable novel, *Beware of Pity*, that I realized what mischief pity could unleash.

For better or worse, my fantasy worked. Overnight, Douglas's disposition brightened; his capacity for affection tempered his capacity for enmity; his tongue lost its awful lacerating edge and became honeyed. There was something that the fairy tale failed to reveal, however: the moment the kisses cool, the Prince turns back into a toad or, in Douglas's case, a bad, bad baby, who requires a lot more affection to be cured of his tantrums. For the next twelve years Douglas would play on my compassion, alternating cajolery with brute force, psychic cunning with infantile bellowing. The tension was often excruciating, but the Tolstoyan bond that developed between us—a bond forged out of a passionately shared experience of works of art—made it all worthwhile. There would be another key aspect to our relationship: that of father and son. My father had been seventy when I was born and I was five when he died. I would miss this doting, handsome, seemingly all-powerful man. Although I did not realize it at the time, my affection for Douglas must have been at least partly filial.

On returning to my mother's flat in the morning, I was pestered with calls from friends who had heard about the Lehmann party—How could you? How was it? What next?—questions I was unable to answer. It was not until Dunhills delivered a box of Monte Cristo cigars, enclosing a note of amorous apology, that I realized I had sparked a blaze that might be hard to extinguish. Even more embarrassing was the arrival of an expensive bunch of flowers. In my family, nobody ever got flowers unless they were very ill or dead. My sister sniffed; my brother sneered; my mother sighed and said in a tiny, woebegone voice, "They're awfully pretty, dear, but what on earth have you done to deserve them? Nobody ever sends *me* flowers." And then came the crunch: a call from Douglas asking me to go to Amsterdam with him. An exhibition of medieval treasures was about to open at the Rijksmuseum, and there were to be three days of festivities: medieval banquets in medieval castles, get-togethers with van Gogh's nephew, trips to the Kröller-Müller Museum, and so forth. What is more, fresh raw herring fillets were just coming into season. Douglas knew how to bait his hook.

No sooner had we arrived at Schiphol airport than Douglas tried to impress me with an embarrassing show of officiousness. A mob of press photographers had surrounded a prosperous-looking American couple—a corporate husband with a hard-faced wife in a mink-lined raincoat—who were brandishing a large rectangular package, evidently a painting. Douglas had instantly realized who they were: Bill and Edie Goetz. "What passes for royalty in Hollywood; he's a producer married to a daughter of Louis B. Mayer. New collectors, my dear, and *very* poorly advised." They had just spent a fortune on a dubious, newly discovered van Gogh, which they had brought to Amsterdam to be authenticated. Douglas puffed himself up like a pouter pigeon and informed me that he was going to advise the Engineer—as van Gogh's nephew was known—to have it condemned and, "as fakes must be," destroyed. Sure enough, a day or two later he pushed his way into the Stedelijk Museum's restoration studio, where the painting was being examined, and tried to muscle in on the proceedings. The Engineer—so frighteningly like his uncle's self-portraits—and the Dutch experts had no need of Douglas's remonstrations. They had already denounced the painting and paid no attention to the suggestion that it be destroyed. Instead, the Engineer steered us to a relic that had been found among his uncle's effects: a ball made up of countless odds and ends of different-colored knitting wool. The artist would juxtapose these lengths of wool in one aleatory combination after another, until he found the one that worked for this or that painting. This was the key, the Engineer said, to van Gogh's innovative color harmonies and dissonances.

In the course of this trip, Douglas rekindled my feelings for van

Gogh. When I was eleven, his *Yellow Chair* in the Tate Gallery had opened my eyes to modern art. All my pocket money had gone on reproductions of his paintings. After discovering Picasso two years later, I had disloyally shut the van Gogh reproductions in a closet, in adolescent shame at having had such a predictable penchant, also at having cried my eyes out over Irving Stone's shlock biography *Lust for Life*. Douglas set me back on the right track. He showed me that what I admired in Picasso—the visceral power of his vision—corresponded to what I had admired in van Gogh. "Why else is van Gogh one of Picasso's favorite painters?" he said. "Take the Dutchman back into your little pantheon, and expunge Irving Stone from memory."

Studying the van Goghs or, for that matter, the Rembrandts or Vermeers, with Douglas on this, the first of so many similar trips, was eye-opening. If Douglas was at his best—didactic, challenging, and refreshingly quirkish—it was probably because he was in love, insofar as someone so consumed with self-hatred could be in love, and I was passionately responsive.

Visits to museums or historic buildings with Douglas were a revelation; on occasion they could also be embarrassing. As a matter of principle, he insisted on being allowed in before or after these places were officially open, or on days when they were shut; allowed, also, into galleries or other such areas that were off limits to the general public. Harassed curators were forever rescuing us from queues or mobs, ushering us into cordoned-off areas or through doors that said Private, No Entrance, or Staff Only. I was mortified by the string-pulling that this necessitated, especially when the exhibit had little or no relevance to Douglas's spheres of interest. In his efforts to impress me, Douglas could not resist putting the museum directors he knew to a lot of needless trouble. He badgered Baron Roël, director of the Rijksmuseum; he badgered Bob de Vries, director of the Mauritshuis; and he badgered Jan Heiligers, a charming, partly Indonesian curator (known in certain circles as "the Chinese Washerwoman") at the Boymans Museum in Rotterdam. Amazingly, none of them seemed to mind.

Back in London, my hitherto humdrum life became a round of pleasure: operas, concerts, plays, dinners as good as postwar shortages allowed. Little by little, Douglas took over my life. He included me in

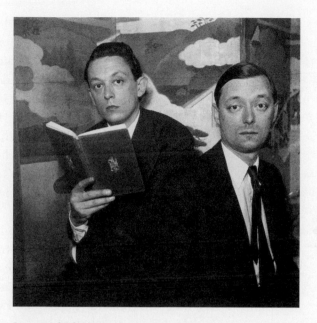

James and John Pope-Hennessy, London, ca. 1950

everything he did: outings in the country, visits to exhibitions, evenings with an assortment of surprisingly loyal friends—mostly art historians of one kind or another—who appreciated his prickly intelligence and Falstaffian jollity and did not necessarily take his malice to heart. Like many another bully, Douglas was careful to stay on the right side of his more formidable colleagues. John Pope-Hennessy, already internationally celebrated for his studies in Florentine and Sienese art, was a case in point. John contrived to be almost as well informed about his friends' fields as he was about his own. In the presence of "the Pope," as he was known, Douglas was unusually circumspect. I was terrified of him. Willie King had told me about visiting John and his brother James when they were barely out of nursery, and finding them dismissing Proust. One of the most daunting things about John was his oratorio hoot of a voice, which brooked no contradiction and could sometimes put a damper on conjecture. And then one day John wrote to congratulate me on a critical review of Nigel Nicolson's *Portrait of a Marriage.*

Nothing could have given my precarious sense of assurance a greater boost. Awe turned to admiration, and admiration to affection.

Douglas would have been delighted by John's eulogy of him in his memoir, *Learning to Look*. "I liked his outré clothes and his malignant and extremely funny sense of humor, and I admired his written work. However mendacious he might be in life, his concern as an art historian lay with truth. Addiction to truth can make one many enemies, especially if it is combined, as it was in Douglas, with a witty and exceptionally astringent tongue. It was to his enemies and not to him that preferment invariably went. An excellent linguist, he was less quarrelsome in Italian or German than in English or French. Difficult as he was, in his own field he represented standards—not only visual standards but intellectual standards too—and in a world peopled with limp critics and sequacious art historians the ruthlessness with which he used the battering ram of talent invariably earned my admiration and almost invariably my support."

John's younger brother, James Pope-Hennessy (the biographer of Queen Mary and Monckton-Milnes), was also a very close friend of Douglas's. From their Malaysian great-grandmother, both brothers had inherited the faintly oriental look—those heavy-lidded, slightly protuberant eyes—that had earned their military father the unfortunate nickname "Puff-adder." In James's case it made for a certain beauty. He was also prodigiously charming: urbane, humorous, and flirtatious with upper-class women and working-class men. Douglas doted on him, as did a number of besotted ladies, whom James allowed to catch tantalizing glimpses of his dark side and its denizens. James's compulsion to tempt fate, the cause ultimately of his death, was a source of prurient amusement to some of his friends, and worry to others, not least his brother. One summer, when he was assistant editor at the *Times Literary Supplement*, James became obsessed by the sight of a bare-chested laborer sweating away in a hole in the road outside the *TLS* office in Printing House Square. Unable to keep his mind on his work, he tore a twenty-pound note in two. He gave the laborer one half, on which he had written his telephone number, and told him to come and collect the other half. The strategy worked.

Over the years, James would gradually do himself in. A disastrous mix of self-aggrandizement and destructiveness would take over his once-beguiling character. So would drink. His sense of reality, such as it was, would evaporate. After having tea with old Princess Alice at Kensington Palace, James would rush to the pubs of Shepherd's Bush and chat up Irish laborers in his languid, supercilious voice. Although so extravagant that he was often reduced to penury, he would titillate them with hints of large sums—advances for a biography of Noël Coward—secreted in his flat. One lunchtime in February 1974, a young Irishman called Sean Seamus O'Brien, who did odd jobs for some of James's grand friends—and was described by one of them as "a beautiful woodland creature who found birds' nests like a water diviner finds water"—called on him with two of his mates. Since James knew O'Brien well, he let them in; whereupon they tied him up, gagged him (there was a police station across the road), and demanded cash. They refused to believe that there wasn't any, and proceeded to torture him. In the course of doing so, they killed him, at which point James's servant returned and set upon a blood-soaked murderer with a kitchen knife. The murderer fled on a bus, but was soon apprehended. Lord Goodman, a powerful lawyer, saw to it that the killing was played down in the press.

I asked a friend who had met "the beautiful woodland creature" what had triggered the violence. He blamed James's *de-haut-en-bas* tendency to pull rank when "the lower orders" got out of hand, and say things like "How *dare* you!"—enough to touch off anyone's fuse. Francis Bacon, who also drank too much and tempted fate in the form of "rough trade," would never have found himself in James's predicament. But then Francis had the nerve of a lion tamer and always managed to manipulate his brutes into doing what *he* wanted.

Another great friend of Douglas's was a charming man called Francis Watson, Keeper of the Wallace Collection. Before Watson's marriage, he and Douglas had had a brief affair, which is probably why when Douglas went off to war he gave Francis the mews house in Belgravia he had been using as a pied-à-terre; also probably why his affection did not extend to Francis's Gibraltese wife, Jane. "If she looks like a monkey," he used to say, "it's because she's the last descendant of the apes of the Rock." I liked Jane: she had the courage of her eccentricity. Francis reveled in his wife's mischief. The first time Douglas and I went to dine with them, we were greeted by the acrid smell of burning rags that I associate with Gypsy encampments and the backstreets of Naples. "Francis has been naughty," Jane announced, "so I'm burning all his hats." And there she stood in front of the fire, poking away at a flaming derby—a scene Magritte would have relished—while dense black smoke poured from the top of a top hat as if it were a chimney. Her infinitely good-natured husband egged her on: "While you're about it, you might as well burn the homburg."

Francis told us with some pride how Jane had recently avenged herself on a neighbor for parking his car outside her door. Finding the trunk unlocked, she had filled it with the kitty litter generated by her numerous cats over the previous month. Jane spent most of his salary, Francis claimed, on housing the strays that she could not resist adopting. "It's not just the cost of boarding them in the cat's Ritz," he said, "it's the cost of all the advertisements she puts in *The Times*." The bedridden gentlewomen, homeless divorcées, and orphaned twins seeking "good homes" for their "adorable pussies" would all turn out to be Jane. As Francis was a leading authority on French furniture, he frequently visited Paris. While he worked away in the Louvre, Jane would be off cat-catching. If successful, she would take the animal to a crooked vet for knockout shots, then would smuggle it back to London in her capacious bag, to avoid quarantine. "It's my old fur," she would say, if questioned by customs officials.

Of all Douglas's women friends, the one who meant the most to him was the utterly fascinating, utterly charming, utterly unscrupulous Baroness Budberg, a hefty sixtyish woman with a large, flat, intelligent face. Moura had been the mistress of Robert Bruce Lockhart (the principal British agent in Russia at the time of the Revolution), Maxim Gorki, and H. G. Wells. She is said to have spied for the British and the Russians, and heaven knows who else. After World War II, she had gone to work for Alexander Korda, the movie producer; she also did translations. Writers and actors and journalists and Russians of all persuasions—Benckendorfs, Ustinovs, Pasternaks—congregated in her large, scruffy flat and talked and drank and plotted as if they were members of the Moscow intelligentsia in a Joseph Conrad novel. When we were in London, Douglas and I would see Moura two or three times a week, and she would pay us regular visits when we moved to France. We were very

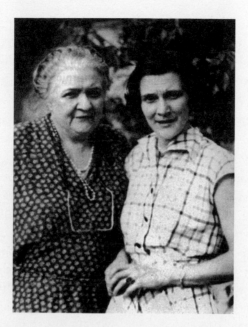

Baroness Budberg and her daughter Tania
Alexander, ca. 1960

fond of her. And then, decades after her death, I met the expatriate writer Nina Berberova, who had known Moura well in her early days and had also written a book about her.

Moura turns out to have played a far more questionable role, politically, than any of us could have imagined. In 1933, when Gorki was about to return to Moscow from Italy, where he and Moura had been living in exile, he entrusted her with his famous trunk, which was full of letters from anti-Stalinist dissidents. She was to hand it over to nobody, not even back to Gorki, if he asked for it to be sent to him in Moscow. Despite these injunctions, Moura seems to have given in to an ultimatum from Stalin. His agents told her that if she wanted to return to Russia to see Gorki before he died, she had better take the private train Stalin was putting at her disposal and bring the trunk with her. If she failed to do so, his goons, who had already taken Kerensky's and Trotsky's papers by force, would not hesitate to seize Gorki's trunk and quite possibly murder her in the process. Although Moura always denied having returned to Russia, she evidently did so, trunk and all, in 1936. Possession of Gorki's papers greatly strengthened Stalin's hand in his show trials of Bukharin and many others. Another fact about Moura that emerged only after her death: She was a direct descendant of Peter the Great. Her ancestor Count Zakrevsky had been a son of the Empress Elizabeth and her morganatic husband, Alexis Razoumovski. It figured.

My friends were an altogether younger, wilder, less academic lot. Douglas made himself as agreeable to them as he could. At first they were not very amenable, but in due course most of them came round to him, except of course Cuthbert, who continued to edit me as dutifully as before. He was as woebegone as ever, thanks in part to John Lehmann, who had taken it upon himself to castigate rich, evil Douglas for taking me away from poor, virtuous Cuthbert. In fact, my feelings for Douglas stemmed from much the same need as my feelings for Cuthbert. I wanted to learn how to write—above all about art. I needed Douglas's knowledge just as I needed Cuthbert's skills. It would be hypocritical to pretend that Douglas's money was not a factor; it made everything much, much easier, but thank God I had a little of my own.

Earlier in the year, Cuthbert and I had planned to go to Italy together in August—to Ischia, to stay with his old friend Wystan Auden, a poet I revered but had never met. After that, I had arranged to spend a couple of weeks in Switzerland with my dearest friend, Geoffrey Bennison. Geoffrey had been the most gifted student at the Slade: a fine academic draftsman with perfect pitch in his use of color. He was also a born comic. Professional actors flocked to his performance as Bottom in an undergraduate production of A Midsummer Night's Dream. Tragically, Geoffrey contracted TB and had to give up being a painter. For the last five or six years he had been a patient in various sanatoriums, culminating in the Waldhaus at Davos, the place that had inspired Thomas Mann's Magic Mountain. He had undergone a pneumothorax, but was now on the way to being cured by the newly discovered antibiotic Aureomycin. Most summers I would go and stay with him and would have a walk-on part on the Waldhaus's sad little stage.

Nothing would induce me to forgo these visits. And so, when Douglas decreed that he and I would spend the summer traveling around Europe together, I explained that I was not all that free. Chuck these people, he insisted. "I've worked out a wonderful Grand Tour for us." I refused: "No Ischia or Davos, no Grand Tour." Douglas grudgingly accepted my terms. For his part, Cuthbert hoped that exposure to Wystan would exorcise the baleful influence of Douglas. Meanwhile, he went on trying to make a writer of me. "Don't let any of Douglas's sneering and backbiting sour your style," he said. "Spite stems from failure."

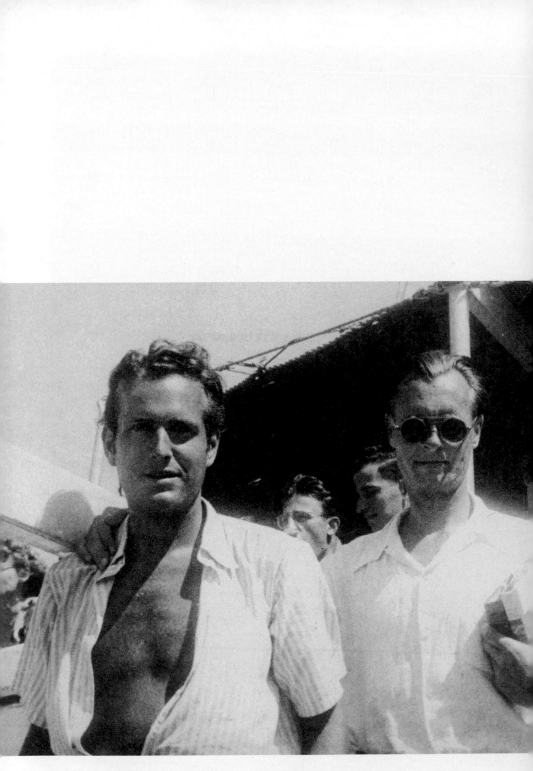

JR and T. C. (Cuthbert) Worsley on the ferry to Ischia, summer 1949

GRAND TOUR

Our Grand Tour, which began in late June and lasted until early October, started grandly enough. Douglas put Basil's old Rolls on the plane from Lympne to Le Touquet. To make the first leg of the journey more congenial, he had asked James Bailey to join us. It was not a good idea. Now that his Gustave Moreauish opera sets were having a success at Covent Garden, James, who was short and squat and hirsute, had started behaving in an inappropriately diva-like way, as if he were Tosca or Thaïs. His misfortune had been to grow up next door to the famously epicene Stephen Tennant, and rather too much of Stephen's stardust and outrageousness had rubbed off on him. Once, when I was staying with the Baileys, James's grim father had returned from buying some of Stephen's land, holding the deed by a pair of tongs. "The closing took place in the feller's bedroom," Colonel Bailey fumed. "The document stinks of Chanel Number Five." James made things worse by correcting him: "Nonsense, Papa, *Arpège.*"

Like Douglas, James had a horror of passing unperceived; and, sure enough, when we arrived at Le Touquet in the wasp-colored Rolls, with Douglas in horse-blanket checks, and James trailing a ten-foot-long angora scarf pinched from his mother, we were noticed. Tourists tittered, and even the *douaniers* raised their eyebrows. The attention—or was it the competition?—was too much for Douglas, and he saw to it that our paths diverged as soon as we got to Paris.

Having spent six months in Paris two years earlier, I thought I knew the city well enough, but Douglas revealed its splendors to me as never before. Every morning we would embark on a round of museums and monuments, galleries and private collections, or we would make

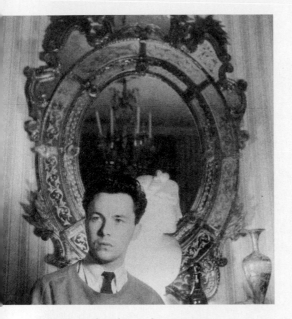

James Bailey, theater designer, 1946

sorties to Fontainebleau or Versailles, or to less obvious places like Ecouen or Champs. The big Gauguin retrospective was only one of many other exhibitions that Douglas was reviewing. The re-opening of the gloriously installed Musée de Cluny enabled him once again to show off his knowledge of medieval art. Douglas shocked me by actually liking an oversized Utrillo retrospective and not liking a beautiful show in honor of Matisse's eightieth birthday nearly enough. "Fiddle-faddle," he said of this first appearance of Matisse's marvelous *papiers-découpés*—"no comparison with cubist ones." Douglas deplored my ignorance of the French classics and would take me to the Comédie Française, or the Opéra, or whatever was of interest at the theater. With the excuse of food shortages back home, we went in for a lot of serious eating and drinking.

Douglas took me to visit such celebrated friends as Léger and, most memorably, Picasso. As early as our second meeting, Douglas had tried to impress me by calling Picasso in Paris as if for a casual chat. The artist did not come to the telephone, nor did he do so on several subsequent occasions. Far from being impressed by Douglas's intimacy with the great man, I felt acutely sorry for him. Why expose himself to these unnecessary rebuffs? A few weeks later, when I accompanied him to Picasso's rue des Grands Augustins studio, we were received warmly enough, but no more so than the other ten or so supplicants—collectors, publishers, photographers, dealers, journalists, fans, and friends—who had arrived, bearing gifts in the hope of a favorable response to their requests. What surprised me was Picasso's smallness and delicacy, also the unassuming courtesy—those radiant smiles—with which he greeted people, who seldom had a language or anything else in common with him and seemed only to want to waste his time. Each of the supplicants needed something from the artist: a charitable donation, a book jacket, a signature on an unsigned work. Simpler requests were satisfied there and then. More complicated ones were listened to and seemingly acceded to. However, as I later discovered, Picasso had as many ways of saying yes while meaning no as a Japanese: "I'll do my very best" or "I'll be in touch" usually implied the opposite. Even when he was interested in a specific project, he would prevaricate for months before getting down to a promised drawing or collaborating on a promised exhibition. The only gratification that Picasso can have derived from these audiences was a papal one: the reassurance that the faithful were still faithful. This need for reassurance would become ever more pressing in the 1950s, when the avant-garde would start melting away in the direction of abstract expressionism or—Picasso's pet hate—neo-Dadaism. "All they have done is change the wrapping-paper," he said.

Above all, I was fascinated by the way Picasso used his huge eyes as a hypnotist might, raking the room for possible subjects. At one moment he turned his eyes on me and held my gaze for long enough to induce a responsive quiver. He was good at spotting susceptible people. When he went on to do the same thing to another new face, I felt slightly betrayed. After getting to know Picasso better, I would be amused to watch him fix his voracious stare on one unsuspecting person after another—regardless of age or sex. The *mirada fuerte,* the "strong gaze"—so highly valued by Andalusians, who believe that the eye is akin to a sexual organ and that rape can be ocular—never failed to work its magic.

The unaccustomed tensions of life with someone as hyper as Douglas were already taking a psychic toll. In Paris I developed a mysterious fever. Douglas claimed to have a doctor friend who could cure psychosomatic ailments, Jacques Lacan. This man had yet to become a celebrated intellectual guru. If Douglas had faith in his powers, it was because Picasso had entrusted Dora Maar to his care after her crack-up five years earlier. When this dandified doctor materialized in our room in the Hôtel des Saints-Pères, my temperature shot up even higher. *"Enlevez votre pyjama,"* Lacan said, and peered at my sweating

torso with distaste. He took a large Lanvin handkerchief from his breast
pocket, laid it over my chest—as doctors used to do before the invention
of the stethoscope—and listened from a safe distance, nodding saga-
ciously as he did so. This diagnostic charade ended with Lacan tearing a
page from his Hermès diary and, after a pensive pause, writing down the
address of another doctor. I subsequently saw Lacan a few times, but
was never able to take this brilliant man as seriously as intellectual fashion dictated. The contrivance was such that he seemed like an actor playing himself.

Basil, who had been attending a parliamentary congress in Paris,
joined us for the first leg of the trip. I was still feverish—pleased to have
a doctor along. In midmorning we broke our journey for a couple of bottles of Pouilly-Fumé on a terrace overlooking the Loire. And then
Douglas sped on to Moulins to look at the great triptych in the cathedral
and treat us to a four-course lunch that would have disqualified anyone
else from driving. Afterwards he wrapped me up in rugs in the jump
seat, where, windblown and sweat-drenched, I slept until we arrived at
Aix-en-Provence. The music festival was a new attraction, and Douglas
had obtained seats, the following evening, for *Don Giovanni* in the
courtyard of the archbishop's palace. I took the precaution of staying in
bed. Unfortunately, Segovia, most revered of classical guitarists, had the
room above mine, and was practicing for a concert later in the week. The
sequence of three nasal notes played over and over again for hours at a
time—ping, pang, pung; pung, pang, ping—was like water torture.
Sleeping pills put me out of my misery, but the aftereffects kept me doz-
ing through much of *Don Giovanni*. All I remember is the Don's missing
fingers—frostbite, I was told.

While we were at Aix, Douglas insisted that we call on old friends
who lived there, Georges Duthuit and his wife, Marguerite, Matisse's
formidable daughter. Marguerite seemed far from pleased to see
Douglas, and arranged to receive us on the sidewalk outside their house.
Later I discovered why. When war had broken out in 1939, the Duthuits
were staying with Douglas in London. As foreign checks were no longer
negotiable, they had run out of money, and had asked Douglas to lend
them twenty pounds for their journey home. Marguerite, who was
exceedingly scrupulous, had left one of her father's drawings, a beautiful
1916 *Vase with Ivy*, with him as collateral. After the war, she had tried to

repay the money and recover the drawing, but Douglas was not prepared to relinquish it. He insisted that she had sold it to him. Marguerite
was too fastidious to pursue the matter further, but it understandably
rankled, which is probably why her majestic, lion-headed husband
insisted on taking us off to a café and plying us with questions about the
friends he had made in London before the war.

From Aix we went on to the in those days privately owned
Mediterranean island of Porquerolles. Basil had been asked by officials
at the Quai d'Orsay whether he would like them to arrange holiday
accommodations for him. Tell them to get us lodgings on Porquerolles,
Douglas said. The island (just across from Hyères) belonged to an
elderly, partly French, partly English woman called Madame Fournier;
and as Douglas suspected, her private house, which abutted the sea,
would be far and away the best place to stay. Sure enough, at the Quai
d'Orsay's prodding, Madame Fournier put the three of us up at her villa,
and we spent our days relaxing on her virtually deserted beaches and
eating langoustes at the one and only hotel. "You are not at all my idea of
official guests," she said. Except for a boat trip to the neighboring Ile du
Levant—a disappointing nudist colony that did not countenance anything more radical in public than toplessness—we stayed on Porquerolles for almost two weeks. Douglas worked intensively on his
Léger book. I lay in the sun and beachcombed and recovered from my
fever.

After leaving Porquerolles, we toured around the Riviera—Saint-
Tropez, Antibes, Cap Ferrat, Monte Carlo—before driving to Geneva
for meetings with Douglas's Swiss publisher. Then on to a succession of
great exhibitions: medieval art at Bern; Rembrandt at Schaffhausen;
Matisse at Lucerne; Bellini at Venice; and a week's total immersion in the
Renaissance at Siena and Florence. Then back to Venice via Arezzo,
Urbino, Ravenna, Ferrara, and Mantua. I was enormously grateful for
Douglas's crash course in Western art, but more than ready to join Cuth-
bert for a few days in Naples—the starting point for our visit to Auden,
who had a house on the island of Ischia, Capri's less spectacular neighbor.

I had another reason for going to Naples. I wanted to see an old
friend from Oxford, the great zoologist J. Z. Young, who spent the summers with his adorable, down-to-earth girlfriend, Raye, in the research
section of the city's famous aquarium, experimenting on octopi. John

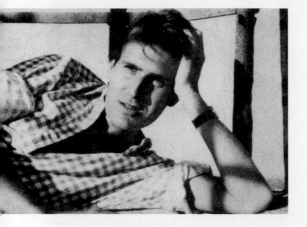

JR at Aigues-Mortes, 1950

allowed Cuthbert and me to watch him at work. The purpose of the experiments was to isolate the area of memory in the brain. John would train his octopi to react to certain electrical stimuli and then remove a slice from this or that part of their brain, to see whether or not they remembered the shock. Thanks to his skill at making scientific procedures comprehensible as well as totally absorbing—a skill that made for the success of his books—Cuthbert and I became so enthralled that we ended up spending our time in the aquarium instead of visiting the great Neapolitan churches and monuments that Douglas had instructed me on no account to miss. John showed us how the octopi, who were kept in separate compartments, tried desperately to find an aperture through which to insinuate their tiny sex-organ tentacles into the neighboring pens. He also showed us how octopi change color according to whether they feel fear, lust, or aggression. Had the aquarium replaced the so-called mermaid that Curzio Malaparte describes in his book *The Skin* being served up with a garnish of mayonnaise and bits of coral as the centerpiece at a dinner given by the American general in charge of starving Naples? "Must have been a manatee," John said dismissively. He and Raye were also leaving for Ischia. We arranged to meet.

A photograph taken on the ferry from Naples to Ischia shows Cuthbert and me looking carefree, although both of us must have realized that the fireworks of Ferragosto—Italy's Fourth of July—would probably mark the end of our attachment. Wystan's house at Forio had been partly destroyed in an earthquake and never entirely rebuilt. Some of the rooms had been left open to the sky. In place of ceilings or awnings, Chester Kallman, Wystan's funny, zaftig boyfriend, had run wires from one wall to another and trained morning glories to grow along them. The effect was charming—heaven knows what happened when it rained. After a month of grand hotels, three-star restaurants, and constant exposure to the West's greatest art and architecture, the sun-baked sparseness of Forio, with its lack of modern amenities, not to speak of ancient monuments, came as a relief. For someone who had overdosed on great art, Ischia provided a wonderful corrective. It had none of Capri's transcendent theatricality. It was unspoiled and to that extent impoverished, but not distressingly so. People seemed content with their lot. Chester told a friend that when he first arrived on the island, "he was taken by a local boy into the family vineyard. Once there, the boy made it abundantly clear that for five hundred lire (less than a dollar even then), Chester could have him and all the grapes he could eat." Cigarettes were sold individually; lighting in most houses took the form of a single, dangling low-wattage bulb; the local cuisine was limited to pasta and pizza. Fine with me: I loved pasta, and pizza was still such a novelty in England that I had never tasted it before.

After a month of Douglas's disconcerting oscillations between bossy affection and didactic showing off, Wystan's steadiness of mind and character came as a relief. It was also reassuring to fall into the quasi-monastic schedule that he managed to impose on his household. Work—exhaustive reading or writing—was the order of the day, but everything stopped at appointed times for tea or martinis or visits to the café. Getting drunk or having sex was fine, but there was a time and a place for it and, as I was to discover, certain unspoken rules. I can still see Wystan, accompanied by his snappish mutt, Moses, on his dusty way to or from the village store, his bare feet as callused as a fakir's and his wonderful face crinkled like a shar-pei's ("We will have to smooth him out to see who it is," Stravinsky had said). I can still hear the jokes— about the village idiot, whom he had nicknamed "Harvard," or about Wagner's confession late in life, "I adore Rossini, but don't tell the Wagnerians." I remember being struck by the wisdom of Wystan's comments, and the way they made one perceive familiar things in sharper, deeper relief.

Also staying in the house was a young writer called Jimmy Schuyler, whom Chester had invited along with his demonic friend Bill Aalto (a former guerrilla warfare expert), to look after the Forio house the previous winter while he and Wystan were back in New York. In the spring, Truman Capote and Tennessee Williams had come to stay, each

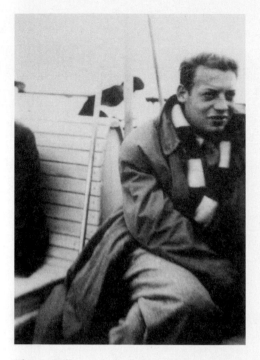

Chester Kallman on the boat to Ischia

with a lover in tow; and there had been a lot of disruptive drinking and shrieking. After they left, Aalto had tried to kill Jimmy with a carving knife, and then fled back to New York. Jimmy had stayed on, typing out Wystan's manuscripts. Though not yet the delectable poet he later became, Jimmy had one of those mesmerizing sensibilities peculiar to schizophrenics. With his short haircut, tight blue jeans, and white T-shirt, he epitomized the fresh American sailor-boy look that would soon become mandatory for young men everywhere. I was dazzled. Chester took us down to the beach to swim and then to have drinks with a gaggle of alcoholic remittance men. Their campy giggles dismayed Cuthbert. He hurried back to be with Wystan, who was good at dealing with psychotic friends. I stayed because Jimmy stayed. I had no thought for anyone else.

The second or third night, Jimmy and I waited until the household was asleep and lugged a mattress out onto the moonlit terrace, where we made frenzied love under a fig tree. For Jimmy this can hardly have been a novelty; for me this wild night turned out to be a Dionysian *rite de passage*. A rustle from within the house indicated that someone was watching. Jimmy pointed into the darkness. Wystan's head could just be discerned peering over the wall of one of the ceilingless rooms. He must be standing on a box, Jimmy whispered. "Don't stop." Moonlight bathed us. Wystan went on watching, maybe Cuthbert, too; we went on with whatever we were doing.

At breakfast I was still too euphoric to look contrite. Cuthbert was wearing sunglasses. Wystan seemed cross and schoolmasterish. Dear Chester, so often in trouble himself, gave me a conspiratorial leer. Jimmy was nowhere to be seen. Without anything being said, I was made to feel that although a guest in an exceedingly permissive household— both Wystan and Chester had Forian lovers on the side— I had thoughtlessly transgressed. I had hurt the feelings of the vulnerable friend who had brought me; I had reawakened Jimmy's demons; and I had offended against Wystan's exacting sense of the right thing. Better go and pack, Cuthbert murmured. After tight-lipped farewells, Cuthbert and I made our way back to the island's principal town, Ischia Porto.

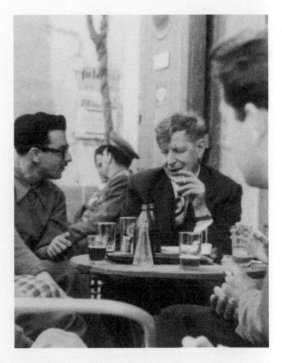

W. H. Auden (center) with Irving Weiss at Maria's Caffè, Ischia

When I next saw Wystan and Chester, two years later, Chester was in disgrace. It was in Venice in 1951. They were there for the opening of *The Rake's Progress*, the opera they had written and Stravinsky composed; Douglas and I were staying with Peggy Guggenheim. Chester had picked up an Italian sailor who pretended to be so smitten that he had to be given "something of value" as guarantee of a further tryst. What did Chester hand over but his precious Parker pen— a Christmas present from Wystan. When Wystan found out, he went straight to the police and insisted that they pressure the naval authorities into pressuring the sailor to return the talismanic pen. The intervention worked.

Ischia Porto turned out to be crowded with Neapolitan holiday-makers celebrating Ferragosto. After several drinks with John Young and Raye, who had come over for the occasion, I too felt like celebrating. In a fit of alcoholic rapture, I ripped off my shirt and shoes and, to the noise of firecrackers, made a wild dive into what I took to be the harbor.

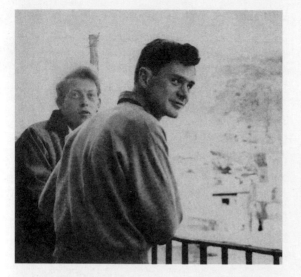

Chester Kallman and James Schuyler, Ischia, 1948–49

The water turned out to be eighteen inches deep; a bit of rusty metal on the bottom gashed my head open. Retribution! Cuthbert took me to the hospital and fed me grappa by way of an anesthetic as the banana-fingered doctor darned the skin on my skull. The pain was intense, but it allayed my guilt, also some of Cuthbert's despair. For the rest of our stay in Ischia, he was less tearful.

Through Wystan we had met the duo pianists Bobby Fizdale and Arthur Gold, who had rented a house on the island with Edwin Denby, most perceptive of ballet critics. They were a vast improvement on Chester's drinking companions. Denby would become Jimmy Schuyler's next lover, only to be replaced, a year or two later, by Arthur Gold. And then, in 1951, Jimmy went temporarily out of his mind. After telling friends that the Virgin Mary had warned him that Judgment Day was nigh, he was confined to a mental hospital. There, thanks to Frank O'Hara's encouragement, Jimmy developed into a poet of great visual sensibility. As he noted in his diary, "I'm a poet / and I know it." He also became exceedingly fat. I never met Jimmy again. After I moved to New York, he and I must often have been at the same party or concert or bar, but Jimmy told a mutual friend that he wanted to be remembered as a beauty, and that indeed is how I remember him.

My next stop was the Waldhaus in Davos, where Geoffrey Bennison told me the good news—Aureomycin had saved his life—and the bad news: his savings were running out and he hated the sanatorium. During World War II, the Swiss had allowed the Nazis to have tubercular soldiers and sailors treated at the Waldhaus; and to believe Geoffrey, there was still a whiff of the Wehrmacht—nurses like Gauleiters. The patients were a different matter. Geoffrey saw their little dramas through the eyes of Vicki Baum (author of *Grand Hotel*) rather than Thomas Mann. Although almost recovered, he still had his meals in bed. I took mine downstairs in the dining room so that I could fill him in on what passed for sanatorium gossip: "Nice Mr. X is no longer sharing a table with awful Fraulein Y"—that sort of thing. At lunch one day there was something more exciting to report. An elegant Italian couple had brought their handsome young son for treatment. The family could not hide their grief, any more than the other patients in the dining room could hide their curiosity. Each of the women patients got a glint in her eye. So did Geoffrey, when I told him what had happened. That evening he insisted on coming down to dinner to meet the new arrival. Geoffrey's warmth was as seductive as his wit, and in no time they became the closest of friends. Enrico, the Italian was called, and he turned out to share Geoffrey's passion for film and theater. Geoffrey did some marvelous drawings of him, and sanatorium life became much more tolerable for the two of them. A decade or so later, they would both make names for themselves: Geoffrey as London's most imaginative *antiquaire* and decorator, and Enrico as a key collaborator in Luchino Visconti's films.

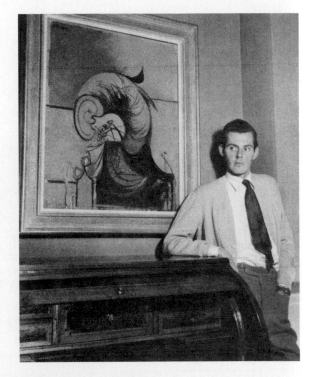

Geoffrey Bennison, London, 1946

While I was at the Waldhaus, I had a mild attack of sinusitis and asked one of the doctors for an antihistamine. Only after giving you a full checkup, he said. I told him I had just had one, but that made no difference. Geoffrey warned me that the checkup would involve X rays, which

were bound to be positive. "They're Swiss," he said. "All they're interested in is your lolly, so they've got the X rays rigged. You'll be here for
life. The only way you'll escape is feet first or by going broke like me."
Just as Geoffrey said, the head charlatan summoned me to his office,
pulled a long Swiss face, and told me I had a patch on my lung. But not
to worry, if I checked into the Waldhaus I would be cured in a year or
two. They had a nice room with a balcony next to Geoffrey's, and they
were ready to start treatment at once. I called Douglas, who was waiting
for me to join him in Venice. I'll drive up tomorrow and rescue you, he
said. This was a mission after Douglas's own heart. The following afternoon he arrived in fierce fighting form and treated everyone to a torrent
of Schwizerdütsch invective. When the head doctor insisted that I was
tubercular and must remain in the sanatorium, Douglas said he wouldn't
dream of leaving anyone in the care of quacks and swindlers. And off we
drove, Douglas berating the Swiss for turning a blind eye to Nazi war
crimes whenever there was a profit to be made; and yet in his paradoxical way he really rather loved them. A few weeks later I had myself
X-rayed again—just in case. There was no sign of lung disease.

The Grand Tour continued until mid-October. I had the feeling
that Douglas did not want to return to London, where he would no
longer have me to himself. After Davos, we moved on to Zürich to see
his friend Gustav Zumsteg, proprietor of that excellent restaurant the
Kronenhalle, where Lenin and James Joyce and the Dadaists had been
patrons thirty years before. Gustav was very proud of the modern masterpieces—Braques, Picassos, Matisses, Mirós—that hung on the
restaurant's walls. He was also very proud of the silk he manufactured
and sold to Paris couturiers, notably Balenciaga, whom he had come to
revere as a latter-day saint of fashion. This irritated Douglas: "I wish
Gustav would stop crossing himself every time he mentions the name of
that lugubrious Spanish dressmaker."

From Zürich we set off on an intensive tour of Swiss private collections, which Douglas knew by heart: Oskar Reinhardt's private museum
at Winterthur, and Baron Thyssen's La Favorita at Lugano, where we
were horrified to find the baron's restorer, a former English guardsman,
scrubbing and polishing the old masters as if they were buttons or boots.
He was about to start on the van Eycks. Douglas implored him not to
touch them. Alas, he did. We also went to collections that were more dif-

ficult of access. Best of all was the handsome house on a hill outside Basel belonging to the Swiss conductor Paul Sacher and his wife, a Hoffmann-LaRoche heiress. Their house was a shrine to modernism. Sacher owned the world's finest collection of modern musical manuscripts; his wife, who was a great friend of Braque's, had put together a wonderfully discriminating collection of contemporary masterpieces. The scariest collection we visited was housed in a sinister *bürgerlich* mansion on the outskirts of Zürich belonging to Emil Bührle, the armaments manufacturer whom Douglas had nailed as a major purchaser of paintings looted from Jews. It was impossible to disassociate the van Goghs and Cézannes on his walls from the carnage that had gone to pay for them. Far more attractive was the vast and varied collection belonging to an industrialist called Joseph Müller, who owned a nuts-and-bolts factory in Solothurn and used to ride to work on a bicycle. Besides great Cézannes, Renoirs, and Kandinskys, Müller's scruffy mill house was jampacked with treasures: cubist paintings in a room furnished with an old treadle sewing machine, racks of Rouaults in a higgledy-piggledy attic, and African masks and blood-stained tribal furniture in a bedroom hung with some of the Swiss artist Ferdinand Hodler's scenes of nude figures copulating by the side of an Alpine lake.

The next year we made a trip to Scandinavia, and in Stockholm spent some time with Douglas's old friend Rolf de Maré, the legendary Maecenas whose adventurous *Ballets Suédois* had given Diaghilev's company a run for its money in the 1920s. Meanwhile, I developed a passion for Gustavian neoclassicism, above all for Gustavus III's miraculously beautiful pavilion at Haga, and the work of Gustav Piló, his court painter. Piló's vast, diaphanous masterpiece of the king's coronation and his portraits in tones of copper sulfate, aquamarine, and ice still strike me as being among the eighteenth century's best-kept secrets.

In Copenhagen we discovered yet more Pilós in one of the royal palaces, not to mention an amazing array of Gauguins and Matisses in various Danish museums. Our only disappointment was a visit to the elegant country house of Baroness Blixen, who wrote under the name of Isak Dinesen. Her early autobiographical book, *Out of Africa* (later made into a horribly hokey film), and *Gothic Tales* had a sizable following, but she had yet to transform herself into a sacred monster on the international circuit. I did not take to Blixen. A friend of mine, who had been one of the first British officers into Denmark after the German occupation, told me that when he drove up in his jeep to deliver a care package from her publisher, the baroness had run off to hide in the raspberry canes at the bottom of her garden. She assumed he had come to arrest her for consorting with the Germans. I was put off by the affectation and contrivance of Blixen's appearance. She asked me to come up with suitable names for the characters in a story she was writing about nineteenth-century London, but I did not think enough of her stories to bother. Years later in New York, I was amazed when Mary McCarthy and others who should have known better touted this self-invented Germanophile pasticheur as a possible Nobel Prize winner.

The shock of twenty-four hours in what Douglas described as hellhole London was such that he insisted that we retire to the peace and quiet of the Bear hotel at Woodstock outside Oxford. The pretext was work—after three months' absence, both of us had a lot to do—but the real reason for this rustic interlude was Douglas's desire to prolong my *éducation sentimentale*. When we were not working or going for long, damp walks in the park at Blenheim, we would visit Oxford friends or inveigle the owners of stately homes to let us in. This suited me fine: I was writing a lengthy, would-be authoritative review of Margaret Jourdain's book on William Kent for the *Times Literary Supplement*. Rousham—one of Kent's finest houses and gardens—was only a few miles away, and the owner provided me with a lot of unpublished information. Despite efforts to the contrary, my Kent article turned out to be all too redolent of Douglas's influence: querulous, academic, and unnecessarily nitpicking. Cuthbert, who was forgiving enough to go on seeing me, was appalled at the snooty tone and implored me not to sacrifice liveliness to art-historical bickering.

Looking back, I can see that Douglas wanted me to turn into one of those tasteful young dilettantes who explore the byways of the decorative arts. He had already picked out the subject of my first book: John Opie, a late-eighteenth-century painter celebrated for his chiaroscuro portraits and quirkish genre scenes executed with an overloaded, bituminous brush. This was preordained, Douglas said, because I had recently discovered *The Fortune-Teller*, Opie's lost masterpiece, in a junk sale. "The lost masterpiece" would soon be lost again—this time for good. I had left it with my disaster-prone family; there was a fire, and nobody bothered to rescue it. Fortunately, no publisher was interested in Opie, but that did not stop me from wasting too much time writing boringly about things that bored me. Douglas did not want anyone—least of all his lover—poaching on what he regarded as his preserves.

While we were at Woodstock, Douglas persuaded Basil to let me move into Egerton Terrace. At last I could get away from my family. Under the terms of my father's will, my mother had the right to move house as often as she wanted, so long as I was the nominal owner of the property. While I was out of the country, my younger brother had persuaded her to sell our house off Thurloe Square and move to a flat where there was no room for me. Basil's generous provision of his one and only guest room and a study on the ground floor was a godsend. Offers to contribute to the costs of the household were brushed aside. Thanks to Basil's goodheartedness, the arrangement worked well. Far from being resentful or jealous, "Our Lord" was most welcoming—anything to keep Douglas happy. It somehow never occurred to me that I might have forfeited my freedom.

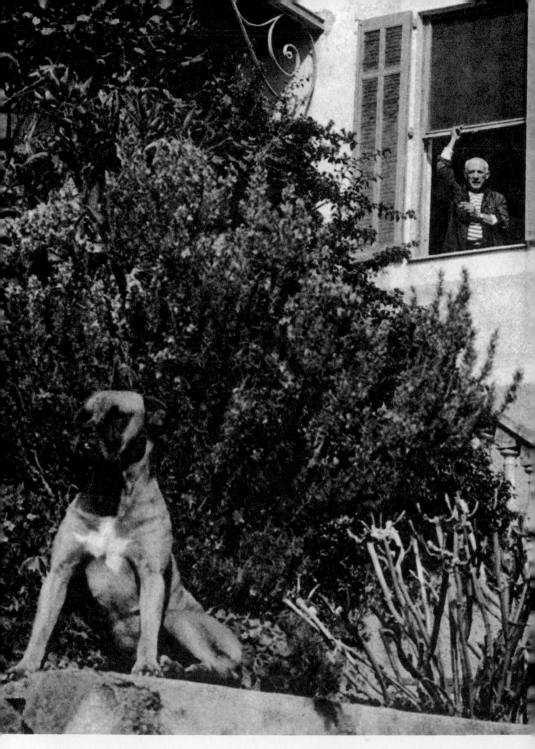

Picasso at the window of his villa La Galloise, at Vallauris, 1953; his boxer dog, Yan, is in the foreground.

BACK ON THE ROAD

Since recognition was what Douglas most wanted in life, I suggested that he try mending a few fences. And so long as I provided the requisite affection, he became much better disposed toward his friends and associates, even his parents. This new trend was encouraging. I liked old Mabel, his bridge-mad mother, and had brought her together with my own bridge-mad mother. Soon they were inviting each other to play cards, and behaving as mothers-in-law should, congratulating each other on each other's offspring, as if their relationship were the most normal thing in the world. Douglas and I seemed "to get on so well," Mabel told my mother, somewhat incredulously. "He's not easy, you know." Most of the time we did indeed get on well, but I had to watch out; Douglas was forever taking liberties. The first worrisome glitch occurred when the Royal Danish Ballet invited a group of British critics, including myself, to Copenhagen for a Bournonville festival. Douglas was against my going. Since he could not talk me out of it, he solicitously insisted on driving me down to Harwich, the point of departure for the Copenhagen boat. Halfway there, he said he had lost his way. By vigilantly watching the signposts, I saw to it that he soon found it again. We arrived on the quay as the gangplank of the *Princess Ingrid* was about to be raised. I realized I was getting a taste of the treachery that Francis Bacon had predicted.

Copenhagen was a delight. Seeing Bournonville's romantic ballets performed as they had been set and choreographed (all that intricate *batterie*) over a hundred years before was like hearing Malibran sing. No less a revelation were the bright northern nights, with people window-shopping at three in the morning as if it were three in the afternoon; the

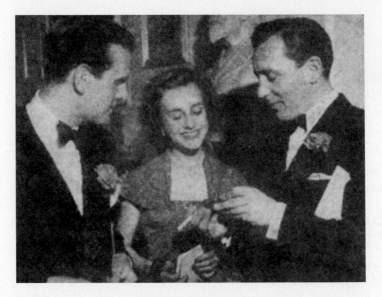

JR and Richard Buckle at the Danish Ballet Gala in Copenhagen

gay discos, where I saw men dancing together in public for the first time in my life; and the gala dinners given for us by prominent brewers and their cigar-puffing wives.

Back in London, there was a lot more ballet to review. Lincoln Kirstein had brought over the company he and Balanchine had founded. I raved about the classical ballets, and panned the literary ones—notably the *Illuminations* after Rimbaud and the *Age of Anxiety* after Auden, which, in my opinion, failed to do justice to the poems that had inspired them. A fellow critic, Richard Buckle, had invited Douglas and me to a party he was giving for the company. Kirstein turned out to be in one of his manic phases. After assailing me for daring to criticize any of his ballets, this massive, bullet-headed man, whom I would later come to know and admire, charged me like a buffalo. A neat sidestep saved me. Kirstein crashed into someone else.

A week later, Douglas swept me off on the second lap of our Grand Tour in a small green car that he had acquired for the purpose and drove as aggressively as he did everything else. Basil joined us at Reims, to celebrate his fiftieth birthday, and then we drove on to Geneva so that Douglas could work with his publisher, François Lachenal. During the war, François's influential father (lawyer to Picasso and various Roth-schilds), had helped his son become Swiss consul at Lyon, where he worked as a courier for the French Resistance. After the war, François opened a small publishing house, where he brought out a series of books on famous painters written by their friends. Hence Eluard's Picasso and Paulhan's Braque, as well as Cooper's Léger, which were distinguished by their insights and intimism. Much of the daily business of François's publishing house was conducted in a noisy brasserie, where we sat around consuming the local white wine, which, according to Douglas, had made James Joyce's bad eyesight even worse.

The brasserie also served as an alternative office for Geneva's other art publisher, the more celebrated Albert Skira, who seemed only able to function on lashings of alcohol. Douglas regaled me with stories about this man, whom he admired, envied, and denigrated. Skira had appar-ently started his career as a professional dancing partner at the Palace Hotel in Saint Moritz. And there he had been discovered by Averell Harriman's second wife, Marie. Skira wanted to be an art publisher, he told her. After many a tango, she agreed to provide the money for what turned out to be two of the most beautiful illustrated books of our time: Matisse's *Mallarmé* and Picasso's *Ovid.* A few years later he would pub-lish *Minotaure*, handsomest of art magazines. Skira had charmed Doug-las, charmed him into allowing his best paintings to be reproduced in the glossy *History of Modern Art* that he was in the process of publishing. At first, Douglas had been thrilled with the results and pooh-poohed my complaints that Skira's overvarnished color plates had a meretricious gleam that was fine for food advertisements but falsified tonal values in works of art. Later, when he realized that the less perceptive visitors to his collection found the originals a letdown after Skira's reproductions, he took to denouncing their "baked-bean sheen."

Douglas was very curious to see the newly consecrated church at Assy nearby in the Haute Savoie: the brainchild of the celebrated Father Couturier, and proof, it was said, that modern artists, whether they were believers or not, had much to contribute to sacred imagery. Doug-las did not subscribe to this view and had worked himself up into a state of hating Assy long before we arrived. I remember the gist of some of his comments: "Unbelievably disgusting—looks like an incinerator—architecture foul and irreligious—two stage boxes for clergy—

confessionals like Swiss telephone booths." As for Germaine Richier's crucifix: "a fake Romanesque Christ on a piece of driftwood—stained-glass windows unspeakable—Rouault's especially—Matisse's Saint Dominique—black swishy lines on shiny yellow tiles." The idea that modern art and the Church could meet struck him as absolute rubbish. And although he would describe Léger's enormous mosaic honoring the Virgin on the church's façade as "Léger's greatest mural success"—presumably to please the artist—Douglas disliked it as much as the rest of the church.

To correct the proofs of his Léger book, Douglas needed to shut himself away, so we moved to rooms above an excellent little bistro run by Spaniards, on the shore of the Lake of Geneva at Bellerive. Except at meals, we had the place to ourselves. Work, swim, eat, was all there was to do. This regime brought out the best in Douglas, quiescent during the day, hilariously funny and childishly affectionate in the evening. I took advantage of the peace and quiet of our lives to tackle Douglas about his and my work: about the academic straitjacket he had imposed on his own style and was now trying to impose on mine. I wanted him to loosen up and write less rigidly. In conversation and correspondence he put across his views so pungently; why did so many of his articles have to be so negative? He was forever chastising culprits for misspelling names, misprinting dates, and misplacing accents instead of pointing out more serious shortcomings. I made little headway. Douglas defended himself by claiming to be one of the first art historians to apply the apparatus of traditional scholarship to modern art. The trouble was, he regarded scholarship as a means of aggression rather than of enlightenment, just as he regarded virtually all other scholars who dared to write about "his" artists (not just the cubists, but most French painters of the nineteenth and twentieth centuries) as frauds and interlopers. Fifty years later, I can see that Douglas's professional vendettas stemmed from a need to distract attention from the fact that although he knew more than anyone else in his field, his ideas seldom transcended formalism. Negativism is its own reward, which is why this former scourge of the art world has been virtually forgotten. Even Douglas's mammoth *Picasso Theatre* does not live up to his own high standards; as he once said of a rival's book, it belongs on the coffee table rather than the library shelf. Far and away his best contribution to art history is his *catalogue raisonné* of Juan Gris, which he worked on for more than thirty years, but it is by his letters, if they are ever published, that he deserves to be remembered. Douglas could turn out to be a twentieth-century Vasari.

After Geneva, we went on to Bern, where we stayed with Rolf and Kathi Bürgi in their Klee-filled *château-de-poche,* Schlössli Belp. The first evening we sat around an enormous white porcelain stove while our host ceremoniously cooked a fondue. Rolf was most meticulous: the proportion of Emmenthaler to Gruyère had to be exactly right, also the hint of garlic, and the all-important dollop of kirsch. The guests gossiped away about the diplomats and wayward foreigners who had washed up in their tight little community: nightfall had once again stranded the British ambassadress halfway up the Matterhorn with a young guide; Benjy Guinness's Rumanian widow was back in jail for fraud, and so forth. The most interesting of the guests, Meret Oppenheim, the beautiful Swiss Surrealist, celebrated for her subversive objects, looked as out of it as I felt. To break the ice, I asked what kind of fur she had used for her icon, the *Fur-Covered Cup and Saucer.* No luck. "Cat," she snapped.

Too much fondue, too many Klees. The whimsicality of the masterpieces on the Bürgis' walls—all those *Twittering Machines*—suddenly became as irritating as the glockenspiels in *The Magic Flute.* And then when the maid asked in a singsong voice whether anyone wanted more *pflümliwasser,* and Douglas started showing off his Swiss German, I could not help comparing the excess of diminutives in Klee's cuckoo-clock imagery with the excess of diminutives in *Bärndütsch* (Bernese dialect). No wonder the artist had felt so at home in this *schlössli,* this wee castle. Much as I admired the courageous attempts to surpass himself in depth and scale and expression that Klee made at the end of his life, and his infinite Mozartean ingenuity, I would always regret his earlier disinclination to embark on anything that he could not already do flawlessly. For me at any rate, flawlessness is seldom compatible with the life-or-death urgency that makes for great art.

Despite my reservations about Klee, I was not going to refuse Douglas's offer of a work from the *Gesellschaft* that Bürgi had set up. I rightly suspected that this burst of generosity was unlikely to be repeated. Fortunately, Bürgi had put very low prices on the Klees: the gouache that I picked out cost little more than a hundred pounds. *Feuerwerke,* it was called: colorful Catherine wheels awhirl against a dense, night-brown sky. Sure enough, its enchantment palled. A year or two later, Braque agreed to sell me a colorful little painting I coveted, called *Firebird*. Its brilliance is in marked contrast to the gathering dusk of the very late work. Douglas sold my Klee to a collector friend called Dave Thompson in order to help me pay for the Braque.

A few years later, the Klee *Gesellschaft* had to be liquidated. Klee's son and heir, Felix, had emerged most inconveniently from a Russian prisoner-of-war camp to claim his birthright. On discovering how his father's Bernese friends had saved the estate from Allied confiscation by appropriating it for their city and themselves, Felix accused them of making off with his inheritance. Bürgi and Co. were outraged. How dare the son be so *ungrateful* to the saviors of his father's oeuvre? Felix had little but the clothes he stood up in; however, he managed to scrape together enough money to sue his "benefactors." In due course he was able to reclaim at least part of his birthright. Douglas's high principles had a way of evaporating when his interests were affected. He sided against Felix—"so unprepossessing." He had a point, but what really pained him was the prospect of no more good, cheap Klees.

After a few days in Zürich and Innsbruck, we arrived in Salzburg for the Festival. We stayed outside the town on Lake Fuschl, not in Ribbentrop's former Schloss, which was already on the way to becoming an *hôtel de luxe*, but at his former guest-house on the other side of the lake, where rooms cost less than a pound a day. For me the high point of the Festival was not Flagstad in *Fidelio*, as I had expected, but Richard Strauss's *Capriccio*, which was having its first postwar performance. Though longish, *Capriccio* is a one-act opera. We arrived a minute after it had started, and were refused entry. Declaring in the noisiest possible whisper that he was not going to put up with any of "their fucking Nazi regulations," Douglas grabbed my hand and yanked me through a posse of attendants to our seats. Thank God he did. The performance (with Bruno Walter conducting) was a revelation, and I have loved this allegorical opera, which pits music and poetry against each other, ever since.

Also attending the Festival was a woman who turned out to have played an important role in Douglas's early life, Ingeborg Eichmann. She was accompanied by her husband, Georg Pudelko, a sympathetic, somewhat seedy man, who looked like a clown in mufti. "Old friends from way back," was how Douglas passed them off. By now I was used to his secretiveness about certain areas of his past, so I was not surprised that the existence of this couple had been kept from me. It was only after I became friends with Ingeborg that I was able to piece together the story of her relationship with Douglas and their mentor Reber and discover the sequel: how, at the beginning of the war, the stateless Ingeborg had settled in Florence, as had Reber—the man who had not only formed Douglas's collection but had tried to marry her off to him. After the Nazis took over Italy, they packed off Ingeborg and her sister Lizzie to an internment camp outside Padua. There they had made friends with another detainee: a seductive, partly Javanese adventuress called Toto Koopman (subsequently the girlfriend of Francis Bacon's first dealer, Erika Brausen), who had become the commandant's mistress. The commandant had offered to release Toto from the camp and set her up in a hotel in Padua. Only so long as the Eichmann sisters could accompany her, Toto said. The commandant agreed.

After the war, Ingeborg had married Pudelko (the first husband of Reber's daughter, Gisela). Meanwhile, the wretched Reber remained exiled in Italy until 1947. On our way through Zürich I had finally met this infamous man, who had played such a Svengali-like role in Douglas's and Ingeborg's lives. Whether the meeting happened by chance or design, I cannot remember. All I do remember is the palpable embarrassment on both sides: Reber was shifty and scared—a ringer for Wagner's Nibelung, Alberich—and Douglas uncharacteristically awkward and tongue-tied. I could only imagine that while working for the Fine Arts Commission, Douglas had learned rather more than he wanted about his former mentor's wartime deals with Goering—shabby things that were not heinous enough to be mentioned in his official memoranda. That Reber had recently sold his last remaining treasure, Cézanne's *Boy in a Red Waistcoat,* to Bührle did not exactly exonerate him in Douglas's eyes. "I need an enormous drink," Douglas said after we took our leave. He mumbled something about Reber's troubles stemming from the Nazi persecution of Freemasons, but that was far from the whole story.

Ingeborg's family turned out to have a pretty house on another of the lakes in the Salzkammergut, and there we would spend our afternoons resting up for the opera, swimming in the lake if and when the local *Schrammelregen* (needle rain) ceased. Douglas had a chameleon-

like ability to take on local color, above all to adapt his accent to his sur-
roundings. In the course of our Salzburg visit, I caught a glimpse of what
he must have been like before the war, when, despite a loathing for
Nazism, he had steeped himself in German culture and learned to speak
the language with such virtuosity that he could have passed as a native
(so German friends assured me) of Vienna, Zürich, or Berlin. Douglas
tried, and failed, to interest me in the German classics—still a blind
spot—but he did not encourage me to speak the language. That was *his*
field of expertise.

After visiting every church, palace, castle, and monastery within
range of Salzburg, we moved on to other cultural areas. The account I
sent my mother of our movements leaves me breathless. Luckily, my
appetite for baroque and rococo proved a match for Douglas's, and he
was such a beguiling mentor. We went to St. Florian, Kremsmünster,
and Wilhering, as a prelude to an extensive tour of Bavarian churches
and monasteries: Die Wies, Ottobeuren, Weingarten, Fürstenfeld-
bruck, and many, many more. We were bowled over by the unexpected
magnificence of Burg Trausnitz, with its Italian Renaissance staircase
frescoed with scenes from the commedia dell'arte. Douglas pretended
to be shocked by Oberammergau—American nuns in nylons, chewing
gum and trying on lederhosen—but loved the Passion-play hokiness of it
all. He was thrilled to meet the Magdalen in the Gethsemane bar but
found Judas a bit of a prig. We did every single one of Mad Ludwig's
wonderfully hideous palaces: Neuschwanstein, more Walt Disney than
Wagner; Linderhof, the Monte Carlo casino in an alpine setting; and
best of all, Herrenchiemsee, Ludwig's Las Vegas Versailles, where the
overblown rococo comes to a sudden shrieking halt in great blank
walls—the king had gone mad.

We then spent six luxurious days in Munich. Douglas was torn
between delight and dismay at the speed with which Germany was recovering from the war. "I was hoping to see many more amputees," he said in
the course of a Lucullan dinner at Walterspiel. "George Grosz would
have found nothing much in the way of subject matter this time round."
Just as well Douglas kept these views to himself, when he prevailed upon
whoever was in charge of Bavarian monuments to let us see whatever we
wanted to see, whether the building was open or closed or being

restored. And then on with the Grand Tour to Ascona, where we spent five days in the company of prosperous Jungian matrons and elderly Weimar Republic intellectuals on the sunny shores of Lake Maggiore. After a day and a night in Torino, we forged on to Vallauris to see Picasso.

Except for a couple of acres of unkempt garden, there was nothing attractive about La Galloise, the little *bicoque* that Picasso had shared with Françoise Gilot and their two children for the previous two years. He had settled on it for no better reasons than that it was available, quintessentially ordinary, and almost impossible to find. It was tucked away in a warren of little roads above this rundown industrial town—the Sèvres of shlock—which the arrival of Picasso was supposedly transforming into a thriving *ville d'art*. Blocking the entrance to Picasso's little property was a garage with an apartment above, which former owners had rented to a crazy old lady, Madame Boissière, who gave lessons in *danse libre*. Local girls were sometimes to be glimpsed cavorting like so many Isadora Duncans in and out of the dusty shrubbery. She was also a painter—a mystical Rosicrucian one—and she loathed Picasso and his work. Signs on the front of her garage proclaimed, "This is where Madame Boissière lives. This is not where Monsieur Picasso lives." And, as Françoise Gilot has described, if these signs did not deter visitors, she would pace up and down on her balcony shouting at people that Picasso was a terrible painter and they should stay away. "The perfect concierge," Picasso would say. Zette Leiris, Kahnweiler's partner and stepdaughter, had told us to disregard the imprecations of the dancing mistress and follow a path around the side of the garage to Picasso's cheerless quarters, which were in keeping with his ironical notion of a Communist way of life. He seemed to take perverse pride in its anonymity.

Picasso was on his own. Françoise had taken the children, Claude and Paloma, somewhere, probably to the beach, but there were reminders of them all over the place. Since there was little space at La Galloise for work, he had recently purchased a derelict factory where essences of jasmine and orange blossom had once been distilled. He took us to see how he had turned it into a series of studios for painting

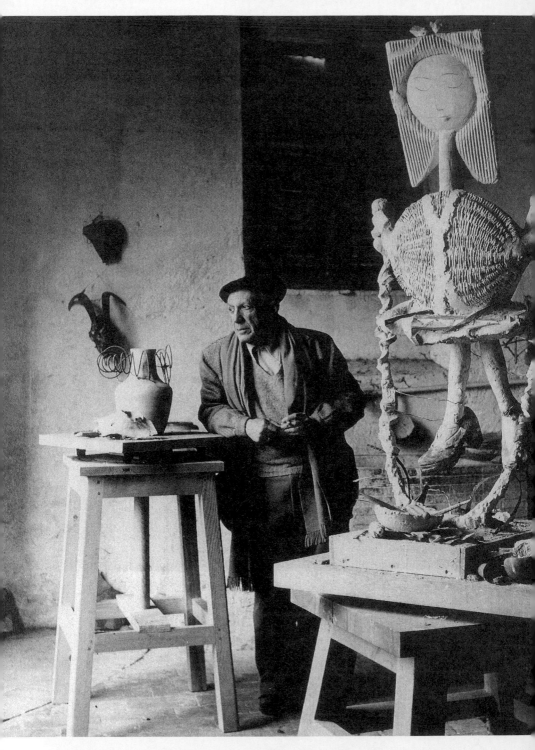

Picasso at his Vallauris studio, Le Fournas, with Girl Skipping Rope, 1950

and sculpture, as well as storage for the hundreds of ceramics which he had fired at Ramié's Madoura pottery. At first sight, Picasso's Le Fournas factory looked abandoned—surrounded by a tangle of waist-high grass, wildflowers, and weeds. He had bought donkeys to control the vegetation, he said, but their droppings had made everything grow even more luxuriantly; and then little Claude had started playing football with the donkey shit. The moment the artist arrived, the rusty, ramshackle place came to life. There was no outside help of any kind, and yet, in the space of little more than a year, the workshops had filled up with stacks of paintings, drawings, prints, and major sculpture and ceramics. Working in this factory had stimulated Picasso to paint, print, pot, and sculpt on an industrial scale.

For me, the greatest revelations were the sculptures that Picasso had recently taken to fabricating out of rubbish. "I am the king of the ragpickers," he told Jean Cocteau. The most spectacular of these was the *She Goat* made of a wicker basket (the pregnant belly), a palm frond (the spine), a pair of broken pitchers (the udder), the top of a tin can (the vulva), and a metal pipe (the anus) into which, he told us, he intended to insert one of those squeakers to be found in animal toys. "She's more like a goat than a goat," Picasso said. I told him I felt I could smell her, which pleased him. There were two other major sculptures: *Françoise Wheeling a Baby Carriage* (a real baby carriage with Paloma, ingeniously constructed out of broken crocks, in it); and *Girl Skipping Rope,* which the artist would work on for two more years. Picasso explained that he had always wanted to make a sculpture that didn't touch the ground, so he had asked the local ironmonger to bend a length of metal tubing into a huge, U-shaped skipping rope. This serves as a kind of armature (exterior instead of interior) and holds together the basket, which stands for the little girl's torso, and the lid of a box of chocolates, which forms her head.

After being exhibited and reproduced again and again over the last fifty years, these sculptures are now taken for granted, but when we first saw them, they were known only to visitors to the studio, hence their shock-of-the-new impact. It was as if Picasso, who fancied himself as Pygmalion, had not only reinvented sculpture but also discovered how to endow his figures with life. Was he going to cast these pieces? Picasso seemed of two minds. They were so fragile, he said; also, he did not want

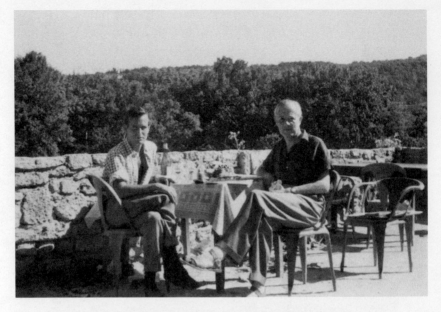

JR with Basil Amulree on the terrace of the Hôtel du Pont du Gard, 1950

to have the originals chopped up into castable sections. And in any case he much preferred plaster to bronze—"so academic and rich looking— *ça fait trop musée.*" Eventually, of course, he did have them cast.

Douglas and I left Vallauris delighted with our visit. A rapport had been established, as witness a poster of a clown in a crown that Picasso did a few months later; he all too evidently had the unwitting Douglas in mind. The artist asked us to join him the following weekend for a bull-fight at Arles; also for a bullfight, the weekend after that, at Nîmes. I suddenly realized how necessary it was for Picasso to have people around who believed in him and his work and could be trusted to follow him wholeheartedly into the future. Henceforth he would welcome us to his studios and show us whatever he was working on. For me this would be the greatest possible privilege, and it would enable me, decades later, to embark on my biography of the artist with more insight and sympathy than would otherwise have been possible.

On we drove to Avignon, where Basil joined us. He turned out to be as exhausted by his parliamentary duties as we were by our touristic ones. All of us needed a rest, so we decided to spend a few days at an inn

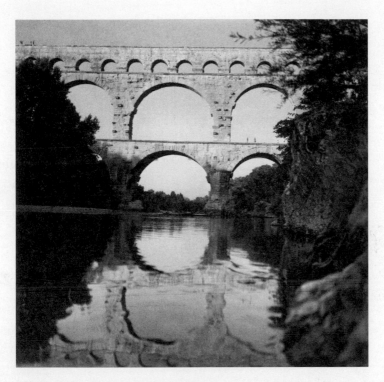

Pont du Gard, the first-century aqueduct over the river Gardon

in the shadow of the Pont du Gard, the Roman aqueduct that bridges the river Gardon and once supplied Nîmes with water. Because it had been constructed of friable sandstone, this handsome bridge had been restored again and again, and it looked much as it must have done at the time of the great Agrippa, who had built it nineteen hundred years earlier. Nowadays the delicate openwork masonry of the three-tier aqueduct, which spans the narrow valley, has the lightness of one of Christo's huge chasmal curtains. At dawn, as the sun turned the sandstone to golden fudge, we climbed up to the conduit and looked down on a group of boys diving off a rock into the river. A lone laundress—"left behind by Hubert Robert," Douglas said—was wringing out sheets.

When I revisited Pont du Gard a year or two ago, the great Agrippa's monument had finally become a hostage to tourism. You now have to leave your car in a concrete parking lot and walk past rows of fast-food stalls, T-shirt vendors, and Portosans before you see the aqueduct. Instead of the lone laundress, picnickers with ghetto blasters had taken over the river's pebbly *plages*, and were egging on rowdy canoeists to a river battle. I thought back to the stillness of the place half a century before; how in the evening the dusty garden of the auberge, where we liked to sit drinking after dinner (as often as not the only people there), would gradually turn into a sacred grove. The silence would be broken only by the cackle of one of Douglas's monologues: "As for Agrippa, my dear, he governed the Roman empire like a Nazi, but fancied himself an architect, Augustus's Albert Speer—aqueducts and amphitheaters all over Gaul." Meanwhile, Basil would be making glottal attempts to inter-ject, while trying to relight a cigar or reinsert an errant monocle. And I would wander off in the moonlight to listen to the cicadas and nightin-gales and wonder what was to become of me.

Each morning we would set forth in quest of three-star monu-ments and meals. Usually we would head eastward toward Arles and Saint-Rémy, and would end up at Les Baux, where Thuillier had recently opened his celebrated Baumanière restaurant. I seem to remember that Douglas's and Thuillier's paths had crossed at the end of the war in the course of some clandestine business: hence a degree of extra attention and the addition, when the season came round, of ortolans, rarest of birds, to our orders of partridges. Douglas, who knew about such things, proposed to follow the ritual established by Brillat-Savarin for eating this delicacy: you put a napkin over your head and devour the little songbird, bones and all, at a single bite. Basil and I dis-suaded him from doing so.

And then, one never-to-be-forgotten day, we took off for a change in a westerly direction, toward the dilapidated duchy of Uzès. En route, we were stunned by the sight of a cluster of golden columns on the edge of a vineyard. We stopped the car and found ourselves in front of a scaled-down version of Bernini's colonnaded peristyle in the forecourt of Saint Peter's. Part of the peristyle, which had been quarried from the same sandstone as the Pont du Gard, had fallen down—in an earthquake some thirty years earlier, we later discovered—but so picturesquely that Pannini might have stage-managed it. What made the place of more than casual interest was a small sign on one of the columns, proclaiming CHÂTEAU À VENDRE. Little did Douglas and I realize that our lives were about to undergo a radical change.

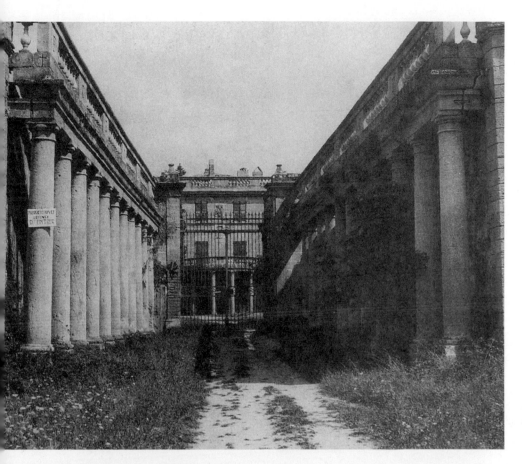

The Château de Castille, up for sale, 1949

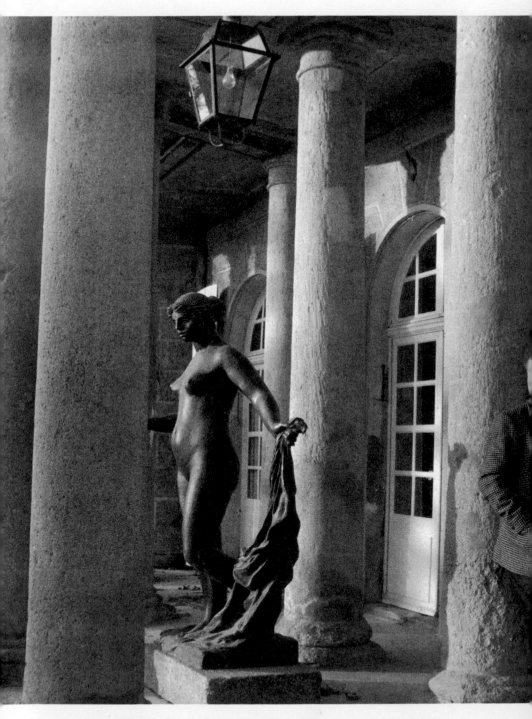

DC with Renoir's Venus Victrix *at the front door of the Château de Castille*

THE REVELATION OF
CASTILLE

The approach to the château, up a short, colonnaded drive, was nothing if not theatrical. Besides concealing two ranges of tumbledown farm buildings, these colonnades were part of an elaborate trompe l'oeil effect. The columns decreased in scale and converged, thereby accentuating the perspective—"just like Borromini's *prospettiva* in the Palazzo Spada," Douglas observed to Basil. This gave the relatively cramped entry a decidedly imposing air. Through the bars of a large, padlocked gate we had our first glimpse of what was to be our house: a moderate-sized building with a turret at each corner and yet another sandstone colonnade running around three sides of it so as to form a balustraded balcony. Incised repeatedly into the balustrade was a large monogram, C.R. (for Castille Rohan, we later learned). "It stands for Cooper/Richardson," I said. "We have to get it." "If I buy the place," Douglas said, "I'll buy it for myself." His acquisitive heart was evidently set on it.

The oxblood shutters looked as if they had been shut tight for centuries, except for one on the ground floor that was slightly ajar: chickens wandered in and out. A mangy hound on a long chain did not bark so much as howl at us, at which a slatternly woman emerged from the house, making angry fuck-off gestures. No, we could not visit the château. Douglas brandished a banknote at her. Yes, she would unlock the gate. Apart from weeds, the courtyard consisted of an elaborate *jeu de buis* (box garden), which was so overgrown that it was unclear whether it had started life as a maze or simply developed into one. Off to one side of the château, overlooking what had once been a formal garden, was a long, tumbledown building with columns at either end, which

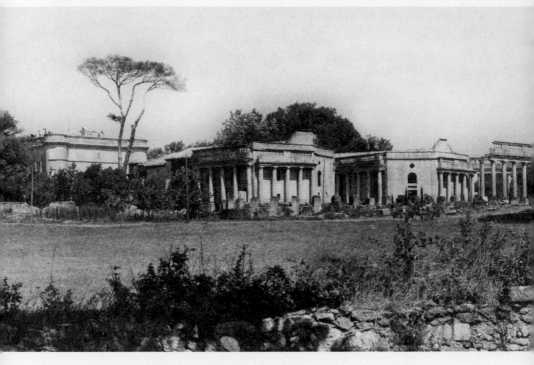

View of Castille and its peristyle from the road

looked as if it might have been an orangery. It turned out to have been a *magnaneraie*, a place where silkworms had been reared.

This, the slattern told us, was the Château de Castille, known locally as *"le palais des mille colonnes."* The building had apparently originated in the fifteenth or sixteenth century as a fortified *bastide*. Shortly before the Revolution, the owner, Gabriel-Joseph Froment, Baron de Castille, had made a grand tour of Italy and had returned to France so enamored of columns that he set about "columnising" his ancestral home in honor of his marriage to a Princesse de Rohan. To judge by a paltry little monument to her in the wooded park at the back of the house, inscribed with the lines *"elle a vécu ce que vivent les roses / l'espace d'un matin,"* his wife did not live very long, but her widower continued to squeeze every last drop of glory out of this illustrious alliance. Another of the baron's sentimental little monuments turned out to be of special interest to Basil: it celebrated the visit to Castille of the elderly Louise de Stolberg, the unfortunate wife of Bonnie Prince Charlie (also known as "The Young Pretender"). Basil's interest stemmed from a historical obsession with the five-year period when this anything-but-"bonnie" prince was on the run from the French as well as the British. Somehow or other, "Our Lord" had discovered the aliases, addresses, and mistresses that the fugitive had used, and solved the mystery of his disappearance.

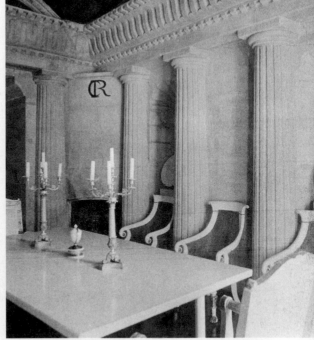

The Doric dining room at Castille, ca. 1970

Another banknote induced the sullen-looking woman and her sullen-looking, peg-legged husband to open the shutters and let us inside the château. Thanks to a roof that had remained in good repair, the fabric of the building was dry and less ruinous than we had feared. Surprisingly, there were no cellars, not even any proper foundations. And since most of the floorboards downstairs had either been burned or stolen or allowed to rot, the chickens pecked away at earthen floors. The rooms, which opened one into the other, turned out to be modest in scale, provincial Louis XVI in style, with good simple moldings and chimney pieces and *plafonds à la française* (multi-beamed ceilings) in good shape.

Mercifully, the walls were not paneled or otherwise embellished— the better for hanging paintings—except for one dramatic little room that seemed imbued with the spookier, more romantic spirit of the Enlightenment—the spirit that had inspired so many other neoclassical follies of the period. Years later I read about the Marquis de Montesquieu's allegorical park at Mauperthuis (destroyed during the Revolution), with its Masonic pyramid, its ruined tower that evoked the Knights Templars, mythic ancestors of Freemasonry, and its paths that signified the successive ordeals Masons had to undergo, and I realized that the Baron de Castille had been out to do something similar—albeit more crudely and on an infinitely smaller scale—in his little park at the back of the château. Topographical engravings done in the baron's lifetime seem to bear out that the miniature pyramid and other numinous relics derive from Freemasonry.

Further evidence of Masonic derivation took the form of an amateurish painting on the ceiling of one of the smaller rooms—a view of the château afloat in a starlit sky—which reminded me ever so faintly of Schinkel's decor for Mozart's Masonically inspired *Magic Flute*. This curious chamber, constructed of the same sandstone as the columns outside, took the form of a small but massive Doric temple. Had the architecture been less rustic and more grammatically correct, it could have been by that other Freemason, Ledoux. This miniature temple, which would become our dining room, would have made a most appropriate setting for the meetings of a secret society (the Baron de Castille would surely have been a friend of his neighbor, the Marquis de Sade), or for the ordeals by fire and water that Mozart's wretched Tamino had to endure. Later, when I mentioned the possibility of a Masonic concept to Douglas, he was indignant. Insofar as his father had ever worked after leaving the army, it was to the greater glory of Freemasonry, and he had reached a position of eminence in his lodge. Freemasonry was anathema to Douglas. "At a very early age," he said, "I made it very clear to my vile father that I was not going to waste my time strutting around in an apron. I cannot believe that the geniuses of the Enlightenment went in for any of that middle-class hocus-pocus."

There turned out to be a major problem with the house: no water, hence no bathroom, lavatory, or kitchen sink—not a tap in the place. The slatternly woman, who was called Madame Grousset, showed us the only well; it's always running dry, she explained with relish. There had been several wells on the property, but these now belonged to *her* family. The Baron de Castille's descendants had apparently been a feckless lot who had allowed the family fortune, such as it was, to dwindle to nothing. Around 1930 the bank had foreclosed, and the Groussets had bought up all the land that was under cultivation, as well as the wells that went with it, and the scruffy farm buildings down by the road, where they now lived. These included a little chapel—a pretext for more of the baron's columns—which they used as a barn. A local businessman had bought the "useless" part of the property: the château, colonnades, outbuildings, and pocket-sized wooded park at the back. He had intended to restore it and sell it at a profit, but all he had time to do before war intervened was repair the roof. During the war a family of Polish refugees had moved in and kept sheep and goats in the little Doric chamber. By rubbing their itchy flanks against the friable stone columns, the animals had transformed more than one entasis into a concavity. The For Sale sign had gone up a year or two after the war, and Madame Grousset had become the concierge. Since the château was going very cheap, for ten to twelve thousand dollars, several people had shown an interest, but lack of water had precluded a sale.

As we emerged from the shade of the colonnaded house into the glare of sunlight and the blare of cicadas, Douglas announced that he was going to buy it. "Ghastly, philistine England" had never deserved his collection and now would never get it. His pictures would be much more at home in life-enhancing France, where most of them had been painted. Castille would be far more conducive to writing about modern art than Knightsbridge. And then think of the *basse cour* we would have—pigs, chickens, sheep, rabbits would provide pâtés, hams, eggs, cheeses. . . . Basil looked put out—hadn't he just bought a house in London to share with Douglas?—until we cheered him up by explaining that Castille would serve the three of us as a kind of Egerton Terrace South. Also, since he was a baron and Castille a barony, Basil could be "Our Baron" as well as "Our Lord." As for water—no problem. As soon as the sale went through, we would simply dig a new well; the river Gardon was nearby, so water would have to be available. "Don't worry," said Douglas, who was optimistic only when pessimism was called for, "we'll go on digging till we find it. If the worst comes to the worst and no water materializes, I will put the château back on the market and take a loss."

It was not, of course, as simple as that. In those postwar days there

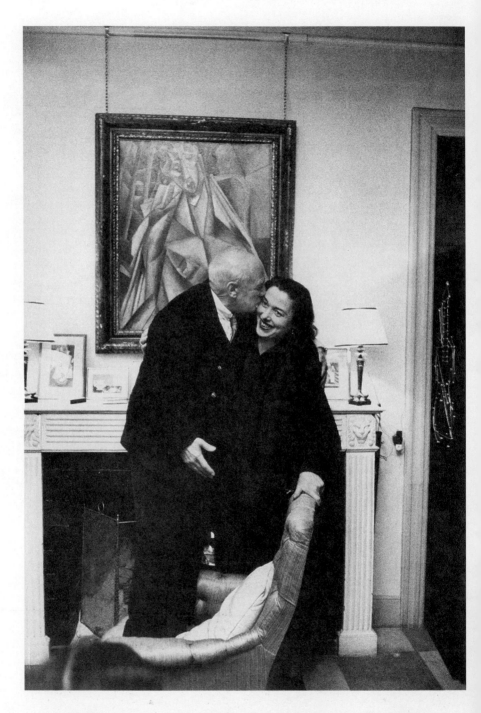

Picasso standing on a chair to kiss Lauretta Hugo in front of his 1909 Nude Woman in an Armchair

were severe restrictions regarding currency and the export and import of works of art. Moreover, French red tape proved even worse than the British variety. Douglas spent most of the next week seeing local lawyers or telephoning London ones. We were lucky in that I had an old friend in the neighborhood, Lauretta Hugo, sister of London's last greenery-yallery dandy, Felix Hope Nicolson—"the Squire of Chelsea," as he came to be known. Lauretta, who was as tall and statuesque as one of Picasso's classical goddesses, had married Victor Hugo's great-grandson and was in the process of bearing him numerous children. Jean Hugo was a tall, famously seductive patriarch with white hair *en brosse*, eyes as commanding as Casanova's, and a fondness for those wide-wale corduroy suits that artists like Courbet and Cézanne used to wear. His exquisitely crisp and delicate watercolors of Provençal life deserve to be much better known than they are; likewise his no less crisp and delicate memoirs. Jean and his ever-increasing family lived some thirty miles to the west of Castille at Lunel in the sprawling, romantic Mas de Fourques, where he produced a delicious dessert wine, Muscat de Lunel, which had been a favorite of Louis XIV. Alas, the family no longer makes it.

Jean dispensed hospitality in the seigneurial style of his forebears. Disdaining the weekend as a vulgar, modern concept, he urged his friends—among them Cocteau and Bérard, Marie Bell and Louise de Vilmorin—to settle into Fourques for weeks or months at a time. Jean Bourgoing, the inspiration for one of Cocteau's doomed *Enfants Terribles,* stayed for years until he finally became a Trappist. Tramps were never turned away, but fed in the kitchen and bedded down in one of the barns. Cocteau, who spent part of the war at Fourques, told me he once found a gigantic tramp installed in one of those miniature cottages known as "Wendy houses," where children play at being grown-ups. The tramp looked like Gulliver, Cocteau said: one foot stuck out of the front door, the other out of a window. Smoke rose from the chimney; he was baking a hedgehog in the little grate.

I had never been to Fourques before, and was intrigued by the antiquity of the modern conveniences: for instance, Jean's Model T Ford, which was about to function again, courtesy of one of Henry Ford II's wives, who had commandeered the necessary spare parts from the museum at Dearborn. Oil lamps looked anything but out of place in the chintz-hung bedrooms lined with Victor Hugo's demonic drawings.

The bathrooms dated back at least a hundred years: antique geysers fueled with *sarments de vigne* that terrified me as much as they would have kindled the spirit of a pyromaniac. I loved the moment at dusk when there was a sudden strange din as of flags or sails unfurling and, one after another, the peacocks would fly up into the great cedar tree to roost. Traditionally, the garden of every Provençal *mas* swarmed with peacocks. "They will destroy your roofs and decimate your garden," Jean said, "but if you are going to live at Castille, you have to have them." And so he had his gardener catch a male and a couple of peahens for us so that we could start up our own flock. Within a couple of years we had a horde of them, much to the delight of Douglas, who seemed to identify with their shrieks and showing off and wanton havoc. Grousset, the one-legged farmer who lived at the bottom of our drive, regarded them as vermin and set his dog on them. The dog killed one peahen, wounded another, and slaughtered ten chicks. Jean duly replaced them.

Dinners at Fourques were as ceremonious as they would have been a century earlier. If a priest was present—and one often was—grace would be said. Certain other precepts had to be observed: that nobody should ever rise from the table during a meal was the most stringent. Telephones could ring, children scream, peristalsis strike: *you had to stay put.* Jean would never even rise to his feet to carve the massive roasts—a *gigot* supplied by the shepherd, a goose from the farm, very occasionally a peacock from the garden—which were set in front of him. He would deftly slice them sitting down. One evening, Basil, the Hugos' mad Russian chef, raced into the dining room brandishing a knife. Nobody stirred. "I'm afraid he's b-been at the v-vodka again; he's p-perfectly harmless. The B-Bolsheviks were absolutely b-bloody to him." Lauretta's breathless stutter never sounded more reassuring.

Basil turned out to be more dangerous than anyone had thought. One day in December 1956, Lauretta telephoned to say that he had had an attack of homicidal mania. He had tried to kill the housekeeper, but Jean had overpowered him. Somehow Basil had wriggled free, climbed onto the roof, and tried to throw himself off. Once more he was overpowered; once more he escaped, and tried to kill Jean, who again managed to get the upper hand. Meanwhile, an ambulance had arrived, but before it was possible to force him into a straitjacket, Basil had run off yet again. He was finally found, stark naked in a flower bed, jabbing himself with a knife, and apprehended. "We can't p-possibly have him back," Lauretta said, "so I have to do all the c-c-cooking."

Jean opened a lot of local doors to us. So would his Amazonian sister, Maggie, who had another great property closer to the Camargue; and his half-brother François, the silversmith, who would later (at Douglas's and my behest) do a line of silver dishes for Picasso; also François's Italian ex-wife, the beautiful Maria de Gramont, who used to tell us how wretched she had been as a duchess, and how she had scandalized Paris by going to a fancy

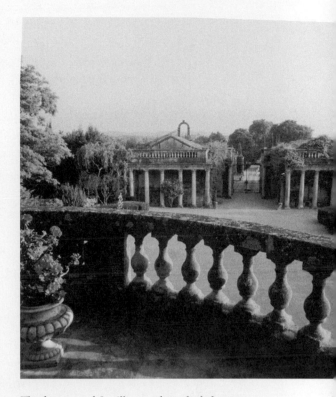

The forecourt of Castille, seen from the balcony

dress ball, when in mourning, all in black, as John the Baptist's executioner, with Jean Hugo and the Prince de Chimay in drag as Herodias and Salome.

Everyone seemed to know about Castille and wanted to help us restore this "sleeping beauty" to life. And not just the locals, either. Diana Cooper told me that she and her husband, Alfred Duff Cooper, had thought they might buy the château and retire there. Douglas soon found important strings to pull; as usual he would pull on some of them so hard they snapped. Our most powerful connection was with the local senator, Suzanne Crémieux, a handsome woman of great allure and down-to-earth good sense, who had been born a few miles from Castille. Suzanne and her newspaper-owning husband, Robert Servan-Schreiber, owner of *L'Express* and a financial journal called *Les Echos*, had established themselves at the Château de Montfrin, most stately of neighboring houses. And it was there that we met all the wheeler-dealers of the department of the Gard. For many years Suzanne had been the *égerie* of the Socialist Party, also, supposedly, the mistress of various prime ministers and presidents—hence her vast clout. She took the cause of Castille to heart, and was a tremendous help with local authorities. Douglas adored Suzanne, and because he was slightly in awe of her, he behaved impeccably when she was around. We also had a very good time with her brilliant daughter, Marie-Claire, but saw much less of her after she followed her mother's political bent and married a former prime minister, Pierre Mendès-France. With Suzanne on our side Douglas felt much more sanguine about the project, and we went back to London to await the closing.

A month or two later we returned to sign papers, apply for residence permits, and comply with other formalities. As soon as the house was ours, we sent for the local dowser. His little stick got very excited conveniently near the kitchen. "No problem," he said. "Dig here and you'll find all the water in the world." No problem? After a few days' work, the *puisatier*, the well digger, had to be brought to the surface, asphyxiated: all he had discovered was carbonic gas. There was a further problem: the local village was called Argilliers for the good reason that the neighborhood was situated on a layer of *argille* (clay) of unknown depth. We would not find water, we were told, until we reached the aquifer below the clay. Our best bet was to drill an artesian well—something that nobody in the locality had done. Lightning struck the drilling equipment twice, but at ninety-six meters—just within the hundred-meter limit that we had set ourselves—we reached the aquifer and found enough water to supply two villages. We immediately set about making plans for the restoration of the house. Estimates from masons, plumbers, electricians, carpenters, poured in. How about a fountain? I asked. Douglas snarled.

In his enthusiasm for all things French, Douglas had assumed that this unspoiled valley of the Gardon would abound in traditionally trained craftsmen—gifted local artisans who would look and talk and carry on as earthily as characters out of a Marcel Pagnol movie. No such luck. Apart from ourselves, few outsiders had as yet chosen to settle in this backward neck of the woods, let alone rebuild a tumbledown château, so there was little demand for any but the most basic construction work carried out in

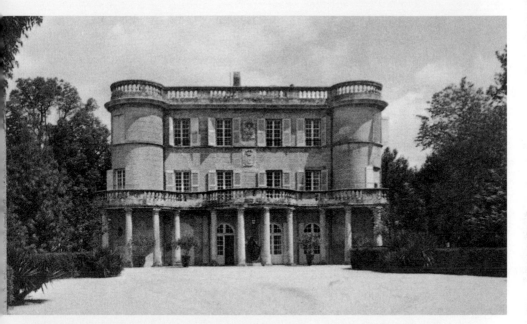

The principal façade of Castille

cheap, ugly materials. To replace weathered Roman roof tiles, we had to go to antique shops: the ones from the local *tuilerie* were too garish and low-tech to use. Same with the hardware. In the wake of the war, the English had adopted the inappropriate word "utility" to denote the poor-quality, badly designed things we were obliged to use. French products were not even up to "utility" standards. When the mistral set doors and shutters slamming, bolts and doorknobs would rattle to the floor. The craftsmen to whom we entrusted the run-of-the-mill restoration work did their sheepish best, but, as Douglas liked to point out, their best was not something in which they, or for that matter their clients, could take the slightest pride. We warmed to the gnarled old rogue of a carpenter: "At least he looks the part," Douglas said. "Let's hope he knows his trade." But when the beams in a new ceiling started to sag because they were made of unseasoned wood, the carpenter had to go.

Shortage of money was another problem. Currency regulations compounded Douglas's tightness. True, he sold his only nineteenth-century painting, a beautiful Courbet of a sleeping woman, as well as his only old master, a French primitive of Saint Roch, to raise extra funds.

But he still insisted that we keep costs to a minimum. Since there was no question of selling any of the cubist pictures, I suggested that Douglas take out a bank loan, the better to do justice to this handsome house. Against his principles, he said. I had to fight to get inexpensive, local stone (*pierre de Vers*) instead of "terrazzo" tiles for the salon floor, but was unable to persuade Douglas to buy anything but the cheapest appliances: rickety plastic shower stalls, a water heater better suited to a bungalow, a refrigerator fit for a doll's house, and, worst of all, a fortissimo toilet that was plugged to the hear-through floor above my study. I did not mind showing guests the not very comfortable *chambres d'amis,* as they were filled with Klees, Légers, and Mirós, but I was ashamed of the one and only guest bathroom, which looked as if it cost even less than it did. Douglas had decreed that central heating could wait, so for the first years we had to depend on coke stoves, which required constant tending and were no match for the mistral.

Douglas likewise economized on the decor. If in the end the rooms had an unpretentious, low-key look that worked with the paintings, it was because I had scoured the junk shops of Avignon and Nîmes for bargains and come up with massive bits of simple provincial furniture of the same period as the columns. I paid for a few of the things, but my funds were limited. Apart from a tiny trust fund from my father, which brought in around $500 a year, the pittance I earned doing prefaces to art books and reviews for the *Times Literary Supplement* was all I had. This was just enough to cover my personal expenses and help out my mother, not enough for me to contribute to the running of Castille. That would be Douglas's responsibility. If I had had the money, I would have splurged on a set of twelve enormous, eighteenth-century *pots d'Anduze* (glazed terra-cotta urns) complete with fully grown orange trees. They cost "nothing"—two hundred dollars each—and would have made the whole difference to our wilderness of a garden. I begged Douglas to buy them. "Certainly not, I'm only buying things I regard as necessities," he said. But give him his due. When he splurged, he splurged with a vengeance. From one of Ambroise Vollard's heirs he bought Renoir's great, life-size bronze, *Venus Victrix,* to put outside the front door. Nearsighted locals spread a story that we had a black maid who went naked.

We spent most of the winter of 1950–51 at the Magnaneraie, a modest, family-run hotel with a garden on the outskirts of Villeneuve-lès-Avignon, a half hour's drive from Castille. Out of season there were very few visitors; it was quiet, and we had the place more or less to ourselves. The rooms were spacious, but the food was simple without being at all good. One day we found a small, newly opened restaurant called La Petite Auberge, a few kilometers away at Sauveterre on the Rhône. The owners, a retired businessman and his wife, were determined to fulfill a fantasy of running a three-star restaurant, and they devoted all their resources and energies to this end. Although their food was sublime, their clientele was as yet minimal. To help keep their business going, we arranged to have all our dinners there. Night after night, the young chef would try out his repertoire of dishes on us; night after night, the restaurant remained virtually empty. Even Douglas was touched. Fortunately, the proprietors' perseverance would soon be rewarded. Within a year or two they got their first star in Michelin; then they moved to larger premises and were awarded even more stars. Fifty years later, La Petite Auberge at Noves is one of the most celebrated restaurants in the region. I still look back on our exquisite dinners with gratitude. They compensated for the freezing days we had to spend in the mud and mess of Castille, supervising the endlessly frustrating *travaux*.

Moving house is said to be one of the most traumatic things in life, but to give Douglas his due, he was remarkably patient with me; he took his rage out on everybody else. Successive sparring partners included the patron of our hotel, who could not abide him, the mason who failed to lay a stone floor to our specifications, the postmistress who supposedly listened to our calls, and most of all the "ghastly peasants," who had temporarily replaced the "ghastly English" as targets for his rage. And it is true, the "ghastly peasants" were difficult, but how could Douglas expect them to be anything else? From the very start he had treated them as if they were his serfs, hectoring them about their hens, accusing them of poaching rabbits in our little wood, telling them where to park their farm vehicles, claiming that the driveway down to the road belonged to him and not them. The ongoing feud over ownership of the drive ultimately culminated in a lawsuit, which solved nothing and made matters much, much worse. Far from trying to defuse this resentment, Douglas derived an infantile kick out of exacerbating it. Rightly or wrongly, he attributed the narrowness and suspiciousness of the locals to their Cathar ancestors, fundamentalist heretics who had imposed their

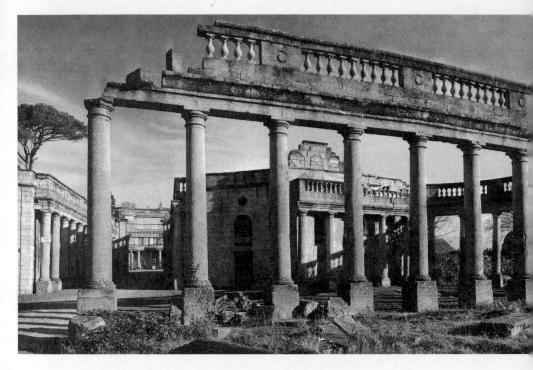

View of Castille from the surviving section of the peristyle

joyless doctrines (three lents a year, and the notion that matter is evil and man an alien sojourner in an evil world) on much of this area some seven hundred years earlier. "Too bad the Inquisition is out of business," Douglas once said. "There are a lot of heretics I'd like to burn." I, on the other hand, was terrified of these inimical people. I would anxiously try to placate them with nervous nods and smiles, which were acknowledged laconically, or with a gob of spit in the dust.

My fears were not entirely without cause. A summer or two after our arrival, a ritual murder had caused panic in the neighborhood. An adventurous English couple called Drummond, with two young children, had gone camping in a particularly primitive area of *la haute Provence*. They had set up their tent half a mile or so outside a small village. Needing water, the father had gone to the local well, but had been refused access by the villagers. After an altercation, he had returned with a bucket and helped himself. For this offense against the commu-

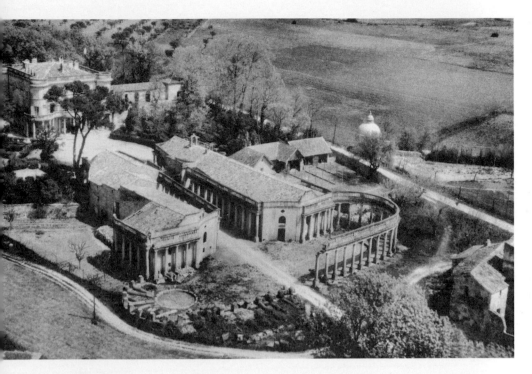

Aerial view of Castille

nity, a village patriarch called Dominici decreed that the Drummonds be ritually killed. Dominici and his sons were soon apprehended, tried, and convicted in a cause célèbre at Aix-en-Provence. The Dominici affair left me very scared. Childish, I know, but as I saw it, Douglas was far guiltier than the unwitting Drummonds of offenses against local susceptibilities, and might well bring vengeance down on our heads. As long as I lived at Castille, I was terrified of this atavistic malevolence, which had never, it seemed to me, been entirely exorcised. On returning home, I was always in dread of finding the guard dog poisoned or the house on fire, or, as happened after I left, the place burgled. And then there would be the time Douglas was stabbed almost to death in the hills above Nîmes. I don't believe I ever spent a night alone in the house.

In the course of this endless winter, we returned to London more than once to make inventories and supervise the packing of Douglas's paintings and books as well as some bits and pieces and family things that I had accumulated. Douglas had even relented and acquired a few goodish pieces of furniture—notably an imposing suite of white and gold Empire chairs and sofas—in keeping with Castille. It was also necessary to help Basil with replacements for the numerous works from Douglas's collection, which had left his walls in a shambles. The handsome Braque still life, Monet harbor scene, early Matisse interior, and 1908 Picasso nude that we found seemed to appease him. Basil behaved with his accustomed saintliness, and showed no sign of the resentment he must have felt.

There was one tedious formality with which both Douglas and I had to comply—for our sake as well as the French nation's. We had to go to the French consulate to have our inventories stamped *"import temporaire."* This meant that for the next fifty years Douglas and I would have the right to take our works of art and other possessions in and out of France as we chose, without paying export taxes or risk having things blocked by the greedy Musées Nationaux. *Import temporaire* was of little significance so far as my things were concerned, but of vast importance to Douglas, as it would allow him to move his paintings around and sell them if he wanted to. In 1949 the collection was already worth around $10 million, but today, judging by the $200 million fetched by the far smaller Ganz collection in 1998, it would be worth almost half a billion.

Twenty-five years later, Douglas's vainglorious pride would bring about the very thing he most feared: the cancellation of the *import temporaire* arrangement, despite the consular guarantee. Douglas would trigger this disaster by pressing an important friend of his, Michel Guy, to visit Castille. This was tempting fate: Guy was Minister of Culture, and in France, sensible collectors are apt to conceal their treasures before letting the Minister of Culture into the house. Douglas showed Guy everything he had, and, sure enough, the minister was so impressed by the sheer size and quality of the collection that on his return to Paris he promptly and most unfairly arranged to have the half-century dispensation, which foreign residents had hitherto enjoyed, reduced to twenty-five years.

That was the end of the friendship with Michel Guy. Douglas switched his rage from England to France. And he forthwith embarked on a campaign to get the new regulation—"aimed specifically at me, my dear"—rescinded, at least in his case. According to Douglas, this could be arranged only if he donated the rarest and most valuable of his Picassos, the great 1907 *Nudes in the Forest*—the equal of which did not exist in France—to the as yet unopened Musée Picasso. Douglas reluctantly agreed to this quid pro quo arrangement, but it soon unraveled. Douglas went and wrote one of his famous *lettres d'injures* to his new friend President Pompidou, saying in effect how much he regretted relinquishing the most precious of his pearls to the swine in charge of the museum— swine to whom Pompidou promptly forwarded his letter. It would be up to Douglas's heir to renegotiate the deal.

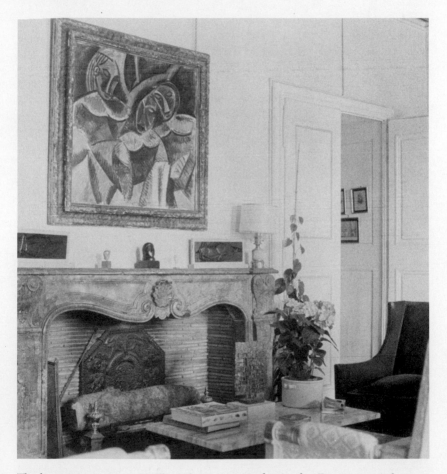

The front sitting room at Castille, with Picasso's Nudes in the Forest *(1907), later given to the Musée Picasso*

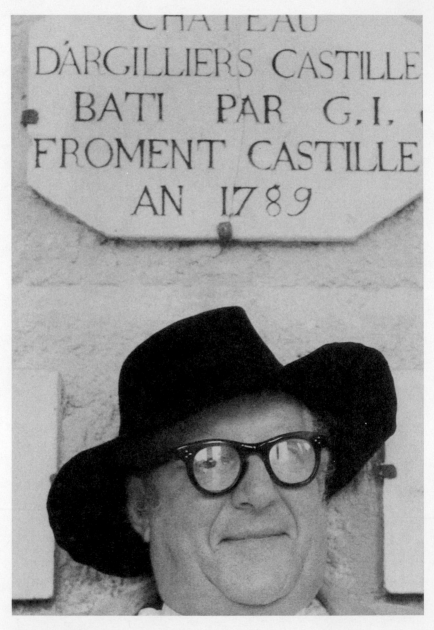

DC at Castille, ca. 1970

MISCREANTS, PETS, AND NEIGHBORS

Shortly before moving into Castille, we had gone to Paris in search of servants and found a seemingly suitable couple, Gaston and Marie Desvignes, with a young son, Jacky, who would attend the village school. Marie turned out to be the perfect person for the job. She was plump, red-faced, feisty, and energetic, and she worked like mad, fifteen hours a day, seven days a week. She cooked simply but well, served the meals, did most of the housework, kept stoves going and sheets ironed. To help her out, we brought in girls from the village, but they were never up to her standards. As she herself was something of a tyrant, Marie approved of Douglas's tyrannical ways; she also stood up to him. She loved me like a son; I loved her like a nanny, also for sharing her cooking skills with me, including her secret for really crisp *pommes frites:* fry them in horse fat. Guests loved them, but I never let on about the horse fat.

The sturdy, fifty-year-old husband—a butcher, who supposedly wanted to switch to domestic service—turned out to be a rogue as well as a drunk. In those days the law entitled servants to several liters of wine a day. The entailed buying wine by the barrel and bottling it ourselves. The job left Gaston little time for his other duties beyond looking after the pig and rabbits and chickens and pigeons that he had landed us with. We had no better luck with our first gardener. Someone had told us to apply to the Foreign Legion's demobilization base for an ex-legionnaire. Douglas liked the idea—"maybe he can wear a képi with a flap down the back and guard the place"—so we drove off to the barracks at Fréjus to interview possible candidates. Douglas had envisioned a glamorous black sheep like Gary Cooper in *Beau Geste.* No such luck. We were

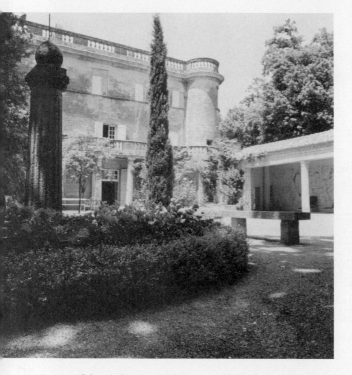

Corner of the garden at Castille

presented with an assortment of criminal types from the ratholes of Eastern Europe: they looked as if they might have been guards at Treblinka or Auschwitz. We chose the wretch who had the cleanest record, and took him back to Castille with us. He was white as a maggot, with small dead eyes set much too deep and much too close together. Oulnik, he was called, and I was terrified of him. So was Marie. His skills were limited to the ax and the chain saw and the disposal of debris. The day after Douglas fired him, Marie served us a dish of zucchini. It tasted bitter, so we sent it back to the kitchen. Marie did not eat it, nor did Oulnik; those that did were quite ill. Weedkiller, Marie said.

I briefly took over as a gardener. Knowing nothing as yet about Provençal horticulture, I limited myself to clipping away at the overgrown box hedges in a futile effort to discover the original topiary layout. What I did come upon was a mysterious bush seemingly alive with tiny, iridescent green beetles. These turned out to be cantharides. Having read in some lubricious novel about the aphrodisiac effect of taking a rest in the shade of one of these shrubs, I returned a few days later, for a siesta, but by that time the cantharides had devoured the bush and flown away. No sooner had we found a skilled gardener than Gaston became a major problem. His drinking took the form of *folie de grandeur*. He thought he was the Baron de Castille. He cooked the household books and spent the proceeds on presents for people he met in local bars and wanted to impress. He also gave *us* presents—vast, unbreakable vases like fairground prizes. In the face of Douglas's wrath, Gaston fled. It transpired that he had swindled a lot of local people and there was a warrant out for his arrest. The police found him at Toulon and brought him back to face charges at Avignon. His jail sentence was a great relief to Marie and her son, Jacky, who wanted only to be rid of him and stay on with us. They became our family.

A year or so later, we had another brush with criminality. While Douglas was away in America, someone telephoned to ask whether he could bring an art student to see the collection. I said yes; in due course, two utterly forgettable people came by. And then, a few months later, Douglas received a call from the art student's father—a doctor or lawyer we had never met—warning us that his son had run away from home with a friend, and that the two of them had been overheard planning an armed robbery of Castille. Douglas was not the least bit concerned, but Marie panicked and insisted we arm ourselves. For the first time in my life, I went to bed with a gun. After the gardener found a large bag (empty except for a white silk mask) in the garden, we took the matter more seriously. We handed the bag over to the police, and they arrested the culprits a day or two later. They had indeed been armed—with a machine gun—and had indeed tried to raid the house, the night before we received the telephone call, but had been driven off by our watchdog. They had hoped to steal enough pictures to finance a trip to South America. Oddly enough, Douglas did not want to prosecute them: "I'm all for enterprise in the young," he said. He should have paid more heed to this warning. Although his collection had become one of the most valuable of its kind in the country, he never installed burglar alarms, or proper locks on windows, shutters, and doors. Fifteen years later, when more professional robbers struck, Douglas would rue his negligence.

Our local town, Uzès, once a stronghold of some importance, seemed to have fallen fast asleep. The pride it took in being the premier dukedom of France had contributed to its eclipse. Out of fear that their feudal peace might be blighted by progress, the dukes of Uzès had refused to allow the diabolical railroad to come near their territory.

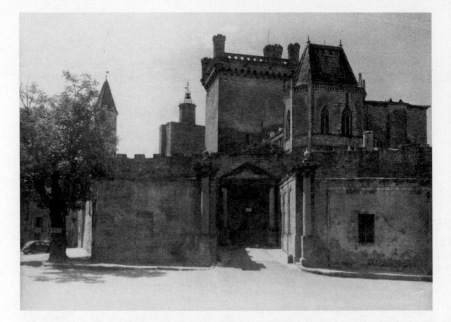

The Duché at Uzès

The handsome town had thus remained a sleepy, smelly backwater. Meanwhile, the ducal family—traditionally a source of patronage—had gone virtually bankrupt. This was largely the fault of Duchesse Anne d'Uzès. Despite literary and feminist pretensions, she had squandered millions of gold francs on studs, stables, hunting lodges, and packs of hounds, and millions more on her lover, General Boulanger, and his disastrous coup d'état—which had triggered his suicide on the grave of yet another of his mistresses. The duchess's dissolute son, Jacques d'Uzès, wasted most of what was left as well as the family jewels on a courtesan, Emilienne d'Alençon, who did conjuring tricks with rabbits. To save him from total ruin, his mother exiled him to Africa, where he died of enteric fever.

By the time we arrived in the neighborhood, the dukes of Uzès had long since shaken the dust of the Duché off their boots. To reguild his escutcheon, not to speak of his bank account, the current *duc ruiné,* Emmanuel, had married a Standard Oil heiress called Peggy Bedford. The marriage had not prospered; the duke opted for Morocco, where the local women were to his taste. Thirty years later, I came upon him in Marrakesh, helping out at the Villa Taylor, Boule de Breteuil's elegant *pension*. For lugging my bags to my room, I gave France's premier duke a tip, which he accepted as a condemned man might accept a cigarette from an executioner.

On the outside, the Duché had remained an impressive medieval fastness, its roof emblazoned with the family's coat of arms in polychrome tiles. On the inside, little of interest or beauty survived. The place had been taken over by the duke's cousin, the Marquis de Crussol, who had married a sardine heiress. The marquise's attempts at refurbishment were denigrated by people who cared about such things. But what else would you expect, they said, from *"une sardine qui s'est crue sole"* ("a sardine who thought herself a sole"—a pun on the family name)?

History seemed about to repeat itself when the son of the marquise decided to marry an American heiress. Douglas and I were invited to an engagement party in a neighbor's Paris apartment. The salon was hung with a collection of eighteenth-century drawings, each of them hidden behind little silk curtains. To protect them from the light? No, to draw attention to their coyly suggestive imagery: effete rakes groping saucy servant girls; naked ladies wagging their bottoms at periwigged doctors clutching clysters. The heiress had good reason to look embarrassed. The nobleman that her family had picked out for her was as vapid as any of the louts in the drawings; and her fusspot mother would insist on tying and retying an enormous bow around her waist. This Edith Whartonish scene—new American money to the rescue of baddish, bluish blood—was the more intriguing in that the girl was clearly too bright and independent to go through with this outmoded charade. Sure enough, nothing came of these *fiançailles*.

Our local telephone service depended on the mood of the village postmistress, who went off duty early in the evening. So we were at the mercy of the mail. Since Douglas was a voluminous correspondent—the sight of his manic, cursive scrawl in bright blue ink on sky-blue envelopes would make pulses race as much with anticipation as with foreboding—there was a mass of outgoing as well as incoming mail.

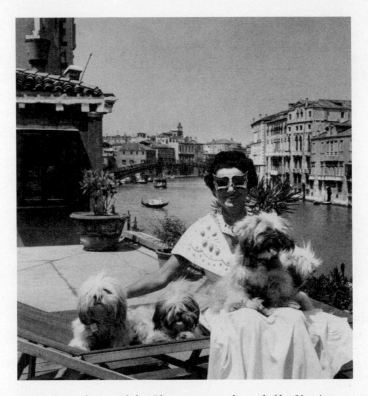

Peggy Guggenheim with her Lhasa apsos on the roof of her Venetian palazzo

And our days revolved around the midmorning arrival of the postman and our late-afternoon walk with the dogs to the post office.

The dogs had been Peggy Guggenheim's idea. In the course of one of our annual visits to her Venetian palazzo, she had decided that something had to be done about Douglas's "vile disposition." It was getting out of hand. She had always thought of him as a friend, but he had written an article denouncing her collection as of interest only insofar as it reflected the modish taste of a mid-twentieth-century American millionairess. Hard knocks had left Peggy with skin as thick as an elephant's—proof against snubs and slights, not to mention rejections—but Douglas had hit her in her raison d'être, her collection, and this had really hurt. With some justice, she attributed Douglas's sneers at her expense to competitiveness; also to homosexual misogyny and bitterness—traits of which she had too often been the victim. "I am furious when I think of all the men who have slept with me while thinking of other men who have slept with me before" is one of several similar *cris du coeur* in her memoirs. Peggy had the perfect cure for Douglas's condition: a dog. "It will bring out the mother in him," she told me. Next time we went to Venice, she presented him with one of the offspring of the famous Lhasa apso that she and her former husband, Max Ernst, had acquired when they were married. The dogs had done wonders for Max's meanness, she said.

Douglas became childishly fond of the dog—Bella was her name—and to that extent she kept him in a goodish mood. In due course he decided that Bella should have puppies. A sufficiently well-bred husband was found. Douglas paid a sizable stud-fee and promised the breeder one of the litter. But there was only one puppy, and Douglas was damned if he was going to relinquish it. The irate breeder sued. Douglas enjoyed that—it quickened the pace of country life and provided yet another outlet for his rage—so he kept the matter on the boil as long as he could. All I remember is that I ended up with the puppy, which I called Jacko—a nickname my father had occasionally bestowed on me—in memory of a favorite monkey.

The dogs loved the daily walk to the post office; so did Douglas, who would be at his best—radiantly happy at the turn his life had taken, at being king of his own little castle. The post office was only a couple of miles away, but we frequently took a roundabout route up into the *garrigue:* the dry, scrubby uplands that take over where cultivation stops and are endemic to the hills back of the Mediterranean from Andalusia to Anatolia. The *garrigue* has superb acoustics. Since there was little traffic on the dusty roads around Castille, distant country sounds—the whack of a carpet being beaten, the rattle of a bucket going down a well on a chain—sounded clear as a gunshot. The cry of a hoopoe to the right, the bleat of a sheep way over on the left, gave the wilderness an added sonar dimension as well as a twinge of the melancholy that lingers on in the wake of an echo in that wonderfully clear air.

Bella and Jacko went crazy in the *garrigue*. They may have looked like animated mops, but they tried vainly to behave like coursers, and would chase anything that moved and come back exhausted, with nothing for their pains except coats bristling with burrs and thistles.

Inevitably they were resented by the locals, who regarded pets as pests. Bella and Jacko did not kill rats or mice; they could not herd sheep; they were not *chiens de garde* or gun dogs; and they were certainly not truffle hounds. Worse, they disturbed game birds in the hunting season; worse still (more money was involved), they bothered the truffle hunters.

Truffle hunting was a very serious, very secret business. Uzès was a major center. Every winter there was a thriving truffle market there—on Saturdays in January and February. Most years we would buy several kilos. In 1955 truffles were fantastically cheap, around fifteen dollars a kilo, and we bought seven kilos. Since the sacks would usually include a lot of earth and leaves and grit and the occasional dud, Douglas and Marie and I would sit around the kitchen table, separating the treasure from the dross. Each of us would take a nail brush and scrub the truffles clean; it took hours, but the wonderful leaf-moldy smell was inspirational. We would set aside the biggest and best truffles to eat that very night, *sous la cendre,* wrapped in dough and baked in the ashes of a wood fire. The remainder would be preserved in Madeira or port, or taken to a local cannery and sealed into small cans with a dollop of white wine. One year our harvest amounted to two huge jars of truffles in Madeira and two others in port, as well as twelve smaller jars and some fifty cans. By the end of the year we would have given many of the *bocales* to Picasso or Braque, Nicolas de Staël or Graham Sutherland— as some return for the drawings and prints they gave us. Meanwhile we would have consumed the rest in omelettes and scrambled eggs, inserted under the skin of a boiling fowl (*poularde demi-deuil*), or stuffed into *pieds de porc,* as well as in any number of pâtés. On special occasions we would have truffle soufflé or soup.

Since the hills back of Castille were so rich in truffles, I was tempted to go hunting for them until I found out what an arduous and tricky process this was. Experienced hunters do not necessarily need a dog or a pig. They know exactly where to search—configurations of three or four mangy ilex saplings on bare-ish patches of *garrigue,* whose location they keep to themselves—and what to look for: columns of small yellow flies hovering at dawn or dusk in these promising spots. People with a highly developed sense of smell are said to be able to sniff out truffles. Less olfactorily sensitive hunters rely on a meat-fly in a matchbox. When released, the fly supposedly alights on the spot where truffles lurk a foot or so below the surface. This method requires an infinite supply of meat-flies and the sharpest of eyes. To mark the place where they have found truffles, hunters plant a combination of seeds known only to themselves; that way they can easily find the same place the following season. Cultivation used to be a matter of luck and patience, and for all I know still is. If soil from a truffle area is spread on calcareous ground and ilexes are planted, truffles should start to materialize after four or five years, but it is by no means certain. And then there is always the likelihood of poachers getting to them first.

On our walks in the *garrigue* we would sometimes come upon men with truffle hounds: skinny, miserable-looking brutes worth a fortune. Training these dogs is long, cruel, and costly. They are starved almost to death, then fed minute quantities of truffle until the smell becomes obsessive. Pigs were seldom if ever used in our area, but that did not stop Marie's drunken husband, Gaston, from deciding that we should get one. He thought he knew someone who would help him train a pig to hunt truffles. If it failed in its duties, we could always eat it. Douglas loved the idea. A pig was acquired forthwith and installed in one of the colonnaded outbuildings. "Such an economy," Douglas said. "We'll not only have free truffles, we'll have free hams." Sheer fantasy! The only thing Gaston knew about a pig was how to slaughter it and butcher the meat. He could not wait to show off his prowess. For a month or so, we ate little but pig—muzzle to tail to trotters. Nothing was left but bones. Gaston's home-curing was a disaster: the hams turned out to be too salty to eat.

When I returned to Uzès a year or two ago, this backwater had transformed itself into a thriving tourist attraction with *antiquaires,* and shops selling lavender bags and folksy artifacts carved from olive tree roots. A further sign of local renewal was the plethora of newly renovated old buildings and fancy restaurants in nearby villages that had never even had a café. Avignon, too, had changed out of all recognition. It was now a sophisticated cultural center, whereas in our day, for all its beauty and its reputation for licentiousness that went back to the Middle Ages, the city was a disappointment: stifling and touristy in the summer and dreary and provincial in the winter. Over the principal public lavatory was a huge sign, STATION DE DÉCROTTAGE, which Picasso remembered from before 1914. Local society kept to itself in the shuttered

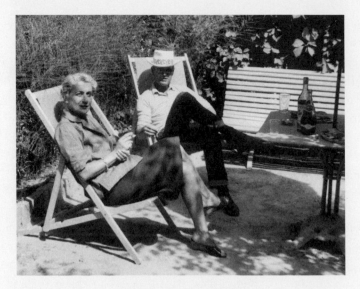

Suzanne Barnier and JR at her farm outside Nîmes

rooms of *dixhuitième* mansions hidden away on tree-shaded backstreets. At a dinner in one of these houses I remember being served a great dish of *alose*. *Alose* is French for shad. Because it had become almost extinct in the Rhône, it was considered a great local delicacy. Douglas saw to it that we would never be asked back again by informing the hostess that the Hudson River swarmed with *alose* and that most of the Americans he knew ate only the roe.

More fun was to be had in the company of Avignon's one and only couturier, the delightful Jean Sully-Dumas, who had resisted pressure from Christian Dior and other *confrères* to make a name for himself in Paris. He preferred to stay close to his local roots and practice his métier on the Avignon ladies. He did so exceedingly well. Jean's muse and model, a beautiful local girl called Eliette, helped him give small, memorably entertaining dinners. Unlike her boss, Eliette went on to greater things. After working as a model in Paris, she married Herbert von Karajan and developed into a celebrity to be reckoned with.

As I was already cataloguing Picasso's portraits, I went around asking people for information about a legendary whorehouse—said to be the most lavishly appointed outside Paris—that had supposedly inspired Picasso's *Demoiselles d'Avignon*. Don't bother, Picasso said, the reference to Avignon was just a joke. However, there was something in Avignon that might be worth tracking down. He told me that when he lived there in 1914, he had always used the same *fiacre*. The driver had asked him to paint a sign advertising FUMIER À VENDRE (manure for sale); and he had come up with a colorful cubist placard, embellished with pointillistic flourishes. "By now it must be worth a fortune," Picasso said, and told me exactly where the stable had been. I made some inquiries, but after forty years the trail had gone cold.

Although we were forever driving into Avignon to meet trains, buy food, frame pictures, browse the antique shops, or wait around while guests toured the Palais des Papes, we ended up finding most of our friends in Nîmes. This came about through our friendship with an adorable Nîmoise called Suzanne Barnier. Besides being the wife of a local landowner who supplied us with most of our wine and the best black Muscat grapes I ever tasted, Suzanne took us under her wing and helped us solve all manner of practical problems. She also introduced us into Nîmes society: progressive, for the most part professional, people— among them her lawyer-brother Paul Carcassonne—who made us feel like honorary Nîmois. Douglas, a linguistic chameleon if ever there was one, even started to tell Marius jokes in a Raimu accent.

Nîmes had more vitality than Avignon. Originally colonized by the veterans of Augustus's armies, the city had been one of the richest of Roman Gaul. Hence its noble classical buildings, among them that miraculously preserved Roman temple, the Maison Carrée; the spectacular second-century A.D. arena where we regularly attended bullfights; and Agrippa's Pont du Gard, which had supplied the city with water. Sacked by Vandals and Visigoths in the Dark Ages, Nîmes became a republic protected by Pépin the Short and a slew of other "protectors," before being absorbed into the kingdom of France. By 1558, three-quarters of the population were Protestants, most of them active in the textile trade. They killed off a great many Catholics, but the Catholics got their own back when the Edict of Nantes was revoked in 1685. Nîmes also had a thriving Jewish community—descendants of Sephardic Jews expelled from Spain by Ferdinand and Isabella. The mix of cultures worked perfectly and kept the place lively and free of chauvinism. The acceptance accorded to two such intruders as Douglas and myself was a measure of this freedom of spirit.

Besides our beloved Suzanne, we saw a lot of a fascinating couple, Jean and Mimi Godebski, known locally as "les God." Jean—a painter of sensitive, self-effacing views of the Camargue—was the son of a Polish sculptor, Cipa Godebski, as well as the nephew of Cipa's sacred monster of a sister, Misia Sert, the flamboyant patron of vanguard art and music, who had been a close friend of Toulouse-Lautrec, Renoir, Bonnard, Vuillard, Debussy, Ravel, Stravinsky, Cocteau, Diaghilev, Nijinsky, and heaven knows who else earlier in the century. Jean was anything but proud of his celebrated aunt, and as I had once been taken to visit her in her ornate apartment on the rue de Rivoli—all mulberry-colored velvet and rock crystal, dud El Grecos and bits of good Boulle—I could see why. Misia was overwhelmingly awful and, according to Picasso, always had been. By the time I met her (1947), she was on her last legs, totally addicted to morphine, which she obtained through her morphinomane attendant, a heavily made-up waif of a man called Boulos Ristelhueber. The two of them seemed to have moved, ahead of time, into one of hell's grander suites. When she died, Misia left Jean and his numerous family nothing. Everything went to Ristelhueber. Jean did not allow his chagrin to show.

Jean's wife, Mimi, came from a very different background. She was the last of one of the most distinguished local families, the Comtes de Bernis, and she and Jean and their *famille nombreuse* lived in the enchanting Hôtel de Bernis, on the rue de Bernis in the old part of Nîmes. In the salon hung the rather too imposing portrait of Misia by Renoir, which Misia had left to Jean's sister, and she had passed on to him. It did not exactly break Jean's heart to sell it. I owed a lot to "les God." On one occasion when Douglas was being difficult, they took me in; and when I finally left Castille, they adopted my dog. Jean was great company. I will never forget our timeless rides around the Vaccarès. He would evoke the *haute bohème* of his youth: the gentleness of Ravel, who wrote the *Mother Goose Suite* for him and his sister when they were kids (how cross Misia was that they couldn't play it for him), the enchantment of life in his father's house on the Seine, and the fun he had with Vuillard, who painted so many of his lamplit interiors there.

The most prominent family in Nîmes were the four Colomb de Daunant brothers. The one we knew best was the eldest, Edmond, a hospitable bachelor who lived—indeed still lives—in a large mansion attached to an even larger *serre:* a botanical-garden-sized conservatory full of magnificent palm trees, where he makes his guests feel very honored to have been invited. Another brother, Denys, an authority on the Provençal tradition of bullfighting, made that beautiful film *Crin Blanc,* about the wild white horses of the Camargue. Denys married a granddaughter of the Marquis de Baroncelli, a leading light of the Félibrige, the society that the great local poet Frédéric Mistral had founded to protect the Provençal language, traditions, and folklore. Such was Baroncelli's passion for the bulls and horses of the Camargue that he neglected his considerable properties in Avignon and went to live in a reed-thatched cabin on an island in the Vaccarès, surrounded by the herds of white horses on which he doted. Denys Colomb perpetuates the spirit of his wife's charismatic grandfather. I recently read somewhere that he had finally installed electricity in his austerely handsome house, Le Mas de Cacharel; otherwise he continues to live and dress much as people did in the days of Baroncelli.

Another Nîmois friend of ours was a burly, half-Russian charmer called Jean Lafont. He was a *manadier,* a breeder of bulls for the village *cockades*—mini-bullfights in which nimble boys in white T-shirts and pants vie with each other to seize a rosette from between the horns of specially bred bulls. Since these bulls are not killed, they become ever more wary and aggressive, and many of the boys get badly gored. Besides bulls, Jean collected chairs—lots and lots of them (preferably nineteenth-century Gothic ones) —and trees. He had a mini-arboretum at his romantically run-down, fancifully decorated ranch (shades of Madeleine Castaing) in the depths of the Camargue. He also collected cowboys. The ranch was a lifetime gift from his admirer Marie-Laure de Noailles—someone whom Douglas and I had known before we knew each other. Since moving into Castille, we saw a lot of her, as she spent much of the year in her house at Hyères.

Marie-Laure was one of the most paradoxical women I ever met: spoiled, generous, sly, fearless, manipulative, impetuous, bitchy, affectionate, childish, maddening, and, not least, extremely cultivated. She was the only child of an enormously rich Belgian banker, Maurice

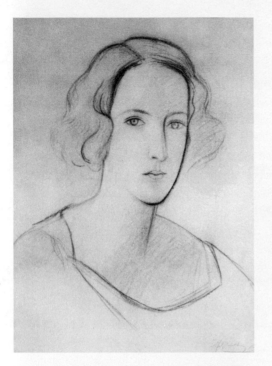

Picasso, Marie-Laure de Noailles, *black chalk,*
1923

Bischoffsheim, who had died when she was eighteen months old. As well as golden, the spoon in Marie-Laure's mouth was prodigiously crested. Her mother was the daughter of the Comtesse de Chevigné (Proust's consummately aristocratic Duchesse de Guermantes) and the great-great-granddaughter of the Marquis de Sade. Marie-Laure had originally contemplated marrying Jean Cocteau, but Proust supposedly suggested that the Vicomte de Noailles would be more suitable. And, it is true, he epitomized the *gratin*. Besides an aristocratic manner, he had impeccable taste in works of art and garden design. He was also, in his distant way, far nicer than most of his peers. In certain other respects he was not unlike Cocteau. Early in their marriage, Marie-Laure had caught the Vicomte (as she always referred to him) in the arms of his gym instructor. She never reproached him; she simply told most of their friends. Thenceforth, they tended to live under separate roofs or at opposite ends of her enormous Paris mansion, not out of any ill feeling—they loved each other and telephoned or wrote every day—but out of a need to lead separate lives. In the 1930s, Marie-Laure had a passionate affair with Igor Markevitch, a handsome, somewhat feral-looking composer and conductor who had been the last great love of Diaghilev and would later marry Nijinsky's daughter. Markevitch cost Marie-Laure so much money that her vast fortune had to be put in the hands of trustees. She continued to fall for good-looking young musicians. At the height of the war she eloped to Evian with a faun-like cellist called Maurice Gendron. They foolhardily took a boat across the Lake of Geneva to Switzerland, where they were promptly arrested and incarcerated in a detainment camp. According to Cocteau, Marie-Laure had to peel the potatoes, while Gendron cleaned out the latrines. After they were repatriated, she did something even sillier: she took up with an Austrian officer.

When I first met her, Marie-Laure was having an affair with a gifted American illustrator, Tom Keogh. Unfortunately, Tom's wife, Theodora, was sleeping with Marie-Laure's chauffeur, Baca, which made the quartet's *cinq-à-septs* difficult to schedule. On the side, she fussed over a bevy of good-looking young musicians, and seems not to have minded that they were mostly homosexual. One of her clique told me that he loved her not just for her generosity and hospitality but for her wonderfully responsive ear and eye and phenomenal memory for English and German as well as French verse. Whether or not she went to bed with her *éphèbes,* Marie-Laure bonded with them and seems sometimes to have felt challenged to outdo them in outrageousness and promiscuity. Ned Rorem, the handsome American composer who lived in her house for seven years, portrays her to perfection in his absorbing Paris diaries.

Marie-Laure did not age well. It was not just that she looked like Louis XIV: she looked like a pregnant Louis XIV—a consequence of a large abdominal cyst that she never bothered to have removed. In the 1950s, she took up with a man of surpassing ugliness, Oscar Dominguez, a satchel-faced surrealist painter from the Canary Isles, whom she called Putchi. Mean people claimed that Oscar was not as nice as he looked. This was true to the extent that he was a bad drunk and anything but scrupulous in his dealings, but I was touched by his desperately clumsy attempts to make his mark—attempts that made not the slightest dent in the icy hearts of *le tout Paris*. Oscar was Marie-Laure's "Elephant Man."

Douglas and I used occasionally to stay at the Mas Saint-Bernard, which the Noailles had constructed on a great spread of medieval ruins on a hillside above Hyères. They had originally approached Mies van der Rohe and Le Corbusier to design a simple Riviera villa but had finally settled for Mallet-Stevens, a designer of film sets, who came up with an enormous house in a modernist style rather too tainted with art deco. There were beautiful exterior spaces—a triangular garden laid out like a checkerboard, with windowlike openings in its walls, a sculpture garden, a rooftop with an open-air bedroom by Pierre Chareau—but the house

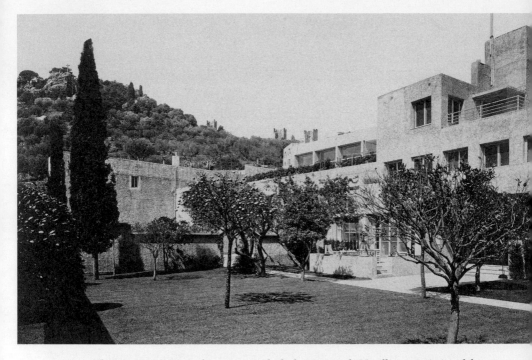

The Mas Saint-Bernard (1923–33), which the Vicomte de Noailles commissioned from Mallet-Stevens

itself resembled the superstructure of a ship, and, notwithstanding its considerable scale, the rooms, especially the bedrooms (of which there had originally been forty), were too cabin-like for comfort. According to Jean Hugo, the Vicomte had originally run the house as if it were a liner and he were the captain issuing orders to a crew of footmen. During the war, the house had been used as a hospital and had subsequently fallen into disrepair, not least the famous swimming pool where Marie-Laure told me she had done her laps on foot, clutching dumbbells to keep herself at the bottom of the pool. The Vicomte, who had financed Dalí and Buñuel's sacrilegious movie *L'Age d'Or*—much to the scandal of the Catholic Church and, worse, his fellow members of the Jockey Club— fancied himself a *cinéaste,* and used the pool as a setting for a 1928 thriller, *Biceps et Bijoux,* which he had also sponsored. A year later, he had Man Ray do an experimental film about the Mas Saint-Bernard, inspired by a famous Mallarmé poem. It was called *Les Mystères du*

Château de Dés. Man Ray had everyone in the house don the dark shorts and striped tank tops that the Noailles issued to their guests, and pull stockings over their faces to give an air of erotic mystery to the scenes in the gym and the pool.

The war had left the Mas Saint-Bernard diminished—in scale as well as allure. Reinforced concrete patinates unattractively. Instead of looking as crisp and white as a lighthouse, it looked a bit grubby, in contrast to the flag emblazoned with the Noailles coat of arms that fluttered feudally above the roof. However, the paintings—Picassos, Braques, Légers, Mondrians, Max Ernsts, and much else—were as impressive as ever. The food was well chosen, and so, except for poor old Oscar, were the guests. Marie-Laure could not abide fools, and her wit and erudition and outrageous flights of fancy brought out the best—as well as the worst, if enough drink had been consumed—in the musicians and writers and luminaries of *la haute pédérastie* she surrounded herself with. Their merciless laughter would have to compete with the braying of the hugely hung donkey—Marie-Laure's notion of a suitable pet—which she kept tethered in the garden below the guest rooms.

After one of our visits to the Mas Saint-Bernard, Douglas and I drove on to see Picasso. He had turned against Marie-Laure. He had recently seen her at a bullfight, he said, and she had looked exactly like Goya's hideous Queen Maria Luísa. Apropos of the famous pass that Marie-Laure had made at him—"You be Goya and I'll be the Duchess of Alba"—Picasso said that she should have cited the Queen of Spain instead. He denounced Oscar for faking his work so flagrantly, but put much of the blame on Marie-Laure. He said that Oscar suffered from acromegaly (an enlargement of the bones of the head, which presses on the brain), and should not be held accountable for his misdeeds. Marie-Laure had no such excuse, he said. She had to be aware of what her "Putchi" was up to.

At the time I could not believe that Marie-Laure did not know. Two years later, when I went to see Klaus Perls, the New York dealer, I realized that she did. Perls had proudly shown me a small cubist Picasso he had recently acquired. When I told him it was a fake, he said it couldn't be: it came from the Noailles collection. Sniff it, I said, you can still smell the turpentine—evidently a recent job. It was easy to work out what had happened. After arranging for Oscar to sell the original to

Heinz Berggruen, Marie-Laure had had him make a copy to hang over her bed in place of the original. That way the Vicomte would not realize it had been sold. And then she had decided to put the copy on the market. According to James Lord's book *Six Exceptional Women,* she had originally asked *him* to sell the fake painting for her. James had offered it to Heinz Berggruen, and was horrified to find that he owned the original. He concluded that Oscar was selling Marie-Laure's paintings and replacing them with copies that he had made; and he describes how embarrassed he was at having to tell Marie-Laure that her lover was swindling her in this way. It never occurred to him that the two of them were in cahoots. Having failed to sell the fake in Paris, Marie-Laure next tried New York. This time she used a jewelry designer called Baron von Ripper, to whom she owed some money. "Jack the Ripper," as he was known, had been given the painting in lieu of cash. Outraged at the deception, Klaus fired off a letter of remonstration to Marie-Laure. Instead of apologizing, she wrote back saying that she should never have been such a fool as to throw her pearls before swine. Her arrogance was going to cost her dearly, Klaus said. How she extricated herself from this mess I never discovered.

On New Year's Eve, 1957, Marie-Laure asked Oscar and a Chilean friend, Tony Gandarillas (a charming opiomane diplomat who had played the drag role of Baroness von Bülop in Cecil Beaton's spoof memoir, *My Royal Past*), to join her for a small festive dinner. Oscar never turned up. Telephone calls went unanswered. They assumed he had passed out. It was not until the next day that he was discovered to have committed suicide by cutting his wrists and ankles in the bathtub. Jean Godebski, who had known Marie-Laure forever, called to tell Douglas the news; also that she had insisted on having Oscar buried in the Bischoffsheim vault in Montparnasse. She was shattered and lonely, Jean said, but he had the perfect solution for her—Jean Lafont. He and Mimi were going to drive Jean over to Hyères the following day and hand him over to Marie-Laure. An inspired idea. Jean proved to be much to her taste. He was sexy and virile-looking, and he liked women as much as, if not more than, most of the men in her life did. But, as the Godebskis well knew, Jean was in possession of a no less important key to her quirkish heart. He had always wanted to follow in the footsteps of Baroncelli and live in the Camargue. Marie-Laure turned out to have a romantic passion for the Félibrige—a passion she had inherited from her mother. The Vicomte approved of Jean, and saw to it that he became the owner of the oldest *manade* in the Camargue. Marie-Laure also gave Jean the wonderful library that had belonged to her mother and stepfather, the playwright Francis de Croisset, who is said to have been the origin of Proust's Bloch. I cannot forget the last time I saw her, somewhere in the Camargue. Marie-Laure was dressed in the flower-sprigged costume of an Arlésienne. She had a cigarette stuck to her lower lip and carried a small, folkloric basket. The effect was odd but authentic.

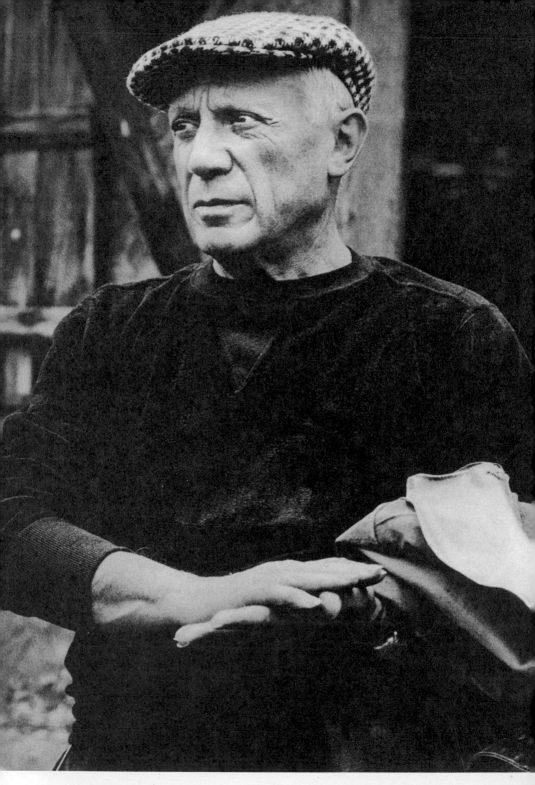

Picasso at Le Fournas, 1953

A TRIP WITH PICASSO

No sooner were we installed at Castille than Picasso dropped by with his son Paulo, who was acting as his driver, to take a look. He liked the place enough to ask whether we would sell it to him—or, failing that, whether he could come and work there, as he was fed up with the pokey little house at Vallauris. He then drove on, probably to Perpignan in French Catalonia, where he was courting an attractive married woman. Come back to Vallauris, he said, I have a lot to show you. Off we went, a month or so later. This must have been in the late summer of 1952. Claude Picasso, who would have been five years old, tells me he remembers our visit—for the sort of disparaging reason that only a child remembers. Douglas and I were wearing shorts. "People who came to see my father," Claude remembers, "wore long pants. We thought it impolite of you to wear shorts. Not that my father cared."

As a future biographer, I could not have entered Picasso's circle at a more propitious moment; the last of the many marital metamorphoses that gave form to his life was under way. Would this one follow the pattern of what Douglas and I had come to think of as "Dora's law"? The astute and perceptive Dora Maar, Picasso's mistress before Françoise, had become a neighbor and friend, and in the course of discussions about her life with the artist, she let us in on her theory that when the woman in his life changed, virtually everything else changed: the style that epitomized the new companion, the house or apartment they shared, the poet who served as a supplementary muse, the *tertulia* (group of friends) that provided the understanding and support he craved, and the dog that rarely left his side. Some of these changes would occur more gradually than others, but sooner or later they would

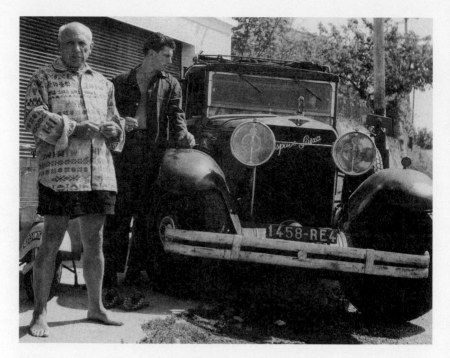

Picasso with his son Paulo beside his vintage Hispano-Suiza, 1953

all come to pass, as Douglas and I would find ourselves well placed to observe.

Picasso seemed preoccupied; things were not working out with Françoise. Paulo, his thirtyish son by his first marriage, hovered around, waiting to see whether *"le père,"* as he always referred to his father, needed to be driven somewhere. Paulo was tall and redheaded: a cross between his Russian mother and his distinguished-looking Andalusian grandfather—nothing whatsoever like his father. Picasso regarded him more as an indentured servant than a son, and it must be said that, apart from chauffeuring, there was little else for which this hapless lover of cars and motorcycles was suited. For his part, Paulo treated his father with a touching mix of loyalty, discretion, and dignity in the face of constant paternal censoriousness. Since Picasso's devoted chauffeur, Marcel, had smashed up his prized Oldsmobile and been summarily fired, Paulo had been driving *"le père"* all over France in the family's prewar Hispano-Suiza: to bullfights at Nîmes and Arles, dinners at Castille, and trysts with women as far afield as Vichy, Fontainebleau, and Perpignan. On this particular morning, Picasso let Paulo go off to carouse with his cronies while he took us down to Le Fournas.

Picasso had a fetish for keys. A key in a centrally placed drawer in a cubist still life invites us to turn it so that we can probe the space and touch the objects. A phallic key in the door of a beach cabana hints at the intercourse that is about to take place inside. A front-door key in the hand of a new mistress coming in from the outside symbolizes her entry into the artist's life and the mysteries she is going to encounter there. And, sure enough, at the epicenter of the Fournas complex was a closet filled with a mass of rusty keys of all shapes and sizes to the sheds and closets, the nooks and crannies, in which Picasso had locked away not only his treasures but the rubbish from which other treasures might one day be made. Apart from Picasso, the only people with access to the keys were a couple of close friends: Edouard Pignon, the Communist painter who had started life as a coal miner, and his Polish wife, Hélène Parmelin (immortalized by Picasso in a couple of spaghetti-haired portraits). The Pignons were spending the summer in Le Fournas's dilapidated attics. "Whitewashed walls blackened with spider's webs," as Hélène recounts in *Picasso sur la Place,* her wonderfully evocative book about this phase of the artist's life. Their host allowed them to use all the keys but one. "Bluebeard's little key," he called it, and it opened the door to the studio, which he had set aside for two huge *War* and *Peace* panels. These were destined for a deconsecrated medieval chapel in the center of Vallauris to be called the Temple de la Paix. Because the Temple de la Paix would inevitably be seen as a riposte to Matisse's chapel at Vence, which had been inaugurated the previous year, Picasso was working on the panels in greatest secrecy. No one, not even Françoise, was allowed in to see them; the only exception was Paulo, who could be trusted to take no interest in what he had seen and never talk about it. Did the artist perhaps sense that the *War* and *Peace* panels would attract a barrage of hostility when they were exhibited at Milan the following year?

Instead, Picasso showed us a group of less portentous, more mocking denunciations of war: images of medieval pageboys dressing up in their masters' baroque armour and going off to battle on caparisoned horses. He had wanted to denounce the medieval grotesquerie and nasty childishness of war, he said. An offshoot of these *Jeux de Pages* was an

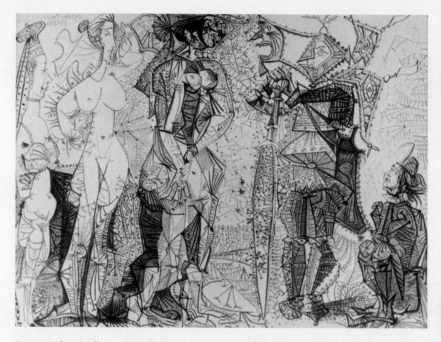

Picasso, The Judgment of Paris, *pen and ink wash, 1951*

elaborately worked-up drawing of a warrior (Picasso in the guise of Paris) encased in ornate armor, confronted by three primping women. We would soon discover how self-referential this was. And then, all of a sudden, an iron-faced matron with the tin-pot air of a village post-mistress bustled into the studio as if by right. Picasso did not look pleased. This turned out to be the famously awful wife of his potter, Georges Ramié, proprietor of the Atelier Madoura, where Picasso made his ceramics. Ramié was a nice enough man, but his wife, Suzanne, was what the French call *"une fausse bonne femme."* Beadiness and calcula-tion belied the cordiality of her shopkeeper's smile. She wanted to be absolutely sure we visited her showroom, where she did a thriving busi-ness marketing copies of Picasso's originals. Suzanne hung around in the hope that Picasso would let her accompany us to the shed that served as storage for his huge holdings of ceramics, but she was out of luck. A sharp look from the artist, and off she swept.

Picasso's ceramics, I had priggishly persuaded myself, were a waste of his time and genius. But then I had not seen any of the originals except in Skira's portfolio of overvarnished reproductions. All I knew firsthand were the multiples churned out by the Ramiés, who seemed to be profiting from Picasso's idealistic desire to make at least some of his work available to the masses. Seen in their hundreds on shelves as dusty as the ones in Tutankhamen's tomb, the one-of-a-kind pieces that he had kept back for himself were a revelation. They bore the same relationship to his sculptures that his drawings bore to his paintings. They were not so much ceramics as *bozzetti*. In this ramshackle shed, many of them had the mysterious look of fertility or funerary figures, or fetishes. I had yet to learn that as a very young man, Picasso had been influenced by Gauguin's mystical approach to earthenware sculpture: If God could make man out of a bit of clay, why couldn't an artist? Years later, I would dis-

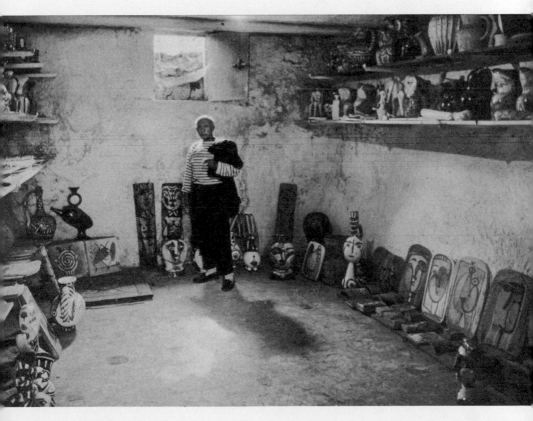

Picasso with his ceramics at Le Fournas, 1952

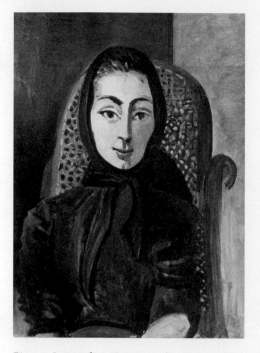

Picasso, Jacqueline Roque, *oil on canvas, 1954*

cover that Gauguin's Basque disciple, Paco Durrio, had been Picasso's ceramics teacher in the early years of the century and had told him of the Cabalistic belief that a lump of clay can be transformed into a golem. However, even without the knowledge of Picasso's earlier involvement with pottery, I instinctively felt that some of the figures in this eerie space—notably a group of terracotta Françoises—had the force, though little of the semblance, of tribal art. Picasso would seldom if ever exhibit them, and if he sold almost none of the great pieces, it was because, like most of his sculptures, they were too talismanic to put on the market.

Henceforth, Douglas and I would get together with Picasso every two or three months, either at Le Fournas or at Castille, where he liked to dine after the *corridas* at Nîmes or Arles. On one of these occasions, in the early fall of 1952, he introduced us to a new attachment: a small, dark, striking twenty-seven-year-old girl with enormous eyes, called Jacqueline Roque, who had lived until recently at Ouagadougou, the capital of Burkina Faso, with her husband, a French colonial official. Bored with the husband as well as Africa, she and her young daughter, Cathy, had settled in a villa at Golfe-Juan called Le Ziquet. Jacqueline had found work at the Madoura shop, replacing the Ramiés' pregnant daughter-in-law as a salesgirl. Hence a rumor that she was Madame Ramié's cousin or niece—a rumor that Madame Ramié encouraged and Jacqueline vehemently denied. Picasso's entourage took a dim view of the new girl—"*Elle n'est pas à la hauteur de la tâche*" ("She's not up to the job"), one of them had said—but I had an immediate rapport with her, and over the next eighteen months of intrigue on the part of her

rivals and their sponsors, we grew extremely fond of one another. I came
to see Jacqueline as far and away the most suitable consort for Picasso—
the right size and shape, extremely submissive and supportive, and
obsessively in love with him. So would Jean Cocteau, who would come
back into the artist's life as his poet laureate after Paul Eluard's death in
November 1952.

In July or August 1954, Curt Valentin, Kahnweiler's New York representative and Picasso's U.S. dealer, suffered a fatal heart attack while
being sculpted by Marino Marini in his Forte dei Marmi studio. Douglas
had been very fond of Curt, and invited his bereft mistress, a well-
meaning but maddening Czech woman called Gertrude Lenart, for a
consolatory weekend at Castille. It was the weekend of one of the year's
big bullfights at Nîmes or Arles. Gertrude cheered up no end when she
found we had seats next to Picasso and his entourage. This included his
son Paulo, and Paulo's attractive new girlfriend, Christine; his nephew
Xavier Vilató; Totote and Rosita, the widow and daughter of Picasso's
friend the Catalan sculptor Manolo; the Pignons; and, of course, Jacqueline. After the *corrida,* we organized a riotous dinner at Castille,
enlivened by the presence of Cocteau and his entourage as well as some
of the bullfighters and their *peons.* Despite his horror of death, Picasso
was ironically attentive to Gertrude. He, too, had liked Curt. Embold-
ened by this, Gertrude was about to launch into the macabre details of
Curt's demise—there had been portents: to Marino's terror, the clay
head kept slipping off the armature—when Douglas shut her up with a
sharp kick. The story was just the thing to put Picasso in a state of superstitious panic.

After the bullfight, Picasso decided not to return to Vallauris and
the debris of his relationship with Françoise, but instead to take the road
in the opposite direction and head for Perpignan. For the umpteenth
time that year, he and his group were going to stay with Totote's patrons,
the Comte and Comtesse de Lazerme, who had a handsome *hôtel parti-*
culier in the old part of Perpignan and kept open house for painters and
writers. Picasso invited Douglas and me to join him on the trip. He
promised to help us console poor Gertrude, although by this time poor
Gertrude was chatting away like a road drill—no longer inconsolable.
What is more, he would take us to Céret, where he and Braque had
reached the apogee of their cubist collaboration forty years earlier, and

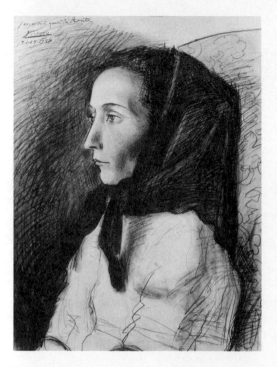

Picasso, Rosita Hugué, *black chalk, 1954*

show us where he had painted the 1911 *Clarinet Player* that was the pride of Douglas's collection and now belongs to Baron Thyssen. What is more, there would be a bullfight, after which we would all dance the sacrosanct Catalan *sardana,* which Picasso liked to demonstrate: "A communion of souls," he told Brassaï, "it abolishes all distinctions of class . . . the servants hand-in-hand with their masters."

On the road we stopped for lunch at a bistro. At the end of the meal Picasso folded and tore and then unfolded the paper tablecloth; it had been transformed into friezes of dancers and dogs. Each of us was given a bit of it; only Gertrude had the foresight to get hers signed. Then on we went to Perpignan, where Picasso proudly introduced us to the Lazermes and their seventeenth-century mansion, with its fifty rooms built around a courtyard. A number of these rooms had been set aside for the artist, but by the end of the summer, when his entourage had swelled from ten to twenty or thirty friends, family members, and retainers, there would be mattresses all over the house. Douglas and I took rooms at a nearby hotel and our meals with the Lazermes. A wise precaution: most of the participants in this spur-of-the-moment jaunt turned out to have a vested interest in supporting or, better still, being the successor to Françoise Gilot. At dinner that night there was a lot of tension. It struck me that the courtly masque on the theme of *The Judgment of Paris,* which we thought we were watching, was turning into a farce along the lines of *Bluebeard's Eighth Wife.* The change of cast predicted by Dora Maar was already under way, but who would be given the apple?

Picasso enjoyed the tension; so did Totote Hugué, whom the artist had taken to calling *La Celestina*—a reference to the celebrated procuress of Spanish fiction, after whom he had named his greatest Blue Period portrait. Totote, a former barmaid who was about the same age as Picasso and had known him for almost fifty years, certainly looked the part: gravel-voiced, conniving, and so tall and gaunt that she only appeared to have any volume, Picasso claimed, when she was holding a broom. This latter-day Celestina had taken it upon herself to find a replacement for the wayward Françoise. For some time now she had been pushing two candidates at Picasso: her adopted daughter, Rosita, a taciturn,

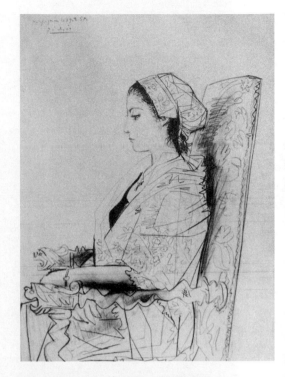

Picasso, Paule de Lazerme, *black chalk, 1954*

squawlike girl who was said to have Gypsy blood and appeared to have stepped out of one of Lorca's tragedies; and Jacques de Lazerme's young wife, Paule—a classic Catalan beauty—as unspoiled and enticing as one of Balzac's provincial heroines.

Patrick O'Brian, the historical novelist turned Picasso biographer, who was also a friend and neighbor of the Lazermes, claims that Picasso had always been very fond of Rosita, but his fondness now turned to "so ardent a desire for her uninterrupted company that it was apparent to his friends . . . that Rosita, by giving him the slightest encouragement, could become Madame Picasso." That may have been the way things appeared to the Lazermes. I had a very different impression. In the first place, as most of his friends knew, Picasso had no intention of marrying anybody so long as his first wife, Olga, whom he had never divorced, was still alive; otherwise he would have to forfeit half his property to her. As for Rosita, he certainly enjoyed talking in Spanish to her and indulging in a kind of teasing, tongue-in-cheek flirtation so as to keep her mother's expectations simmering. However, to us and above all to Jacqueline, Picasso made sardonic jokes out of the other side of his mouth about the girl's lack of allure. Douglas attributed this behavior to the proximity of the frontier: "The nearer he gets to Spain, the more sardonic he becomes."

As for Paule de Lazerme, Totote's pimping had worked to the extent that (to quote Françoise Gilot) "Picasso was flattered to feel that he was attractive to such a charming and handsome young woman." She and her husband had been traveling all over the place with Picasso: back and forth to Vallauris, to bullfights, even to Paris. As a result, Françoise was not alone in assuming they were having an affair. Why else would Picasso have done such loving portraits of the comtesse in Catalan costume? Why else would he have given her such a magnificent gold necklace—a succession of bull's masks linked by a chain of bull's bones—which he had cast with the help of the Vallauris dentist, Dr. Chataignier: "the only person I know who works in gold," he said.

Was Paule's nice, gentlemanly husband one of those men who enjoy being cuckolded by celebrities? I don't think so. Jacques de Lazerme turned out to be consumed with local piety. Perhaps because he had no children, he had focused his passions on his book collection, which covered the whole gamut of Catalan culture and filled the shelves and tabletops of his handsome eighteenth-century library. Like his pride in his Catalan wife, Jacques's pride in his Catalan books had rubbed off on Picasso, who gave little grunts of excitement as he came upon memorabilia of the all-but-forgotten painters, poets, and musicians he had known when he lived at Céret. A special bond between them was the memory of Totote's irrepressible Catalan husband—"the greatest *blageur* I ever met," Picasso said. Manolo was probably the only person Picasso had ever permitted to mock him, criticize him, or contradict him. No execution squad would have been able to kill Manolo, Picasso claimed; he would have had them laughing too hard. Too bad that his anarchic high spirits went into mischievous pranks rather than work. Manolo's Maillol-like sculptures are disappointingly academic—lacking in the temperament for which he was so famous.

As promised, Picasso took us to Céret. There we were joined by another of his oldest friends, Frank Burty Haviland, the half-French, half-American painter who had lured Picasso to Céret forty-three years earlier and now seemed determined—if anyone so frail and shadowy could be described as determined—to persuade him to return to French Catalonia on a more permanent basis. Local authorities were rumored to have offered Picasso a fortress or château in the neighborhood, in the hope of inducing him to do for them what he had done for Antibes, when he turned the Château Grimaldi into a tourist attraction by filling it with his *Antipolis* paintings. The artist seemed to be as

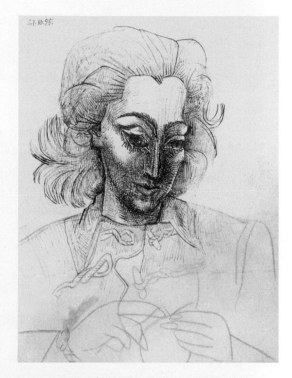

Picasso, Jacqueline Knitting, *pen and ink, 1955*

undecided about moving back to the Roussillon as he was about everything else at the turning point. Fond as he was of the region, he did not strike me as being overjoyed at the thought of returning to the scene of past triumphs, especially under the auspices of the town's Communists, who had political reasons for luring him back.

For Picasso, the proximity of Spain was as painful as it was pleasurable. This became all too clear one afternoon when we drove to the frontier town of Port Bou and stopped at a café that faced into Spain. While the rest of us sat under a tree drinking pastis, Picasso walked off to the end of the terrace and stood still as a sculpture for ten minutes or so, glowering at the beloved country, a few hundred yards away, which he had been unable to visit for almost twenty years and would never visit again. When he rejoined us, he looked older and colder—wizened with anger and frustration. We went back to the Lazermes' house in heavy,

heavy silence. That evening he took his feelings out on Jacqueline—a sign, I suspected, that he was testing her nerve and her resolve. I felt sure that she was the one he would choose.

We returned to Castille the following day, leaving Jacqueline with a lot more ordeals to endure before becoming Picasso's official mistress. She was at a disadvantage in that Paule de Lazerme had decreed that she and her daughter could take their meals with the Lazermes, but had to put up at a local hotel. In Jacqueline's place, Picasso moved his nineteen-year-old daughter, Maya, into his bedroom, according to O'Brian, for "his loneliness had bitten deep and he hated to be alone, especially at night." It was only when Maya left toward the end of August that Jacqueline, who was on her own now that she had sent her daughter to a *pension* in the mountains, was allowed to move into Picasso's room. Two nights later, a blazing row broke out between the two of them. Patrick O'Brian tells the story in some detail. Jacqueline "came down to breakfast much upset, wondering whether she should go or stay." Receiving little encouragement to stay, she drove off back to Golfe-Juan. Every hour or so she would stop and telephone and ask to speak to Picasso. He did so reluctantly. By the time she got to Béziers, she had worked herself up into a suicidal state. If she was not allowed back to Perpignan, she was going to kill herself. " 'She can do whatever she likes, so long as she leaves me in peace,' " Picasso said. In the evening, Jacqueline returned: " 'You told me to do whatever I liked; so here I am.' " Picasso took her upstairs. When they reappeared some hours later, he was in more of a rage than ever. "During the next weeks Picasso's attitude towards her was embarrassingly disagreeable, while hers was embarrassingly submissive—she referred to him as her God, spoke to him in the third person and frequently kissed his hands."

When I asked Jacqueline about these events, she said that the Lazerme house had become a snake pit, that Paule de Lazerme resented her and had done what she could to break up her romance, and that if Picasso was upset, it was primarily because Derain—a very old friend of his whom he had come to despise as a collaborator—had been knocked down and killed by a motorcar on July 14. According to Jacqueline, this rift had made Derain's death all the more painful for Picasso. What exactly did happen chez Lazerme? My own view is that Picasso was testing the limits of Jacqueline's devotion. This time around, he could not afford to make any mistakes. It was up to her to prove by the sheer force of her love that she was the best candidate for his hand. She knew that none of the other contenders had anything like her appetite for self-sacrifice. Sure enough, when Picasso returned to Vallauris at the end of the summer, Jacqueline had won out over the competition. She was the *maîtresse-en-titre* and would never leave his side until his death nineteen years later.

Before Christmas, Douglas and I drove up to Paris to do some shopping. One of my objectives was a present for Jacqueline. And at Christian Dior I found a large red silk wrap like a bullfighter's cape. This turned out to be the first sign of affection that any of Picasso's friends had shown her. She was touched; so was Picasso, to the extent of returning the box, as we will see, with a drawing in it. In a matter of months the formerly carping members of the artist's entourage would be vying with one another to find appropriate offerings for the new *inamorata*, but it was too late. "I had better beware of them," she said, "they are bearing gifts." In years to come, Jacqueline would make a point of wearing this wrap if Douglas and I were going to be present. It became a kind of talisman.

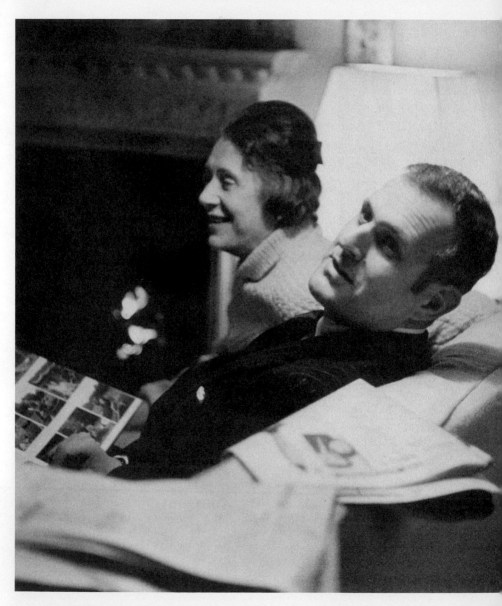

JR with Lil, ca. 1950

THE VISITORS' BOOK

Castille was only fifteen miles off Route Nationale 7, and so within all-too-easy reach of friends traveling from Paris to the Riviera (or, for that matter, from Switzerland or Italy to Spain). No sooner had we settled than we found we were running a hotel. Friends were curious to see our house. Many of them also wanted to visit the music and drama festivals that had popped up all over Provence: Avignon, Nîmes, Orange, Vaison-la-Romaine, Aix-en-Provence. That first summer (1952) our musical guests included the composer Benjamin Britten and the tenor Peter Pears. They had recently returned from a trip to Japan, where they had fallen under the spell of the Noh theater. Ben had been fascinated by the famous Noh scene in which a forlorn mother (played, of course, by a man), in search of a lost child, crosses a bridge in slowest possible motion, while making an exquisite show of stylized grief. This scene had left such a deep impression on Ben that he decided to write a Noh opera with Peter as the protagonist. Did we think this would work? Since Peter was tall, with large, well-defined features, I wanted to say no, but thought it more diplomatic to agree that Peter would indeed make a perfect Noh mother. Just as well I did. The resultant opera, *Curlew River*, was a triumph. (In New York in 1998, it was performed in tandem with the Noh play that inspired it.)

Although he was forever vilifying the House of Windsor, Douglas was delighted that same summer when another pair of musical luminaries, the Queen's first cousin George Harewood and his wife, Marion, paid us a visit. George's musicological expertise put Douglas in mind of his uncle Gerald Cooper, the Purcell scholar—the only member of his family in whom he took any pride. Douglas was all the more admiring of

George for the way he had assimilated the contents of Grove's exhaustive *Dictionary of Music and Musicians* while a prisoner-of-war at Colditz. "At last someone whose knowledge deserves the epithet *encyclopedic*," Douglas said. "Had the rest of the royal family been half as studious, I might never have decided to get the hell out of ghastly England."

Douglas also made many of my friends welcome to Castille, among them the aforementioned James Bailey—not exactly an easy guest. James liked to tipple away to the strains of *Turandot,* turned up full blast, while he mimed the mannerisms of the prewar divas—Caniglia, Gina Cigna, Marguerite Sheridan—whom he revered to the point of identification. James complained of having "blood rows" with Douglas, but deep down they were surprisingly tolerant of one another. To my delight, Douglas developed a great liking for another of my closest friends, the philosopher Richard Wollheim, and his first wife, Ann. Richard would prove to have one of the brightest and most protean minds of his generation, as his writings on art history and psychology as well as philosophy would confirm, and for over fifty years he has played a pivotal role in my life.

Another lifelong friend and a frequent visitor to Castille was James Joll, most cultivated of modern historians, whose knowledge of art and music and literature gives an added resonance to his historical studies. With his very fair hair, bright blue eyes, and reddish face, not to mention his spring-heeled gait, James looked as if he were about to "blow his top"—and indeed he sometimes did—but to those of us who knew him well, he was one of the wisest, kindest, most astute companions one could wish for. While staying at Castille in 1952 or 1953, James embarked on a romance with a fellow guest, a painter and student of art history called John Golding, whose thesis on cubism was being supervised by Douglas at Anthony Blunt's behest. Douglas was thrilled at his pupil's exceptional insights into a subject that had not as yet been done to death. He also took proprietary pride in having sponsored John's relationship with James—a relationship that would outlast the marriages of most of our friends.

Sadly, Douglas's admiration for John turned all too soon to resentment and pique. After opening up his memory and archives to him and overwhelming him with help, Douglas suddenly realized that his pupil was writing the definitive account of cubism that he should have been writing. And from one day to the next he went into reverse and did whatever he could to destroy John and his work. After trying and failing to deny his pupil his doctorate, Douglas made ferocious attacks on his thesis, when it was published, but as usual his brickbats boomeranged and left only their instigator discredited. Forty years later, Golding's history of cubism is still the standard book on the subject, whereas Douglas's contributions to cubist scholarship are mostly forgotten. James died a few years back, but John and I remain close friends. What happened to him would eventually happen to me. And as former comrades in arms do, we ruefully compare the psychic scars Douglas inflicted on the two of us and the pain and the glory they conferred.

The list of these early visitors would not be complete without mention of our up-and-coming-publisher friend, George Weidenfeld, who had recently married Jane Sieff, a Marks & Spencer heiress. Castille was one of several stops on their honeymoon. Jane's seriousness did her credit. She told us how relieved she was to have exchanged the social round dear to her mercantile family for the world of ideas, as represented by George. "Poor Jane has jumped out of the frying pan into the fire": Douglas's verdict proved all too prescient. She would soon leave George for someone less worldly.

In those days, ideas gushed from George in such profusion that most of my writer friends regarded him as a publisher-cum-impresario who would shape their careers. And indeed he soon had a number of highly important writers to his credit, among them Vladimir Nabokov, Eric Hobsbawm, and Saul Bellow, but the company of the rich and powerful exerted a gravitational pull he could not resist. Tycoons outnumbered writers at his gatherings. He once announced he was giving a party for me. I accordingly invited my mother and a few friends, but the party turned out to be in honor of at least one other person—a controversial moneyman—and the resultant gathering surpassed Strauss's *Ariadne auf Naxos* in its comical confusion. The plot of that opera, which hinges on the decision of a would-be patron of the arts to have the two entertainments that had been arranged for his guests (a tragic opera about Ariadne and a comic harlequinade) performed simultaneously, seemed to be a metaphor for George's social life.

For publishing books by prominent politicians and vigorously promoting Anglo-Israeli ties, George would be made a peer. Meanwhile, he was in the course of establishing himself as a social lion. Nobody else entertained on such a professional scale; nobody else cast such a wide-meshed net. At first, snobs held aloof, but most of them would soon join the throng in George's Eaton Square drawing room. Many a social figure would thrill to hear that she had a book, maybe even a best-seller, in her. After signing a contract, a friend of mine was taken aback at one of George's parties to find how many of her fellow guests had similar contracts. Few of these books materialized; besides being unable to write, socialites had little to say.

I have remained fond of George despite his occasional lapses of memory. For instance, in his memoir, *Remembering My Good Friends,* he describes me as "the son of a colonial official . . . educated at Westminster . . . [who] lived on his wits as a young man about town." As I described earlier, my father was a soldier; I went to Stowe and the Slade School of Art and later earned my living first as an industrial designer, then as a journalist. George goes on to describe a famous incident involving Picasso, as well as a farcical incident involving myself, as if he had been present. He was not, and in both cases misremembers.

In due course George asked Douglas and me to edit a series of artists' monographs, and each write one of them. I eventually dropped out. George struck me as too conceptual in his approach, more interested in fanciful schemes than the end product, actual books. Projects had a way of turning out to be mirages. Douglas would be luckier. Some years later he would have considerable success with his pioneer coffee-table books *Great Private Collections* and *Great Family Collections.* There was a bonus: entrée to some very grand houses.

George thought that our roster of London friends needed upgrading and diversifying. "You mean you don't know Princess so-and-so?" he said in a concerned voice. The only princesses Douglas knew were his sister-in-law and her mother. Apparently Albanians didn't count. George's concern gave way to dismay. He promised to lay on "some glamorous people" next time we came to London, as if he were Elsa Maxwell, Douglas said, and we were a couple of pushy bumpkins. However, to his credit and my eternal gratitude, George introduced me to two women whose friendship would be one of the joys of my life. One of them is averse to seeing her name in print; were she alive, the other would, I am sure, prefer to be known simply as Lil. Much to Douglas's rage, Lil would turn out to be one of my longest-lasting loves.

Like most upper-class women of her time, Lil was uneducated, but she had an inherently sharp mind and wit and an idiosyncratically forceful way of expressing herself that gave the simplest things she said— "Let's go for a walk"—an air of comical urgency. This was a refreshing change from the bantering archness and affectation of so many of her contemporaries. Lil loved men, but had not been lucky with them. Her first husband—one of the richest men in England—had been a tyrant; her second would be a toady and a bore. Because she was tall, good-looking, and forthright, she could seem daunting. In fact she was surprisingly vulnerable; she was also immensely good-hearted and great fun. When she divorced him in 1937, her first husband settled what seemed like a very generous income on her—£10,000 a year, tax-free—but when war broke out, tax-free settlements were disallowed and never reinstated. This left Lil what she described as "penniless," and she had to stoop to all manner of stratagems to make ends meet and pay for what she regarded as the necessities of life—opera and ballet seats, airline tickets to romantic places, and the good food and drink she liked to serve her friends. Lil became something of a Robin Hood in that she regarded rich people as ripe for the picking, and would usually include poor people like me in the treats she managed to extort from well-heeled well-wishers; hence a complicit side to the enjoyment we took in each other's company. Years would go by before either of us realized that we had been born on the same day, fifteen years apart. Hence, astrologers might say, our instinctive closeness and deep affection.

At first, Douglas had liked Lil a lot. He liked her intelligence and curiosity about people and places, which made her such a popular guest. Because she was very ignorant about modern art and at the same time very curious about it, we took Lil to see our neighbor Nicolas de Staël. Lil warmed to this genial Russian giant and the minimal landscapes he had recently brought back from Sicily; and she was intrigued when one of the de Staëls' guests, a professor of psychiatry, proposed to demonstrate the role of fingerpainting in his diagnosis of nervous disorders. He asked Lil to dip her finger in a pot of paint and make random marks on a sheet of paper. As she did so, she declared in her overemphatic way that psychiatry was "the most awful bunkum." As if to deny this, her finger went ahead and made a squiggle that could be interpreted only as a large red penis. Concluding that she was out to make a mockery of the process, people laughed. When the significance of her drawing dawned on her, she assumed they were laughing at her, and looked so mortified I thought she was going to weep. "Join in the laughter," I hissed. "That way the joke will be on the shrink and not on you." It worked. From then on, Lil trusted me. This embarrassing incident became a bond.

As Douglas liked to swim, I had assumed he would want to install a pool, but he was adamantly against the idea. Pools, he said, were vulgar, hideous, and expensive. "Provence is not Long Island," he said. "No turquoise eyesores, please." His refusal even to consider a pool had been exacerbated by the discovery that an academic painter of nudes, Sir William Russell Flint, had been in the habit of coming to Castille in the 1930s and using the colonnades as a backdrop for water-colors of topless women sashaying around a balustraded cistern envisioned by the artist. "You wouldn't want the place to look like one of those awful Russell Flints, would you?"

The lack of a pool was all to the good. It obliged us to go to the sandy beaches of the Camargue, which used to be as idyllic and deserted as any on France's Mediterranean shore. The sea was not that far away—thirty-five miles or so—but it was difficult of access: fenced off against poachers and Gypsies and above all campers, who were beginning to pose a major threat. In those pre-paddy-field days, the wetlands back of the beaches were mostly uncultivated. They were either game reserves or bird sanctuaries, and patrolled by mounted *gardians* (cowboys who still wear traditional nineteenth-century outfits: black velvet jackets lined in red, and very tight, slightly flared moleskin trousers). When they got to know you—a bottle or two of Pernod at the beginning and the end of summer saw to that—the *gardians* would let you through the barbed-wire gates onto the winding, dusty tracks that led past lagoons fringed with flocks of flamingos toward a beach called Le Grand Radeau. As we drove along these tracks, a cloud of white dust in our wake, we would sometimes be treated to the sight of another, more distant cloud, pinkish in color, as the flamingos took off (in Evelyn Waugh's unforgettable phrase) "like dust beaten from a carpet."

At the height of summer the light on the Camargue's lagoons and beaches would play surreal tricks. Near at hand, everything would be in eerily sharp focus, like the details in those early paintings by Salvador Dalí, which he described as "handpainted photographs of dreams." Farther off, the heat haze would cause the infinite expanse of sand and waveless sea to quiver and melt into each other. There would be mirages and metamorphic

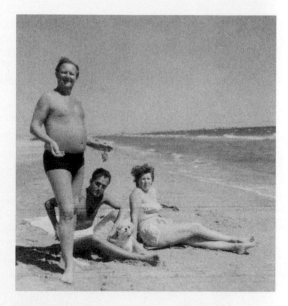

DC, JR, and Alfreda Urquhart on a Camargue beach, ca. 1953

effects—double images that Dalí termed "paranoiakinetic"—which the Surrealists exploited so ingeniously. Walking down the beach, we would look back at the car we had parked in the shade of a tamarisk and watch it melt into one chimera after another—a boat, a donkey, a fat woman looking for shells—before turning back from meltdown into a Citroën. From far away, Douglas's rubbery form would do much the same: change from a biomorphic blob into his all-too-palpable self.

Apart from ourselves, the only traces of human life on these beaches took the memento mori form of things washed up by the sea: cork lifebelts or orange plastic life preservers, which had all too evidently failed to fulfill their purpose. Waves had patinated the rusted innards of wrecks into works of art far more effectively than an artist we knew who used to acquire bits and pieces from shipyards, slice them up, paint them, and sell them as minimalist sculptures. And then there were the bits of driftwood, which Douglas was forever adulating at the expense of Henry Moore. "So much more expressive than Moore's oversized, over-polished, overpriced artifacts," he would say of some gnarled, blanched stump. And he would launch with relish into a denunciation of the man

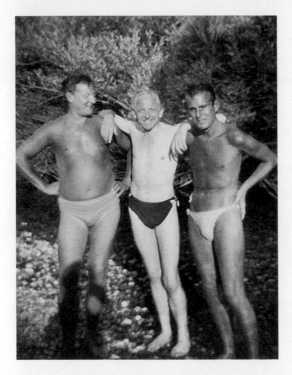

DC, Angus Wilson, and JR in the Camargue, 1952

the British then revered as the acme of modernism. To believe Douglas, Moore had so little visual imagination that he had to pack his assistants off to wastelands and beaches, "not to speak of the streets, my dear, to seek out sticks and stones and bits of pig-iron for their master's delectation." The great man would then decree which of these *objets trouvés* lent themselves to Moorification. Later, according to preferences expressed by art-world VIPs, assistants would blow up the resultant maquettes into something airport-sized, or shrink them into salable *Kleinkunst,* or slice them, eye-catchingly, in half. I was surprised to be told by one of Moore's former assistants that Douglas's malicious hypothesis was not far from the truth.

Douglas and I felt proud of "our" beach, and assumed that our guests would enjoy picnicking there. Most did, among them the then celebrated English novelist Angus Wilson, who spent a memorable day there, recorded in a bizarre photograph of the three of us in bathing suits. Angus had recently graduated from writing brilliant if catty short stories, which I had been one of the first to review favorably, to turgid *romans à thèse.* I might have been more enthusiastic about the novels if Angus had not based one of his characters, Terence Lambert in *Hemlock and After,* on me. We had this out on the beach, Angus claiming that, insofar as it was inspired by me, the characterization was flattering. According to Angus's biographer, Margaret Drabble, he saw me as "a somewhat improbable hero of the postwar world . . . a powerful portent

of social change . . . strong, shrewd, witty, and sympathetic despite—
perhaps because of—his fixation on worldly success." I told Angus,
huffily, that he had misunderstood me, that far from being strong and
ambitious, I was vulnerable and insecure, now more than ever, given the
complexities of life with Douglas. As a polemical novelist, he had every
right to come up with a cast of new characters who reflect changing
social attitudes; however, as an old friend, he was a shit to "out" me.
Forty-five years ago, that could make for trouble.

"Didn't I send you the manuscript in case you might object?"
Angus asked. "Yes, but I never recognized myself in it," I replied, not
daring to admit that I had found his novel too caricatural—too close in
spirit to Ronald Searle's grotesque drawing on the cover—to finish. "But
weren't you just the wee-est bit flattered, dear?" Angus cooed in his
auntie-ish voice. Come to think of it, I just might have been, but I did
not want him to think that I accepted his analysis of my character. My
life would have been so much easier had it been true.

Any residual animosity soon evaporated in the meridional sunlight.
A shrill streetcorner orator when discussing politics or gay lib, Angus was
a scream when he regaled us with stories in his countertenor's voice
about the British Museum Reading Room, where he worked as a librar-
ian: Indian students who liked to lick the plates in medical manuals and
use cheese sandwiches as bookmarks; dirty old men posing as sexolo-
gists, who did such improper things in the North Library, where the
museum's arcane erotica was stored, that they had to be invigilated by
guards. It seemed as if Angus was out to turn our stag picnic into a Girl
Guides' outing, with himself in charge. In this respect he resembled a
celebrated female impersonator of the day, Arthur Marshall, whose
records included such lines as "Brenda sat on her billycan and damped
her enthusiasm." Douglas giggled a lot. Later he said he hated "that sort
of thing." He found it threatening, although heaven knows he could on
occasion outcamp anybody.

The visit of another, less lustrous literary star was a bit fraught.
Nancy Mitford—"that infernal twitterer," Douglas called her—invited
herself and a woman friend to stay. She intended to administer a rebuke.
In reviewing one of her brittle little novels for the *New Statesman,* I had
called her the Emily Post of our time on the grounds that she had set

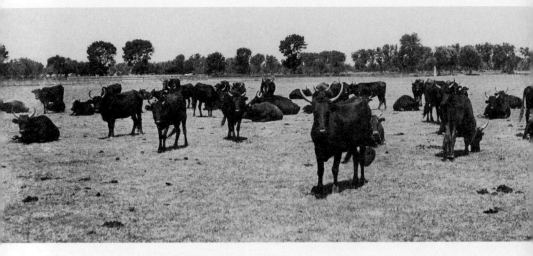

Bulls grazing in the Camargue

herself up as an expert on "U" and "non-U"—upper-class and non-upper-class—usage. Evelyn Waugh had told her that my comparison of her to the author of *The Blue Book of Social Usage* was not flattering, but that did not stop this pretentious goose from proving me right. At some point I had overfilled her glass with red wine, whereupon she looked at me ever so archly and said, "The French have an expression for your little accident, '*coup de concierge*,' " and then treated me to a sample of what one of her brothers-in-law described to me with a shudder as "the hard, tinkling laughter of the Mitford sisters." Douglas was intensely

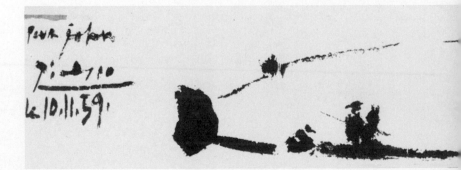

Picasso, Bullfight Scene, *ink wash, 1959*

irritated by Nancy's thirtyish affectations: "Who is she to talk for the aristocracy? She's dainty as a doily, and I wish she'd stop saying prit-ty." Her companion turned out to be a much more down-to-earth and authentically grand woman, who talked intelligently about the paintings and knew about gardens.

Hot on Nancy's heels came the writer she always referred to as "Smartyboots" (a nickname she had pinched from Virginia Woolf): Cyril Connolly, in those days the leading light of English letters. We were surprised that he should invite himself. He and Douglas had never been able to stand each other. Mutual envy had led to mutual resentment. Douglas resented Cyril's wonderfully supple style, Wildean wit, and sense of mimicry—qualities that had endeared him to London's social arbiters, who tended to follow Nancy in regarding Douglas as an "Australian booby." For his part, Cyril, who saw himself as embodying French culture, resented Douglas's instinctive understanding of avant-garde French art and literature, and his rapport with French intellectuals, who tended to regard Cyril as a lightweight. And then, compared to Cyril, who was always whining about money, Douglas was certifiably well off.

Notwithstanding their mutual dislike, Cyril had a penchant for eighteenth-century follies and was keen to take a look at Castille. Douglas was flattered that he should want to do so. I, too, was full of curiosity. Ten years earlier, Cyril's *Unquiet Grave*—that intricately wrought "word cycle" in which the author discourses nostalgically on books, love, food, places, flora, fauna, everything except art—had captivated me. And then, as youthful enthusiasts often do, I had a change of taste. Cyril's

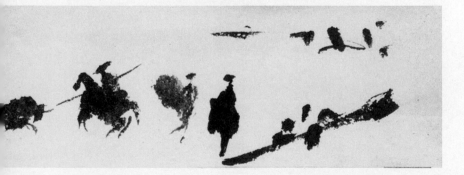

world-weary sensibility came across as a bit of a sham. Now that he was coming to stay, I had reread *The Unquiet Grave* and, except for the fin-de-siècle flourishes—"pale water streaked with sapphirine sea-shadow," or "the sea-purple cicada kingdom of calanque and stone-pine"—had been won over once more.

To my disappointment, Cyril's mandarin sensibility did not measure up to the surreal minimalism of our beaches and lagoons. Here we were at the heart of the region he had lauded above all others, and he didn't seem to have any real feeling for it. All he could do was bang on and on about grand food. Could we sell him some of our truffles? The answer was no. The only achievement in which Cyril seemed to take any real pride was his membership of White's Club. This gesture of acceptance from on high evidently meant every bit as much to him as being a *membre de l'Académie* might mean to a French writer.

Cyril shocked Douglas by turning out to loathe art. "I could do without all painting": this announcement was not a pose; he really meant it. Paintings appeared to be of interest only if they evoked a great name, a great house, a great fortune, or, best of all, a great spread of food. His acquisition of minor bits of food-related Meissen and Sèvres suggested that Cyril lacked the eye as well as the means for the Rothschild look. These ineffectual status symbols merely made those of his friends who knew about such things titter or wince. Douglas could not resist needling Cyril on his taste. "People who inherit the sort of stuff you go in for," he said, "usually sell it and acquire something less aesthetically compromising. Only socially ambitious Parisian queens actually buy it."

We must have been even more of a disappointment to Cyril than he was to us. He had expected to be driven from one exquisite château to another. There were some fine houses in the neighborhood, but Douglas was damned if he was going to take Cyril to any of them. We had thought of trying him out on our local duke—in fact a pretentious marquis who called himself a duke—but he turned out to be away. Cyril's other passion, three-star restaurants, was not one that Douglas was prepared to indulge: too expensive and too full of tourists. Cyril had to make do with dinners at home and a picnic lunch on the beach—chicken, ham, pâté, hard-boiled eggs, local cheeses, melons from the garden, and lashings of local rosé. Marie had run out of the right wrapping paper, so the food emerged from assorted plastic bags and bits of newspaper. Before Cyril had time to sneer, Douglas gave his garish Hawaiian shirt and leopard-patterned bathing suit an evil-queen glare: "By the way, don't worry about the way you're dressed. We are not *going* anywhere."

In the end the beach worked its magic. After a playful splash in the sea, the two egomaniacs relaxed, and Cyril treated us to what he did best: impersonations. Much of Cyril's genius lay in the coordination of an exquisitely acute ear and a beguilingly soft and supple voice. This made for the brilliant mimicry of his literary parodies—among the best things he ever wrote—as well as for the hallucinatory dazzle of his impersonations. For the rest of the afternoon he conjured up friend after friend—Brian Howard, Alan Pryce-Jones, Maurice Bowra—so vividly that they might as well have been sitting on the sand beside us. We were totally appeased. I suddenly understood why Cyril claimed in *A Georgian Boyhood* that being funny had been his "defense mechanism" at school. Too much of his life, it seemed, was tainted by public school hangups. He was still using the same strategy to placate the bullies: bullies personified on this occasion by Douglas. Whereas Douglas used his wit to wound, Cyril used his to seduce. Otherwise they were too alike, I realized—too bullied and bullying, bossy and babyish, vain and self-hating and fat—to stand each other for long. At least Cyril could assume other people's identities; Douglas was stuck with his.

Douglas was at his best—warmest, funniest, and most amenable—with a favored few in his field with whom he could "talk shop": exchange art-world conjecture and inside news and have endless discussions about the paintings on his walls and the modern movement in general. In his cups, Douglas would sometimes become a bit too defiant in his use of cubism as a yardstick with which to belittle virtually all contemporary artists of any merit, except for Klee, Miró, and Giacometti. This would irritate many of his friends, myself included, who admired abstract expressionism. An exception was Anthony Blunt, who tended to share Douglas's narrow view of modernism, and was therefore a welcome guest. In our early years Anthony came almost every summer. He was usually accompanied by his brawny boyfriend, a genial Ulsterman who worked in a Burlington Arcade jeweler's shop, called John Gaskin.

Anthony must already have fallen under suspicion of masterminding the recent defection of the British spies Burgess and Maclean, who were rumored at one point to have been buried—or so Douglas told Stuart Preston—"in the funerary urns dotted about the park at Castille." However, neither of us would have any inkling of the trouble Anthony was in for another twenty-five years. All that he admitted to was exhaustion from overwork as director of the Courtauld Institute, as Surveyor of the Royal Collections, and from his duties on any number of prestigious committees and learned societies. It never occurred to us that his exhaustion stemmed from the pressure of relentless investigations—pressure that would trigger a stroke and partial facial paralysis. However, when the news finally broke that Anthony, too, had been working for the Russians, I was surprised only at not being more surprised.

Because Anthony made no secret of his early commitment to Communism, it was no surprise that he carried this commitment a stage further, but then what sort of spying did his commitment involve? To believe John Le Carré, espionage has become a gray area where nothing is very sharply defined. That Anthony had saved his traitorous buddy Burgess is easier to condone than the help he gave the far more dangerous Maclean. What I still find painful to accept is the fact that the Anthony I knew—compassionate, humorous, affectionate, altruistic, albeit supremely Machiavellian—should have knowingly shared any responsibility with Philby (the fellow spy he vehemently claimed to loathe) for the torture and death of all those operatives at the hands of Stalin's KGB.

Although Anthony seemed all of a piece, I sometimes suspected him of suffering from some kind of multiple-personality syndrome. He reminded me of one of Douglas's Klees, *The Ventriloquist Shouting in the Marsh,* a watercolor of a whimsical creature whose body contains a number of other whimsical creatures. The same with Anthony. Inside this apparent paragon lurked a no less disparate cast of characters: a mathematician who had transformed himself into an art historian; an active homosexual who dodged nimbly in and out of the closet; a brilliant teacher who was revered by pupils and colleagues alike; an accomplished traitor who went on betraying his country long after there was any ideological excuse for doing so; a consummate courtier who not only took excellent care of the royal treasures, but on occasion served the monarch as an effective secret agent; and, not least, an agreeable companion who drank far more and laughed far harder than most people realized.

People who wrote about Anthony or impersonated him on TV portrayed him as snooty and humorless—a bent square. None of them discerned his sardonic sense of mischief. I suspect that he derived enormous, naughty-boyish gratification from being so overtly good and so covertly bad: from presiding over a seminar on Poussin, and looking ahead to a briefing from his Soviet "control" (seemingly a Hungarian publisher we all knew); from taking some visiting head of state round the picture gallery at Buckingham Palace, knowing that he would end the evening in a gay pub with a compliant soldier or sailor who would accompany him back to his flat on the top floor of the Courtauld Institute. Only someone who had been born and raised in the icy bosom of the British Establishment would have worked so tirelessly in both its service and its disservice.

Anthony was a model guest. Mornings he would toil away at some recondite paper in his curiously unformed handwriting. Afternoons we would go on art-historical forays, avoiding tourist attractions in favor of more arcane objectives: a putative Claude in a local château, a Romanesque chapel on the banks of the Durance. Evenings, Anthony and Douglas would discuss museum politics: how to rid the Tate Gallery of its inept director, or how to deed Castille and its contents to the Courtauld or its parent, London University. Later, depending on the amount of scotch consumed, Anthony would regale us with glimpses of royal life: how much he admired the Queen for her "good sense and professionalism." She always made the right decision about the disposition of her paintings, unlike the Queen Mother, who aspired to taste and was apt to suggest changing the traditional hanging of certain pictures

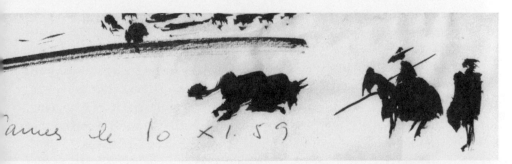

Picasso, Bullfight Scene, ink wash, 1959; heading of letter from Jacqueline Picasso to JR

for no better reason than that they might look prettier in the Blue Drawing Room. Anthony's liking for the Queen seemed utterly genuine. He enjoyed her dry humor. On official tours of the Buckingham Palace picture gallery, the visiting head of state would usually ask her at least once who had painted this or that painting. Since she seldom remembered, the Queen always had the same recourse. In a small, high, not-to-be-contradicted voice, she would say "Dutch," and move rapidly on to the next painting.

I remember Anthony telling us how he had informed George VI over tea at Buckingham Palace that he wanted to resign from his service. So put out was the monarch that he had one of his attacks of stammerer's rage and knocked the spirit lamp over onto the silver tea tray. The tea tray and everything else on it had burst into blue flames like a Christmas pudding, whereupon a courageous footman stepped forward, grabbed the flaming tray, and walked slowly backward from the royal presence. The King was so astounded by the man's sangfroid that he recovered his temper and never referred to the proffered resignation again.

My last glimpse of Anthony was the more haunting for taking place shortly after his final disgrace. The owner of a renowned collection, with whom I had been staying, told me what a huge help Anthony had been with curatorial problems—conservation, loans to exhibitions, and so forth. Now that Anthony had been stripped of his knighthood and other honors, my host wanted to reassure his former adviser of his gratitude. However, by virtue of business duties, he could not have any communication with a traitor. In the circumstances, would I go and convey his sympathy verbally to Anthony?

Back in London, I had to wait a few days. The newspapers were full of reports that John Gaskin had been so traumatized by what he regarded as a personal betrayal that he had jumped out of a window of the flat he shared with Anthony. Luckily, his fall had been broken and, apart from a few fractures, he was recovering in hospital. After the scandal subsided, I went to see Anthony. He looked shaken, but perked up when I passed on the supportive message from our mutual friend. Although it was early spring, the weather was abnormally hot and the top-floor flat stifling. Could I open a window? Of course, Anthony said, indicating a French window that gave onto a tiny balcony—"if you can unjam the door." When it opened without any difficulty, I wondered whether this was the door out of which John had jumped. In my confusion, I asked how the authorities were fending off the reporters, who had been using all manner of ruses to get to John's bedside. Fine, Anthony said, and in his most urbane manner described how he had paid him a visit the day before, and got in and out of the hospital without the press being any the wiser. He had shown the same dexterity when he had gone to Germany at the Royal Family's behest in 1945, and spirited the papers of Queen Victoria's daughter, the Empress Frederick, out of one of the Hohenzollern castles without being caught. He had certainly not lost his amazing nerve.

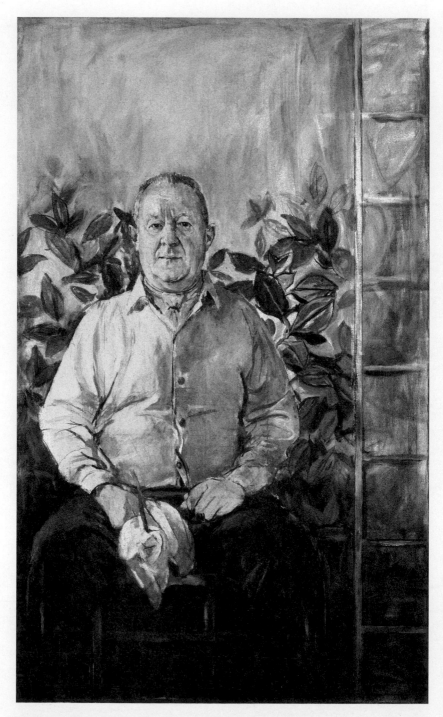

Graham Sutherland, Douglas Cooper, *oil on canvas, 1966*

GRAHAM SUTHERLAND
AND THE TATE AFFAIR

Graham Sutherland—in the 1950s England's most celebrated painter—and his wife, Kathy, were probably our most frequent visitors. They had rented a villa at Roquebrune, which belonged to the ornithological artist Simon Bussy and his wife, Dorothy (Lytton Strachey's sister and a renowned translator). They had then moved into the dismal guest quarters of Lord Beaverbrook's villa, La Capponcina. Later, in 1955, they would buy a small house—a mini-temple to modernism— which the designer Eileen Gray had built for herself in the hills above Menton. Heaven knows why. Graham disliked the modernist look of the house and tried and failed to exorcise it with bits of eighteenth-century grotto furniture. On their way to or from the Riviera, the Sutherlands would usually spend a night or two at Castille. On our trips to the coast we would usually stay with them. For better or worse, we became close friends.

When I first met Douglas, he and the Sutherlands were not speaking. Graham had recently embarked on a successful new career as an Establishment portrait painter. Douglas was derisively skeptical. That British artists were unable to draw was one of his sillier prejudices; hence Douglas's myth that Graham was such a poor draftsman that his wife had to block in his sitter's features for him with an eyebrow pencil. True, drawing was not Graham's forte, but he had a knack for catching a likeness. He was also adept at concealing weaknesses and making the most of strengths: for instance, the way he harnessed his picturesque vision of nature to portraiture. His first and best portrait, the one of Somerset Maugham, stemmed from Graham's concept of Maugham as being "old as the hills," his face crevassed with wrinkles. Douglas's denunciation of the portrait was a measure of his irritation at the success of a painting he had hoped would fail. His Anglophobia decreed that all modern English art be perceived as bad.

As I said earlier, I had been a teenaged admirer of Graham's. The fact that his father had once been my tutor endeared Graham to me. Why attack one of the very few British painters who were any good, I had asked Douglas in the early days of our relationship. It made him, rather than Graham, look a fool. Why not mend this particular fence? Douglas saw that the fence-mending would be to his advantage; the Sutherlands saw that it would be even more to theirs. Just as well, since what would come to be called "the Tate affair" would make Douglas and Graham deeply—much too deeply—indebted to one another. Each would become the other's albatross.

The Tate affair, which dragged on for two years of public recriminations and epic farce (October 1952—December 1954) and triggered endless rows in Parliament, endless fulmination in the press, deserves to be remembered because it stands as a landmark in the British Establishment's painful and long, drawn-out surrender to modernism. Now that Nicholas Serota is transforming the modern foreign section of the Tate Gallery into one of the liveliest and most progressive museums of modern art in the world, it is heartening to look back at the institution's fuddy-duddiness in the early 1950s and rejoice at the transformation. The issue was supposedly maladministration on the part of the then director, Sir John Rothenstein, but that was more of a pretext. In fact the affair turns out to have been yet another skirmish in a fight that goes back to the opening night of Victor Hugo's *Hernani,* the first clash between the vanguard and the old guard. Not that there was anything heroic about the Tate affair. This time round, the principal avant-gardistes were an odd trio: Douglas, Graham, and a devious South African rogue called LeRoux Smith LeRoux, each of whom had a different agenda. The old guard was represented by Rothenstein, the academic son of an academic portraitist, whose taste in contemporary art was parochial and genteel and whose administrative lapses had deservedly come under scrutiny.

The Tate was already steeped in scandal when Rothenstein was appointed director in 1938. The previous director, J. B. Manson (of whom it was said that "he had grown gray in the service of art and purple in its disservice"), had been obliged to resign: at an official luncheon to celebrate the great 1938 exhibition of British art at the Louvre, Manson had drunkenly heckled the speakers and crowed like a Gallic cock. Unfortunately, his deputy, an Evelyn Waughish character called D. C. Fincham, stayed on to perpetuate Manson's mess and harass his successor. When World War II closed the Tate, Rothenstein decided—most unwisely—to take off for a lecture tour in the United States. Anyone who asked for the new director was told by Fincham that he had fled. To refute these

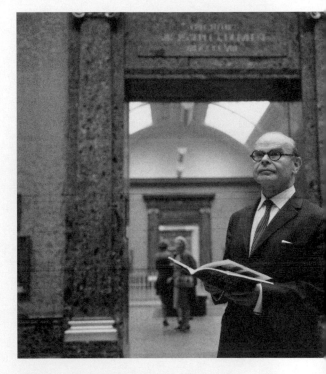

Sir John Rothenstein at the Tate Gallery, London, ca. 1955

rumors, Rothenstein raced back to London. Whereupon it was Fincham's turn to vanish—supposedly to work for military intelligence, keeping tabs on fascists in Chelsea pubs. Nobody believed him, and he went the way of Manson.

At first Rothenstein had difficulty finding qualified curators willing to work for £300 a year. One promising young man decided he could not live on this pittance; another, our friend Humphrey Brooke, found his boss so arrogant and incompetent that in a fit of despair he donned a top hat and went to 10 Downing Street to present the Prime Minister with a formal petition for the director's removal. And then, on a trip to South Africa in 1950, Rothenstein came upon an apparently perfect candidate, the genial, youngish LeRoux Smith LeRoux, who conned him into making him deputy director. A more treacherous underling would have been hard to find. From the very start, this artful manipulator devoted his energies to betraying his benefactor so that he could step into his shoes. At least this is the story Rothenstein tells in his memoir, *Brave Day Hideous Night,* which includes 150 pages of exculpatory whining about the Tate affair. Granted, the memoir establishes LeRoux's villainy; it also establishes the author's innate silliness and lack of authority in allowing his deputy to spend months in the archives digging up evidence of his boss's lapses. LeRoux's sleuthing had the encouragement of Douglas, who had discovered, in the course of cataloguing the great paintings given to the Tate by Samuel Courtauld, that the director had allowed a Renoir from this donation to be deaccessioned (purloined, Douglas said) without the usual procedures being followed. Since Rothenstein's malfeasance stemmed from sloppiness and not dishonesty, these infractions could easily have been rectified. However, his humbuggery had antagonized the powerful outgoing chairman (a former Lord Chancellor), as well as some of the trustees, notably Sutherland, and much of the staff.

Rothenstein's failure to do justice to such major twentieth-century art movements as fauvism, cubism, futurism, and surrealism had the small, mutually mistrustful band of British modernists up in arms. Of these, Douglas was by far the most vindictive. Despite the Tate's refusal to employ him, he had tried to work with Rothenstein. He had lent the gallery paintings from his collection; he had helped him obtain loans for exhibitions and notified him whenever works of museum caliber came on the London market at an affordable price. But the director seldom if ever acted on his tips; and so Douglas passed them on to Alfred Barr of New York's Museum of Modern Art. Barr was thus able to acquire the two greatest twentieth-century landmarks in British hands: Matisse's magnificent *Red Studio* from David Tennant's Gargoyle Club (Douglas bought Tennant's other masterpiece, Matisse's *Study with Nude,* for himself) for around £10,000 and Severini's futurist tour de force, the *Bal Tabarin,* from the estate of Richard Wyndham, for £200. (Today the *Red Studio* would be worth at least $50 million and the *Bal Tabarin* at least a tenth of that.) Even in wartime, an enterprising director should have been able to save these masterpieces from leaving the country.

In an uncharacteristically generous gesture toward the institution he despised, Douglas agreed to lend most of his Klees to the Tate's 1945 retrospective. He also helped the gallery obtain major loans from Swiss collections. To my generation, who had seldom seen a Klee in the original, the show had been a revelation. To Douglas it was a revelation of a very different kind: a revelation of the incompetence and bad faith of the gallery's director. After the show was over, the Tate failed to return his loans despite repeated requests to do so. Mystified and wrathful, he drove Basil's wasplike Rolls down to the Tate. Rothenstein was nowhere to be found. Eventually a terrified underling confessed that Douglas's Klees were being held in the director's office because they were being submitted to the trustees for possible purchase. But they are not for sale, Douglas shrieked. The imputation that he was a dealer was the more offensive since he was ashamed of having been one. "I am empowered to make a citizen's arrest," Douglas told me he told the underling. "If my property is not instantly returned, your criminal director is going to jail for theft."

Douglas got his Klees back. Henceforth he would never miss an opportunity to torment Rothenstein, but the intensity of his malice blinded people to the justice of his cause, so his attacks never prevailed. In the end the Tate Gallery, not Rothenstein, was the loser. "They'll never get anything out of me," Douglas was forever reiterating, and he meant it. Even after Rothenstein had retired and been replaced by someone more progressive, Douglas never relented; he simply changed the thrust of his game. Instead of rattling the bars of Rothenstein's cage, Douglas rattled his will at the Tate trustees. He led them on, helping them organize a magnificent cubist show and letting them have two of his most important paintings on extended loan, but that was all. "Such a good tease, my dear. They think I've forgiven them, but they're never going to get a thing." The Tate should, of course, have made Douglas a trustee. The Prado, which elected him to its Patronato, was left two of his finest paintings.

While serving as a Tate trustee, Graham Sutherland had come to share Douglas's concerns about the gallery; he had also fallen under the sway of LeRoux. The three of them agreed that "the Japanese parachutist" (Douglas's nickname for the small, orientally eyebrowed Rothenstein) had to go. And to this end they formed a cabal. Supporters materialized on all sides, from scholars such as Sir Denis Mahon to critics like Denys Sutton, and members of Parliament and the press. A public-spirited woman friend of ours, who knew Rothenstein to be a Lothario, even offered herself as bait in an attempt to entrap him.

Another important ally was Graham's friend, patron, and sitter, Lord Beaverbrook, who kept the pages of his newspapers, the *Daily Express* and *Evening Standard*, filled with the transgressions that LeRoux dredged up in the Tate's files. However, the more LeRoux dredged, the more Douglas and Graham began to suspect that his motives were not as selfless as theirs. The trustees finally fired him, whereupon Lord Beaverbrook gave him a job. Once again, LeRoux disgraced himself. After swindling this formidable employer out of £40,000, he took to drink and art-dealing, and ended up dying mysteriously after yet another scandal.

Back, however, to winter 1953. On December 21, Douglas triggered the Tate affair by writing a letter to the *Times* assailing the gallery for having mislaid a Renoir. Despite a seemingly satisfactory explanation by the chairman of the trustees, Douglas managed to keep the fire he had started going—principally by encouraging LeRoux to feed more and more inflammatory material to the Beaverbrook press. Two or three weeks later, the Sutherlands broke their journey for a few days at Castille on their way to Roquebrune. Hours were spent discussing whether or not Graham should resign his Tate trusteeship. Douglas finally persuaded him to do so. There was an implicit quid pro quo. Graham wanted Douglas to devote a monograph to his work. He apparently believed that the stamp of Douglas's approval would upgrade him from an insular *petit-maître* to an international star. Eight years later Graham would get his monograph. It failed to validate his work in modernist circles, and did in Douglas's reputation as a progressive pundit.

At the end of January, Douglas and I joined the Sutherlands on the coast. The time had come to detonate the bomb that would supposedly remove Rothenstein from the Tate. The Roquebrune villa, so redolent of Bloomsbury, became a command post. Douglas was at his happiest helping Graham draft letters of resignation to the Tate's chairman as well as his fellow trustees. Had Graham been less assiduous in courting the press, his gesture might have been more effective. Unfortunately, before his letters reached London he had confided the news of his resignation to his friend and neighbor (on the Riviera), Lord Beaverbrook. A foolish move. Beaverbrook jumped the gun and published the story in the *Evening Standard.* The chairman and trustees of the Tate were understandably furious: most of them were every bit as keen to get rid of Rothenstein as Graham was; besides, protocol required that resignations be made to the Prime Minister. Graham was accused of exploiting a delicate situation in order to get his name in the papers. "Now that Graham and Douglas had built up this appalling vendetta in public," the new chairman, Sir Dennis Proctor, said, "we simply couldn't have thrown [Rothenstein] to the wolves." Lady Proctor put it differently: "Graham has kicked the ball through his own goal."

Calls for Rothenstein's removal might have met with more success if the gallery staff had not been civil servants (the Civil Service frowns on firing); also if LeRoux had been more trustworthy, and Douglas less childishly keen to rattle the bars of Rothenstein's cage, "a dank beleaguered flat half underground below the Tate," which he shared with his nice, long-suffering American wife and, it was rumored, a Jesuit priest who ministered to them.

As usual, Douglas's mischief came home to roost, leaving its target relatively unscathed. What saved Rothenstein in the end was the venomous letter Douglas wrote to congratulate him on receiving the Order of the Mexican Eagle: "Now that the Mexican president has provided you with the beak and talons of the Mexican eagle you may perhaps feel better equipped to face me in open contest. But do not deceive yourself into thinking that, because your continued disservices to art bring you in Knighthoods and ribbons, I shall . . . weaken in my attack. There are still more than ten years in which to hound you out of Millbank—and it shall be done." This letter and the copies that Douglas sent to trustees, members of Parliament, journalists, and other interested parties enabled spokesmen for the Treasury in both Houses of Parliament to claim that Rothenstein was the innocent victim of a spiteful vendetta. As if to confirm the existence of this vendetta, Douglas went ahead and made yet another vainglorious attack on the director—one that left the civil servants at the Treasury more than ever inclined to protect rather than fire him.

The second attack occurred at the opening of Richard Buckle's sumptuous Diaghilev exhibition—so sumptuous that the Maison Guerlain sprayed the galleries with the celebrated impresario's favorite cologne, Mitsouko. The evening began with a festive dinner in honor of Lord Harewood and his wife, Marion, who opened the exhibition. After dinner, according to Rothenstein's memoir, Douglas followed him from room to room, "shouting taunts from a distance in a French accent." In fact, Douglas and I were talking to the Harewoods in one of the smaller galleries when Rothenstein suddenly materialized. Douglas, who was drunk, cackled, in an accent more camp than French, "That's the little man who is going to lose his job." The "little man" could hardly be blamed for flying at him.

The "Tiger of the Tate," as one of the newspapers described Rothenstein, boasted that his right hook left Douglas crawling around on the floor. Bunkum! All Rothenstein managed to do was knock off his opponent's glasses. Since Douglas was taller and heavier, he had no problem holding off his attacker, laughing as Rothenstein's little arms flailed ineffectively. Although the Duc de Mouchy took credit for separating the contestants, it was in fact a subeditor from the *Observer* who did so. Madame Massigli, the French ambassadress, claimed that she had come upon Douglas, after the incident, all by himself in a room lined with Benois decors, doing *"un pas seul et victorieux."* She must have been hallucinating. When a journalist asked if he was hurt, the Humpty-Dumptyish Douglas hooted with delight, "Just look at me, I'm bleeding from every corner." The presence at this fracas of members of the Royal Family (George and Marion Harewood) had to be kept out of the press; otherwise it was lengthily reported. Both contestants claimed to have behaved heroically. Rothenstein said he had received a letter of congratulation from a painter he greatly admired, Winston Churchill; Douglas told the press that he had received telephone calls from Picasso, and floral tributes from unknown admirers. I don't know that I believe either of them.

The Tate affair may have sputtered out in farce; thanks, however, to the diplomacy of Sir Dennis Proctor, the conspirators eventually achieved much of what they set out to achieve, except for the expulsion of Rothenstein. In a letter to Stuart Preston, I wrote that "the incident has had the best possible results: Douglas has become a bosom friend of the new Chairman of the Tate trustees, who is appalled at Sir John's behavior. . . . Douglas's new line is to arrange with the Chairman loans and purchase for the Tate over the Director's head; this is the bitterest blow yet to the Japanese parachutist's pride. It seems that the little man is ultimately due to go. The Chairman tells us to be patient." Once again, Rothenstein managed to ride out the storm, but he was stripped of his authority. Under Proctor's aegis, the gallery shed its fogeyish image and set about acquiring significant examples of twentieth-century art. Having won each other's hard-to-win trust, Proctor dispatched Douglas to Paris on a buying trip, which resulted in the Tate's acquisition of two fine Picassos: a major cubist figure painting and a harrowing 1952 still life with a bull's head.

Graham's role in the Tate affair should also be seen in the context of the most illustrious and ill-fated commission of his career: a portrait of Winston Churchill, who was then Prime Minister, to be offered to him on the occasion of his eightieth birthday by both houses of Parliament. The portrait was to remain in Churchill's possession until his death, when it would revert to the

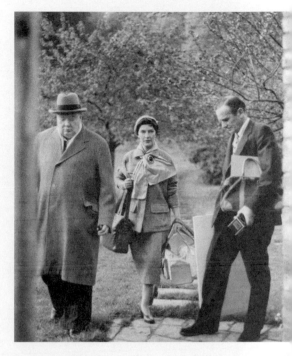

Graham and Kathleen Sutherland with Winston Churchill at Chartwell, 1954

House of Commons. The agreement was signed on July 14, 1954, with sittings scheduled to start at the end of August. Since the Tate affair was still rumbling on, Graham hoped that in the course of the sittings he would be able to sway the Prime Minister (at whose discretion the director and trustees serve) against Rothenstein. No such luck. Churchill turned out to like Rothenstein. Graham, who was nothing if not ingratiating, took refuge in deference. So deferential was he that Lady Churchill declared him to be a "wow."

Graham bombarded us almost daily with pessimistic progress reports. The members of Parliament responsible for the commission had decreed that Churchill be portrayed in his normal parliamentary clothes: black jacket and striped trousers. However, Churchill had set his theatrical heart on being commemorated in the stately robes of a Knight of the Garter, as the savior of Europe, like the conquerors of Napoleon whom Sir Thomas Lawrence had portrayed with such panache for the

Waterloo Chamber at Windsor. Unfortunately, a grand bravura manner was out of fashion; it was also beyond Graham's powers. Besides, the electric blue and scarlet of the Garter robes ill accorded with the ominous mustards and purples he had filched from Francis Bacon. And so, Graham told us, he had done a large, flamboyant sketch of Churchill in full Garter fig, which he kept on the easel and used as a screen to conceal the surreptitious sketches he was doing for a less formal portrait. Like it or not, the old bulldog was going to be memorialized as the great commoner, the pugnacious parliamentarian rising from the front bench to crush some adversarial pipsqueak. This concept was intended to neutralize the more philistine MPs; all it did was antagonize the sitter. Churchill was very difficult to paint: in the morning too busy dictating and telephoning and eternally fussing with his cigar; in the afternoon too drowsy and brandy-sodden. It was impossible, Graham said, to conjure a feisty bulldog out of an old soak desperately trying, and inevitably failing, to stay awake.

Douglas and I arrived in England at the end of October 1954, to attend the fateful Diaghilev show described earlier. We were summoned down to the Sutherlands' house in Kent to see the finished portrait. Graham was understandably in need of reassurance, and Douglas did what he could to provide it, masking his disappointment with fulsome compliments. I took refuge in a dumb show of fake respect to hide my shock at realizing that Graham had based the portrait's format, pose, sartorial details, and egregious lack of feet on Francis Bacon's headless, footless *Figure in a Landscape* (1945) in the Tate Gallery. The fudging of the feet—Francis liked to fudge extremities—was the giveaway. I did not want to draw Douglas's attention yet again to the increasing influence of Francis on Graham's work; it would have triggered yet another tedious row. Years later, I did talk to Bacon about it. "Such a petty pilferer," Francis said. "She never had the nerve for grand larceny."

Instead of keeping his promise to show Churchill the portrait before the presentation, Graham prevaricated and showed him only a photograph. Churchill predictably loathed it and threatened to cancel the official ceremony. He found the ambivalence of the pose particularly offensive—was he sitting down, or struggling to rise to his nonexistent feet? It made him, he told Graham, look like an old man "who couldn't sit on the lavatory." And to others he said, "Here sits an old man on his stool

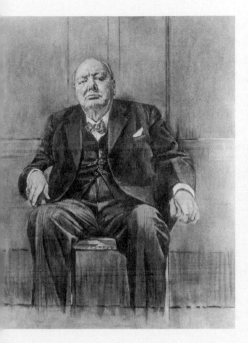

n Sutherland, Sir Winston Churchill, *canvas, 1954 (destroyed)*

Francis Bacon, Figure in a Landscape, *oil on canvas, 1945*

straining and straining." Graham could only assume that his sitter suffered from some shameful geriatric condition. There was also a political angle. Many of the younger conservatives wanted Churchill to step down as Prime Minister; hence his concern that the portrait should pay tribute to his strengths rather than hint at his weaknesses. In the end the sitter allowed the presentation in Westminster Hall to take place. This was the first and last time the portrait was publicly shown. It met with little but hostility. After the ceremony it was delivered to Chartwell, where it was consigned to the boiler room. One of Churchill's daughters-in-law told me that Lady Churchill had developed an iconoclastic hatred of Graham's painting. For all that it was destined to hang in the House of Commons, she cut the canvas up and instructed Ted Hiles, the handyman, to consign the remains to the incinerator—much to her husband's satisfaction.

Despite the Churchill debacle, Graham was deluged with commissions. And Douglas, who had once been so dismissive of his portraits, took over as his Svengali. Graham was flattered; I was worried. His ready acceptance of Douglas's amateurish advice as to a color or a pose or an anecdotal detail seemed to reveal a fundamental lack of faith in his own artistic judgment. Meanwhile, at Douglas's behest, Graham, like Sargent before him, worked hard to cultivate social connections with a view to lucrative commissions. The Sutherlands' taste for high life dated back to the beginning of World War II, when they had taken shelter from the bombing in Kenneth Clark's country house. The Clarks became their exemplars. Graham was too deferential by nature to carry off Sir Kenneth's air of patrician urbanity with any conviction, however. Kathy's impersonation of Lady Clark —a dedicated clothes horse who had little to pass on to Kathy beyond some vintage frocks and a taste for champagne that would eventually do in both of them—was an improvement on the original.

The Sutherlands were soon on the friendliest terms with most of the top froth of the Riviera. Douglas was a bit miffed at their success, especially when they took up with the frequently widowed Australian adventuress Lady Kenmare, who had married into his family. The Sutherlands were also thick with the manipulative Daisy Fellowes, who loved to play humiliating tricks on her guests, though you would never realize this from Graham's bland characterization of her. Another of their new friends was said to have been Goering's *homme d'affaires,* Arpad Plesch, a character out of Ian Fleming who collected rare books and erotica and bred racehorses (including two Derby winners) and served up exquisite exotic food cooked inside coconuts grown in his greenhouses. Café society took to the Sutherlands, and vice versa.

Now that Graham's prices were soaring, Kathy could buy her own Balenciagas. Her haute couture outfits were a matter of great pride to them both, despite Graham's protests that he would rather she dressed the simple way she used to. "Smart clothes give her such a boost it would be cruel not to indulge her," he would say. "Do tell her how great she looks." I would seek out poor Kathy, who would be trying not to seem upstaged by some ultra-smart dress. "Glad you like it, darling. It's a bitch to wear. All those weights and pads and underskirts." (She would tug awkwardly at some asymmetrical flange.) "I'd be much comfier in one of my old caftans. But now Graham is so famous he likes me to look posh. I only do it to please him. Yes, I'd love a bit more champagne. . . ."

Who was one to believe? At dinner one night, Lord Beaverbrook lectured Douglas and me about Kathy: "frivolous, vapid, socially ambitious, such values as she ever had contaminated by Café Society." Douglas agreed. I, on the other hand, felt that insofar as this applied at all, it applied as much to Graham as to her. He was not the only artist I knew to set his wife up as a catalyst for his own shortcomings. Graham's increasingly slick portraits and modish subject matter—toads that look sequined, eagles that have the meretricious glitter of costume jewelry— were his fault, not hers. No wonder people with a serious interest in modern art turned away from Graham's work in distaste and hailed his former friend Francis Bacon as the great hope of British painting. As a source of inspiration, low life had a lot more to offer than high fashion.

The final bust-up with the Sutherlands was suitably farcical. Michel Guy, the French Minister of Culture, had asked Douglas to organize an exhibition, *Masterpieces by European Artists, 1900–1950*. This was to include fifty-four paintings by the greatest artists of the first half of the twentieth century (ten by Picasso, eight by Matisse, six each by Braque, Gris, and Léger, one each by a number of other artists, including Graham Sutherland). The list came in for some vituperative abuse, notably in the French magazine *L'Express,* which published an article on September 9, 1974, entitled "Le Choix Insolent de Douglas Cooper," by Patrick Thévenon. Thévenon felt that Sutherland and many others should have been omitted. Seeing the word *"omis"* applied to Graham, and not understanding French very well, Kathy concluded that he had been omitted from Douglas's list. Without bothering to check, she sat down and wrote Douglas a furious letter. As she told a mutual friend, she then read it through, had another drink, and wrote an even more furious version, which she signed "An outraged wife" and mailed. Douglas, who was only too aware that his support of Sutherland did him little credit, was delighted to receive the letter—delighted, as well, that it was Kathy and not he who had trampled the flowers of friendship underfoot. "Lady Proctor was right," he said. "Trust those silly Sutherlands to kick the ball through their own goal."

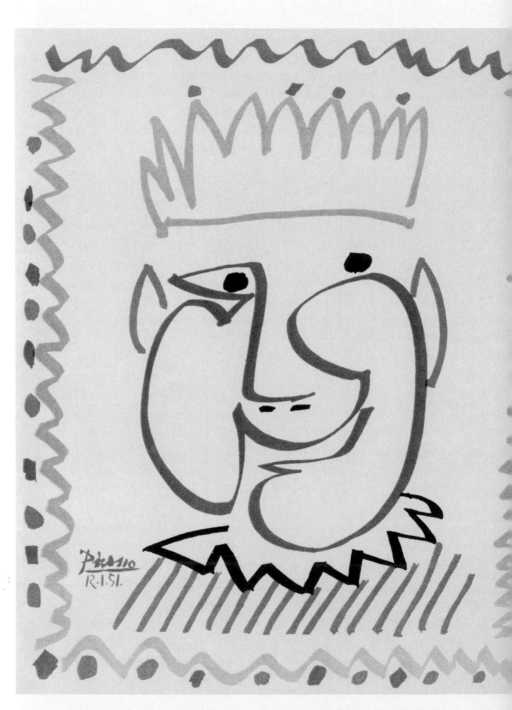

Picasso, Clown, lithographic poster, 1951 (the likeness probably inspired by DC)

GOD SAVE THE QUEEN

D ouglas's political opinions were ambivalent to the point of farce. When I first met him, he was doing his best to be perceived as a Communist: an affiliation that accorded with the mad, bad, and dangerous-to-know image he cultivated. I soon realized he was nothing of the sort. In private, he was a moderate—a highly opinionated old-fashioned liberal not unlike Basil. In public, especially if he had had a few drinks, he would take whatever line would make the biggest splash, or give the most offense, or he would indulge in a show of apoplectic radicalism, which, I like to think, he had inherited from his Wyldbore antecedents. Although he professed to admire the severity of Marxism, Douglas had no use for its dogma. When questioned about his Communist involvement, he would take refuge in eulogizing the artistic and intellectual energy of French Communists: "Except for Braque, *all* the painters and writers *I* know are party members." French Communists were geniuses; English ones were "clods and louts and nitwit commissars." Suspecting that his Communist stance was a sham, Lucian Freud told me that he had once challenged Douglas to prove it. With a mysterious grin, Douglas had flicked the underside of his lapel so subliminally that Lucian was unable to see whether or not it concealed a telltale hammer and sickle.

This pseudo-Communist stance was inspired by Picasso's espousal of the party's Congress of Intellectuals for Peace, for which he had devised his famous emblematic dove. Apart from signing a manifesto, Douglas did nothing about it. He failed to attend the initial conference at Wroclaw in 1948, where Picasso made his first and last speech. He likewise failed to attend the second one at Sheffield in 1950, although he and I were in England at the time. Indeed, Picasso had told the immigration officials at Dover that he was going to stay with Basil at 18 Egerton Terrace, although he would actually stay with Roland Penrose. In those politically fraught days, it was presumably easier for a Communist Party member to enter England under the auspices of a member of the House of Lords than under the auspices of Roland, who made no secret of being an anarchist. Douglas announced that the prospect of sitting through hours of ideological twaddle and playing second fiddle to Roland was too high a price to pay for the privilege of sharing Picasso's company "with hundreds of nonentities." Besides, we had had a foretaste of what the Sheffield conference might involve at a party given by the Polish draftsman Feliks Topolski, in honor of Picasso's visit to London: journalists in search of a story, hacks with autograph albums, and hordes of what Douglas described as "gormless gallery-goers." A crowning insult was the behavior of that "burnt-out has-been" Jacob Epstein, who took advantage of the party to inform the press that Picasso's genius was not a patch on his. "You see what happens when things are left to the likes of Penrose and Popski," Douglas said. "Scum forms."

Douglas's Communism was almost as much of a sham as his mad hatred of the British Royal Family, the Queen in particular. His hatred of her stemmed from Anglophobia—the only form of patriotism that Douglas could permit himself, as I said earlier. Envy is what his resentment was really about. Douglas felt *he* should be monarch. To my embarrassment, I was with him on two occasions when he gave vent to his feelings. The first time was at the coronation; the next time was at the opening of Parliament.

In both cases, Basil was the innocent cause. As a Liberal whip in the House of Lords, he was able to get us special seats for special ceremonies. Given his dotty hatred of the Royal Family, Douglas was not going to miss the coronation for anything. And he was thrilled that "Our Lord" had promised us seats in a stand overlooking the entrance to Westminster Abbey, reserved for the families of the peers inside the Abbey. The evening before the great day, Douglas contracted a high fever. On coronation morning, it had come down to 102 degrees. Despite weather that was phenomenally cold and wet, even for London in April, Douglas persisted in attending the ceremony. For the occasion he had dug out an antique fur-lined overcoat with a sumptuous sea-otter collar and pockets crammed with a pharmacopoeia of pills and drops and linctuses as well as a thermometer and a brandy flask from which he took abundant swigs.

Douglas had insisted that we arrive as late as possible, the better to irritate others in the stand—for the most part nice, sensible Land-Roverish people muffled up in nice sensible garments, such as they might wear to a point-to-point. Many of them had brought picnic hampers and thermoses full of hot sustaining drinks. There was a gasp of polite horror when Douglas arrived with a thermometer sticking out of his mouth at a jaunty angle and proceeded to kick his way past them to our seats. I followed, murmuring apologies—"I'm afraid he's not very well"—and doing everything short of tapping my temple to suggest that he was a bit . . . well, loony. Out of the corner of my eye, I caught sight of an oafish bully I had been to school with. He glowered at me, as if to confirm how right he had been to make my young life hell. I gave him a surreptitious finger and sat down, grimly, next to Douglas, who had finally removed his thermometer. "It's come right down, it's only 103 degrees," he lied, and then, with a nasty, sansculottish cackle, announced that he was going to pretend he was a *tricoteuse* at the guillotine—"I'm here to bring the woman bad luck. When is her tumbrel due?"

The next hour or two were torture. We had a perfect view of the arriving guests: ambassadors, members of the government, celebrities, court officials, and foreign royalties (the only one Douglas cheered was Queen Salote of Tonga, who was as tall as a ballplayer; her ancestors had eaten Captain Cook, she had told the Queen, hence British blood flowed in her veins). Finally the cars and the carriages of the British Royal Family drew up, culminating in the golden coronation coach carrying the dazzling, diamond-studded girl who was about to become Queen. Everyone in our stand had risen and was cheering for all their worth—everyone, that is, except Douglas. He was booing, loud as he could. I was horrified; our immediate neighbors looked as if they might lynch us.

After the Princess had entered the Abbey, we had hours to wait before she emerged as Queen. Douglas rushed out of the stand before anybody else, declaring that he had to see his doctor. This was true to the extent that Basil *was* a doctor and had a seat in the Abbey, but there was no way of getting in touch with him. Instead, Douglas decided to bluff his way into the House of Lords and have a bottle of champagne at the bar. A friendly barmaid was about to open the bottle, when an aged flunky stopped her. "Why are you serving these people? They've no right to be here, do *you*?" He rounded on Douglas. "I thought they were new creations," the barmaid explained. "Well, they're not," said the flunky. "I'm waiting here to see my doctor, who was in the Abbey." Douglas brandished his thermometer at him. "Well, you can't wait here," the flunky said, and threw us out. "New creations! Fucking flunky!" Douglas fumed.

I cannot remember whether we ever got a drink. By the time we returned to our seats, the newly crowned Queen was climbing back into her coach, and the great procession of royal personages in their carriages and the magnificently caparisoned Household Cavalry and the mounted regiments of what was left of the Empire were parading in front of us. To my relief, Douglas did not boo; he stood up and cheered as fervently as a patriotic schoolboy—not the Royal Family but the Bengal Lancers. This was the climax to what for Douglas had been a most fulfilling day, except of course for the weather and the nasty flunky in the House of Lords. By the time we arrived home, his temperature was normal. When I went to bid him good night, he was still euphoric about the Bengal Lancers. Next time we saw Picasso, Douglas told him all about them. Picasso turned out to share this penchant. Bengal Lancers even appear in one or two of his drawings.

Despite Douglas's seditious behavior at the coronation, Basil continued to ply us with seats for royal ceremonies. That kindly Scot did not share Douglas's anti-royalism, so I can only imagine that he derived a vicarious kick out of his friend's anarchic naughtiness. Why else would he propose, a year or two later, to get us places in the canopy of the throne for the ceremonial opening of Parliament? True, there was a condition: we had to be quiet as mice. The first time we went, Douglas was so chastened by the pageantry and the presence in the canopy of a mother of a royal page that he behaved with all due decorum. The successive processions—the royal heralds in their playing-card regalia, the members of the Royal Family in all their finery, the Lord Chancellor with his black-robed attendants—were magical. When the Queen entered with the Lord Great Chamberlain walking backward before her with his white wand, the peers and the peeresses "rose with a sort of feathered, silken thunder," to quote Benjamin Robert Haydon on George IV's coronation. And then the dramatic moment when the Commons barge their way democratically into the upper House. After the ceremony was over, we went down and mingled with the mob of peers in their camphor-smelling velvet and yellowing ermine. Douglas loved every minute of it, but pretended not to.

At the next opening of Parliament, Douglas behaved as badly as possible. As we entered the Houses of Parliament, he swelled up like a blowfish—a bad-baby glint in his good eye. He was wearing one of his more eye-catching suits and a disconcerting neon-pink bow tie. This time we were alone in the canopy, so Douglas felt free to bob up and down and play "I spy" through the finials: "I spy with my little eye something vile beginning with A—Lady Astor." By the time the Queen had taken her place in front of the throne to address the nation on her government's policies, Douglas had discovered that he could peep over the edge of the canopy and read her speech before she could, because it was typed out in big letters to obviate glasses. In a stage whisper, which, in my paranoia, seemed audible throughout the chamber, he hissed, "God save us, she's going to nationalize *fish* next." This triggered an attack of nervous laughter, which I had to bite my lip to control. I was terrified that we would be apprehended and tortured like Guy Fawkes, 350 years earlier. Still shaking, we went down to join Basil and the rest of the peers and peeresses, including the "vile" Lady Astor in an emerald tiara and stomacher. Douglas could not take his evil eye off her; whereupon she glared back at him. "What are you doing here? You don't look like a peer to me. You look like a journalist. Off with you!" And off he went, looking as sheepish as Billy Bunter. That was the last time we were allowed to attend the opening of Parliament. Henceforth, the canopy of the throne would be off limits—to us at least.

Picasso was so amused by Douglas's description of his anti-royal exploits that he came up with one of those rocambolesque spoofs that Spaniards, Catalans especially, enjoy thinking up and elaborating. Now that he was the owner of the grandiose villa La Californie, the artist claimed that he was going to acquire a suitably grandiose bride. Since La Californie had previously been rented to Queen Geraldine of

Albania, he had decided that she should be of royal blood; and since Douglas was related to the royal family of Albania, it was only right that he should represent the artist in this matter. No, an Albanian wife would not be acceptable.

There was only one possible bride for him, Picasso said: Princess Margaret, who had been much in the news. She corresponded to his physical type—on the short side, beautiful skin and good strong teeth. Presumably she had an adequate dowry. Would Douglas go to the Queen on his behalf and ask for her sister's hand in marriage? This would have to be done with suitable ceremony. Picasso would draw up a formal document, on parchment in French or Spanish or Latin, and Jacqueline would make a red velvet cushion on which Douglas would present it. I could accompany Douglas as a page or herald with a trumpet, suitably dressed, of course. If we didn't have the right clothes, Picasso would make them for us: cardboard top hats—or would we prefer crowns? He called for stiff paper and hat elastic and proceeded to make a couple of prototypes. His tailor, Sapone, would help him cut a morning coat out of paper. As for Jacqueline, she would have to go to a nunnery—married off to Christ. "You'd like that, wouldn't you?" Picasso turned to Jacqueline. "No, Monseigneur, I wouldn't. I belong only to you."

Picasso went on elaborating this spoof for the rest of the day. In the end we profited from his fantasy. To show off his prowess as a costumer, he gave each of us a tie as well as a crown out of cut paper emblazoned with colorful arabesques. "Now you look ready to be received by the Queen," he said. "Let's see if you know how to bow." We bowed. Douglas took charge of the ties and crowns Picasso had made for us. He never gave mine back to me. In due course, the son he adopted late in life inherited my regalia. He told me he was donating the items to the Musée Picasso, but failed to do so.

Many years later I told Princess Margaret the story of Picasso's quest for her hand. Like her great-great-grandmother Queen Victoria, she was not amused; she was outraged. She said she thought it the most disgusting thing she had ever heard. "But think of the portraits he would have painted," I could not resist saying.

Next time Picasso, or rather Jacqueline, landed us in a royal situation, it was for real. While married to a colonial official stationed in Ouagadougou, she had been upset by the lack of respect shown to African kings and tribal chieftains by colonial administrators in Paris. Every year a deputation of these notabilities would be invited, Jacqueline said, to make a "state visit" to France. Minor officials would bear-lead them around the country, subjecting them to tours of sewage farms and other such municipal facilities. "Poor wretches," she said, "they are at the mercy of low-level functionaries, who never miss an opportunity to demean them." She told us she was arranging for them to attend an official luncheon at Castille in order to see some good modern art for the first time in their lives. "Be nice to my *'rois nègres.'*"

Douglas was thrilled at the prospect of this royal visit. He immediately drove into Avignon to buy a hundred yards of carpet to roll across the courtyard from the front door to the gate. (The carpet would later prove useful on the stairs.) And he took trouble to devise a menu that would conform to the group's religious and dietary requirements. One of the dishes we served was "Coronation Chicken," which Constance Spry had invented for the delectation of the Queen's multinational, multiracial guests after the ceremony in Westminster Abbey. The French officials were resentful of the attention we paid to their magnificently robed royal visitors—"just like the Magi, my dear"—as well as the interest they showed in the paintings. Were we English out to subvert their vassals? To some extent, yes. Douglas suggested all kinds of pleasurable things for the *rois nègres* to do—things that would tax the power and the patience of the officials to the maximum. "I told the big sexy one from Gabon," he said, "to insist on being taken to visit Madame Claude's—she would introduce him to some suitable girls." Our African guests seemed grateful and presented us with colorful woven garments and a small metal object that Douglas claimed was a medal.

Years later, friends who had long since become inured to Douglas's attacks on the monarchy were disgusted when he took to championing the cause of that disreputable royal, the former King Léopold of the Belgians and his morganatic wife, the Princesse de Réthy. Douglas was foolish enough to eulogize them at a dinner that Stephen and Natasha Spender gave for Philippe de Rothschild at their house near Les Baux. In the August 23, 1974, entry of his journals, Stephen says he asked Douglas, " 'Do you mean the Léopold who killed a million people in the Belgian Congo, or the Léopold who betrayed his allies in 1940?' D. said that Léopold was quite right to stay with his people in their darkest hour, etc. Philippe asked, 'What about his relations to the Nazis?' D. said they were very limited. Philippe said, 'All I ask is that you don't tell that to a Belgian Jew.' " Douglas's penchant for these raffish royals was all the odder given his habitual denunciations of anti-Semitism and his chip-on-the-shoulder rejection of other notabilities. When an attractive neighbor called on Douglas with a friend who wanted to see Castille, he instructed the manservant to tell them he was out. "But we just caught sight of him," the neighbor protested. "Please say I am here with Mrs. Onassis." After checking, the servant returned with Douglas's response: "*Monsieur ne connait pas cette dame.*" By the end of the day Douglas had telephoned friends as far afield as Paris, London, and New York to boast of his rudeness: "The Onassis woman tried to invade my house, but I sent her packing."

Even more puzzling to the neighbors was Douglas's reaction to the Queen Mother's tour of Provençal houses. While proclaiming that he had reinforced the gates of Castille with barbed wire to keep her out, he begged Charles de Noailles, the instigator of the tour, to bring his royal charge to dine. In his wisdom, Noailles arranged for the Queen Mother to make what is called a "standing visit"—minimal refreshments, no dawdling or sitting down. "We queens are at the mercy of a very tight schedule," Her Majesty supposedly told Douglas, apropos the brevity of her visit. Ironically, Douglas was captivated by her. But by that time, the fires that had once consumed him were going out.

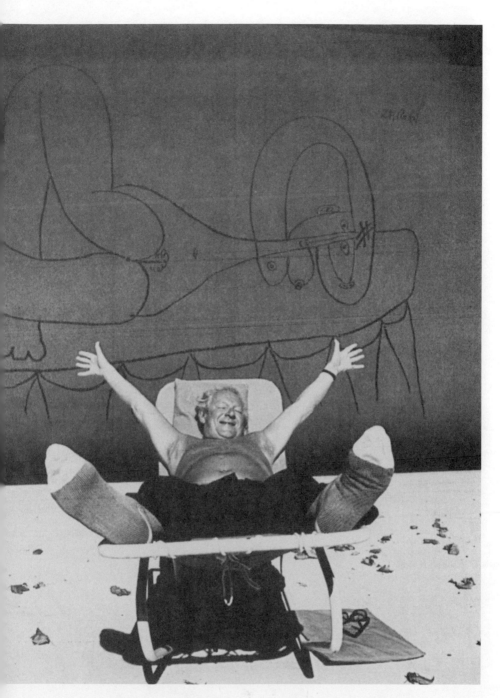

DC in front of Picasso's mural at Castille, 1963

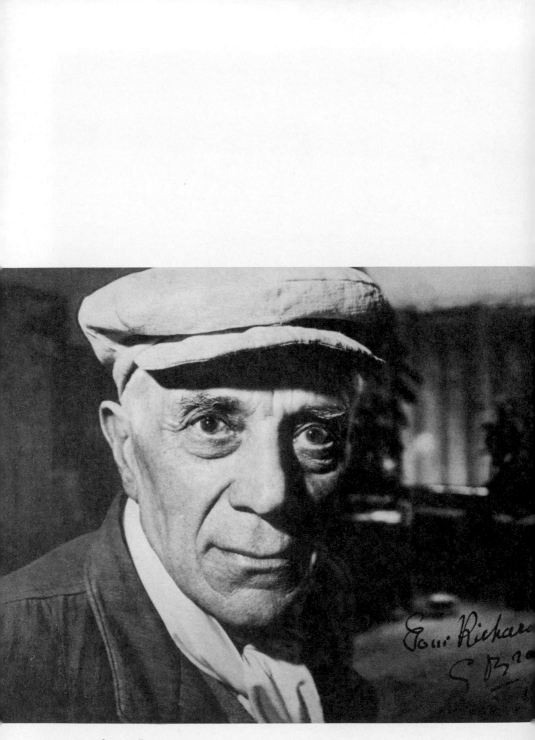

Georges Braque, 1955

PAINTERS AND
PAINTINGS

D ouglas had been reluctant to let me write about his four favorite artists, but I went ahead and adopted Braque as my special concern. I had always loved his work and soon came to love the man, who was the antithesis of Picasso—cool, meditative, at peace. He not only looked like a saint, he behaved like one: a saint of painting. Unlike Picasso, who desperately needed admirers to feed his voracious ego, Braque was self-sufficient, but he enjoyed discussing his work and his vision of art, which he would do with a wonderful metaphysical clarity. Over the next few years I would devote a couple of books and several articles, including a lengthy analysis of his great *Atelier* series, to his work. There was an advantage to doing this at Castille; my study was lined with some of Braque's finest paintings and they permeated the room.

At first Braque came across as daunting and withdrawn. However, once he realized that I understood his "difficult" late work, he opened up. So did his wife, Marcelle—small, fat, wise, and funny, not least about Picasso, whom she enjoyed putting down with a mixture of exasperation and affection. I remember her reminiscing about the time (1912–13) she and Braque and Picasso and Eva had settled at Sorgues, near Avignon. The four of them would take long walks together in the *garrigue*. If the mistral was blowing, they would assume Indian file: first big, brawny Braque, then plump Marcelle, then frail Eva, and finally little Picasso, cowering in their shelter. Picasso was less of a hero outside the studio than inside, she said. I suspect Marcelle never entirely forgave him for referring to her husband as his "ex-wife." Apropos this famous old slight, I always wanted to, but never dared, tell them a story (circa 1938) told to me by Dora Maar. Hearing that Braque had been hospitalized, Picasso rushed off to see him. He returned home in a rage. The

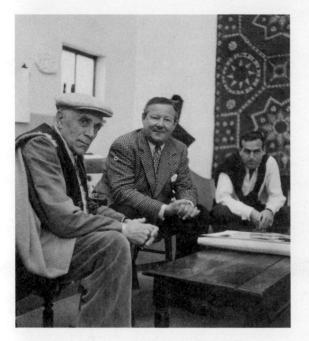

ABOVE: *DC and JR with Braque in his studio at Varengeville, ca. 1955*
OPPOSITE: *New Year's cards, pen and ink and watercolor, done by Braque for his friends*

nurse had refused to let him into his room because Madame Braque was in there with him. "Don't they realize that *I* am Madame Braque?" Typical of Picasso to stand his original joke on its head. *Au fond,* his most abiding male friendship had always been with Braque, Dora said. It was Braque who distanced himself, in part for ideological reasons. While he had drifted to the right—he sympathized with the fascistic *Croix-de-feu*—Picasso had been drawn more and more to the left.

Whenever I saw him, Picasso would ask for news of Braque. Braque *never* asked for news of Picasso, and on the very few occa-sions I saw them together, he would sooner or later do or say something to needle his old friend. One day, when we were all together at La Cali-fornie, Picasso asked us to come up to the studio and look at his recent work. Only Braque said no: he had arranged to take a ride in the photog-rapher Dave Duncan's hot new Gullwing Mercedes. Picasso was furious. He told me that when he had offered his old friend a studio at La Cali-fornie so that they could work together again, Braque had said he pre-ferred to stay at Saint-Paul-de-Vence with his dealer, Aimé Maeght, a man Picasso loathed. Another slight: Picasso had sent Braque one of his ceramics—a suitably Braque-like dinner plate decorated with fish bones and a slice of lemon—and never received any acknowledgment; would I find out what had happened? Braque had indeed received it, but thought it was *une blague*—a joke. "Picasso used to be a great painter,"

Braque liked to say. "Now he is merely a genius."

By the mid-fifties, Braque had turned into something of a hermit, much as Picasso would ten years later. His studio had become the center of his universe; it was also the primary subject of his work. If the light was curiously palpable—what Braque called "tactile"—it was because he kept his studio skylight veiled with thinnish, whitish material, which filtered and seemingly liquefied the light. In this penumbra the artist would sit as hieratically as Christ Pantocrator in a Byzantine mosaic, his great big Ancient Mariner's eyes devouring the paintings set out in front of him. The monastic hush would be broken only when he got up, wheezily, to make a slight adjustment to one of the many canvases arrayed in front of him. On my first visit to the artist's studio, I felt I had arrived at the very heart of painting. I never quite lost that feeling.

Braque accepted visitors from the outside world as a hermit might, without ceremony or curiosity. Unlike Picasso, he did not mind having people in the studio when he was painting. One afternoon in 1956, he let me stick around for a couple of hours while he worked on *A Tir d'Aile* (*In Full Flight*), his eerie painting of a sleek black bird crashing into a cloud as if it were a Stealth B-2 bomber

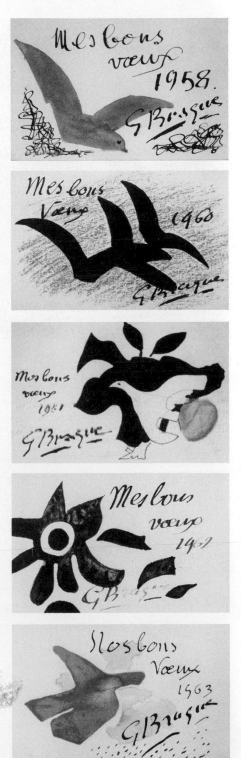

183

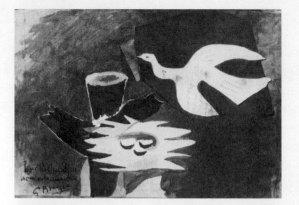

Georges Braque, Bird Returning to Its Nest, *oil, ink, pencil, and cut paper on cardboard, 1955; given by the artist to JR*

breaking the sound barrier. For weeks, Braque told me, he had been adding layer after layer of paint to the grayish-bluish sky to give it an infinite tactile density. As a result, it was so heavy he could no longer lift the canvas on or off the easel. Compared to the weightiness of the sky, the bird and cloud have as much substance as shadows. Braque had been reading about black holes: hence the concept of the cloud as a black void with a gravitational force that nothing can escape. It has been suggested that this blackness might also signify death. And indeed, by the late 1950s Braque was in very fragile health. Mortality held fewer fears for him that it did for Picasso; if anything, it challenged him, as in this painting, to bring *le néant* within his grasp, and to that extent within ours.

Apropos another bird painting, Braque talked to me about his visits to the Camargue, where our mutual friend the ornithologist Lukas Hoffmann (heir to the Hoffmann-LaRoche fortune and son of that perceptive modernist collector Maja Sacher) had established a vast bird reserve, La Tour du Valat. Douglas and I used to drive around in a jeep with Hoffmann, who would point out that the distant streak of quivering coral color ringing the vast Vaccarès lagoon was in fact flock after flock of flamingos. I also used to go riding there with our bull-breeder friend Jean Lafont, helping him round up the wild bulls that graze the salt marshes. Like the bulls, the wild but gentle horses we rode were native to the marshes; they are still never shod and their mouths are too soft to pull on, their flanks too soft for spurs—just a flick of a rein against their beautiful white manes, and they respond. Anything stronger and they throw you in the mud. Braque told me how the apparition of a heron flying low above the marshes had inspired his large 1955 *Bird Returning to Its Nest,* of all the late paintings the one that meant the most to him. Maybe because I shared his feelings for the Camargue, Braque gave me an oil study for this haunting work. I remember him saying how, on still, gray days, the sky seemed to reflect the lagoons rather than the other way round, and the birds seemed to swim through the air. Nor could he forget the swarm of mosquitoes.

I stayed close to Braque because I wanted to keep track of the nine large *Ateliers* he worked on from 1949 to 1956. Their subject is nothing less than painting itself, as practiced by the artist in the seclusion of his studio. They constitute a microcosm of Braque's private universe. There is no trace of a human presence, except insofar as Braque's Zenlike spirituality suffuses them. Until I came along, nobody had studied them in depth. To understand these *Ateliers*, it is necessary to evoke the carefully contrived clutter of Braque's studio: a space that was divided in half by a cream-colored curtain, in front of which numerous recent and not so recent works were arrayed on easels, tables, and rickety stands. Some of the paintings were barely started but already signed; some looked finished but lacked a signature; others dated back five, ten, even twenty years—"suspended in time," the artist said. "I 'read' my way into them, like a fortune-teller reading tea leaves." Sketchbooks ("cookbooks," Braque called them) lay open on homemade lecterns. Pedestals contrived out of logs and sticks picked up on walks were piled high with materials: palettes galore, massive bowls bristling with brushes, and containers of all kinds of paint, some of it ground by the artist and mixed with sand, cinders, grit, even coffee, to vary the texture. On the floor were pots of philodendrons, which Braque liked because the shape of their leaves "rhymed" with the shape of his palette, as well as simplistic sculptures carved from chalk—fishes, horses, birds—all of which make fragmentary appearances in the *Ateliers*. Elsewhere a shelf was set with tribal sculpture, musical instruments, and the large white jug that dominates *Atelier I*.

The presence of an enormous bird in these paintings is less enigmatic than it might seem. It does not represent a real, live bird but a "painted" one, an image that has detached itself from its canvas ground. When Braque embarked on the series, there was a large painting of a bird in flight (later destroyed) in the studio, and it is this image that appears in different guises in all but one or two of these paintings. Braque pooh-poohed suggestions that the bird might have symbolic sig-

THE SORCERER'S APPRENTICE

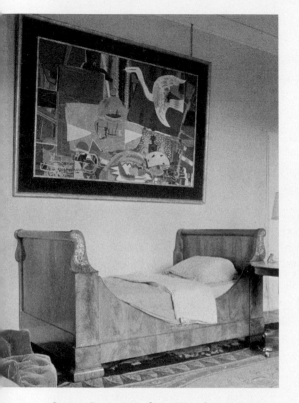

Georges Braque's Atelier VIII, *oil on canvas,*
1954–55, over DC's bed at Castille

nificance: an ectoplasmic material-
ization, a sacred Egyptian ibis, a
Picasso-esque dove of peace (the
journalist who made this suggestion was asked to leave), or, silliest
of all, that a real bird might have
flown in through the window.
These birds materialized on their
own, Braque insisted. "I never
thought them up; they were born
on the canvas." In a long interview
I published in the London
Observer, Braque went on to
explain: "I have made a great discovery, I no longer believe in anything. Objects don't exist for me
except insofar as a rapport exists
between them or between them
and myself. When one attains this
harmony, one reaches a sort of
intellectual nonexistence—what I
can only describe as a sense of
peace—which makes everything
possible and right. Life then
becomes a perpetual revelation. *Ça, c'est de la vraie poésie!*"

Every summer, Braque would dismantle the studio clutter and
reassemble it on a more modest scale in the studio of his country house
at Varengeville in Normandy, so that he could work away at his paintings
in his studio, or simply study them until he was ready to return to Paris in
the fall. The artist took pride in the artisanal ingenuity with which he
rolled up his canvases and stacked them onto the roof of his car. "No
rope," he said. He also took pride in his skill at driving very fast cars; how
he enjoyed the Rolls-Royce that his dealer had provided for him. He
wished he had learned to fly a plane.

On their annual visit to Saint-Paul-de-Vence to stay with Aimé
Maeght, the dealer Picasso disliked so much, the Braques would stop off
at Castille. They loved the Avignon area, because, as Braque said, "the

sky always seemed higher there than anywhere else," and because it reminded them of Sorgues, the ugly suburb where he and Picasso had rented houses in 1912. It was there that Braque had stolen a march on Picasso by making the first *papier collé*, when he was off in Paris, thereby taking cubism a crucial stage further. This *papier collé* was the core of Douglas's cubist collection, and he enjoyed having Braque tell the story of how he had found the wood-grained wallpaper for it in an Avignon shop—"Maybe they still have some in stock"—almost as much as Braque enjoyed reexamining this work, which can be said to have changed the course of modern painting.

In the summer of 1956, Braque had a specific reason for visiting Castille; he wanted to see how we had installed his *Atelier VIII*—the culminant painting of the series, into which he claimed to have put all the discoveries of his life. I had done everything I could to persuade Douglas that this *Atelier* was a kind of belated apogee of Braque's cubism, and that it belonged by right in his collection; and everything I could to persuade Braque, including an appreciation of the painting in *L'Oeil* magazine, that its rightful place was on the walls of Castille. Douglas was very keen on the idea; Braque was too, except that he wanted an undertaking that this work, which he regarded as his masterpiece, would remain in France. Douglas gave him a promise to this effect, a promise he gave in good faith (at this point he had decided to leave Castille and its collection to the Courtauld Institute). In view of this promise, the price was extremely low, around 7 million old francs (in those days about $20,000). As things turned out, *Atelier VIII* did not remain in France. On Douglas's death, it went to his adopted son, Billy, who had it shipped to Los Angeles. After Billy's death in 1992, it came up at Christie's in New York, where it fetched $7 million.

Braque seemed to like the way *Atelier VIII* looked above Douglas's bed. Picasso had difficulty coming to terms with it. Whenever he visited Castille, he would seek it out and scrutinize it and kind of growl at it. Each time this happened, I would try to draw him out. "*Comprends pas, comprends pas*" was all Picasso would ever say. I suspect that it challenged him more than it baffled him. There were still things Braque could do that Picasso couldn't. This must have rankled. Sure enough, two years later Picasso came up with a response—an oblique one that took the form of the most important of his variations on the

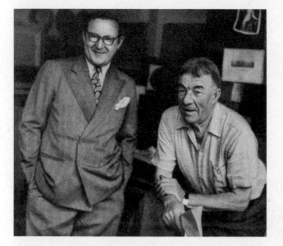

DC with Fernand Léger in his Paris studio, 1949

greatest of all studio pictures, Velázquez's *Las Meninas*. Picasso did not draw on Douglas's colorful *Atelier,* but on one of the earlier monochrome versions. He envisioned Velázquez's studio in the gray light and tactile space of Braque's *Ateliers.*

Of the four cubists Douglas had chosen to collect, only one, Juan Gris, had died—too soon to meet the man who would devote much of his life to studying his work. Douglas's scholarly *catalogue raisonné* of Gris's oeuvre is the publication that does him the most credit. Rightly or wrongly, he felt he would have disliked Gris—"a wonderful artist, but a humorless whiner with terrible chips on his shoulder"—however, Douglas was fond of his widow, the beautiful Josette, who worked as a *vendeuse* in a French fashion house. She had also been the model for the magnificent 1916 portrait (bought for less than £100 at Christie's in the late 1930s), which was the *clou* of Douglas's Gris collection. Picasso, who had done much to encourage Gris when he was a poor illustrator, and quite a bit to discourage him when he became a successful cubist painter, regretted that he had never acquired any of his work. Hence his repeated efforts to persuade Douglas to sell him the *Portrait of Josette*—to no avail. Douglas left this masterpiece to the Prado.

To my surprise, Douglas's eyes turned out to have been opened to modernism not by Picasso but by Fernand Léger: specifically Léger's one-man show at Paul Rosenberg's Paris gallery in 1930, when Douglas had been nineteen. He did not actually meet the artist until May 1933, when Carl Einstein—the pioneer historian of modernism and primitivism, who committed suicide when the Nazis invaded France—took him to Léger's studio. Painter and patron became instant friends. For Douglas, this stalwart, outgoing, left-wing modernist from Normandy, with his tough-minded, architectonic theories and total lack of preten-

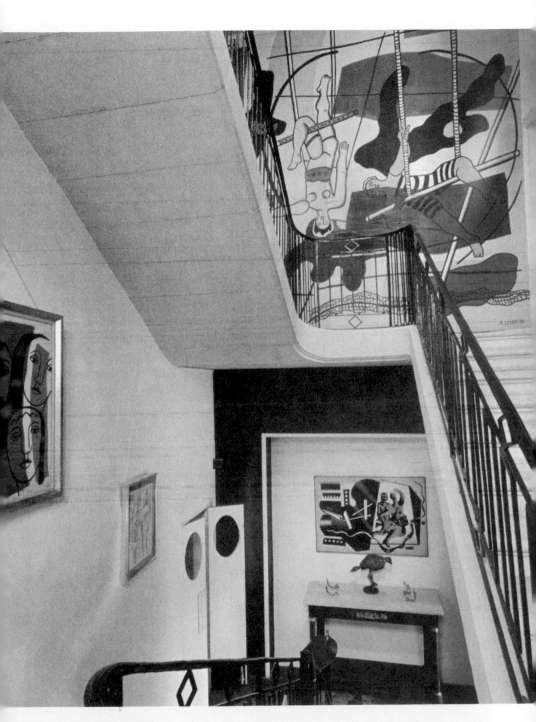

Léger mural, Les Trapézistes, oil on canvas, 1954, on the staircase at Castille, with two other Léger paintings below

sion, would remain Douglas's *beau idéal* of a modern artist. For his part, Léger was delighted to have a new patron (the economic slump had wiped out his biggest collector), above all one who not only understood his work but bought it, wrote about it, and exhibited it. Léger's intrepid wife, Jeanne, also took a shine to Douglas, as he did to her. She was one of the first of his Parisian friends I met; and it took me some time to realize that this frizzed, peroxided old lush had been a heroic Montparnasse beauty—famous in World War I for disguising herself as a *poilu* and, at the risk of being arrested as a spy or shot by a sniper, making her way to Verdun to have sex with Léger in the trenches. Her voice was as evocative as an old Edith Piaf record. Jeanne died a year later (1950), only to be succeeded by a bride whom Douglas described as "a totalitarian turnip."

In the course of putting together the world's finest collection of Léger's early work, Douglas had come to deplore the artist's failure to find patrons for some of his more ambitious projects. To believe Douglas, many of Léger's larger paintings of the 1930s had been conceived as murals—murals in which the tensions and collisions between identifiable objects and abstract forms would "destroy" the flatness of the wall on which they were painted. After buying Castille, he decided that Léger should paint a mural that would "destroy" the large wall on our staircase. On the occasion of his second honeymoon, which he spent with us in February 1952, the artist agreed to do so—in exchange for one of Douglas's many *Contrastes de Formes*.

The only problem was that Douglas could not abide the artist's second wife. Nadia was forever boasting about her important past: her closeness to Malevich—or was it Mayakovsky?—and the fact that she had been able to pee farther than any of the girls or boys in her village. Years later, Nina Berberova told me that Nadia was one of several Soviet women (another was the wife of the famous French novelist Romain Rolland) who had been encouraged to marry important cultural figures so as to keep them in the Communist camp. When I carried Nadia's suitcases upstairs, she told me off. "You carry suitcase, you spoil domestic. You not porter. You fool." Overhearing this, Marie, our cook, asked what Nadia wanted for breakfast. Orange juice: "Sorry, Madame, no orange juice." Well, then, fruit: "Sorry, no fruit." Bacon: "Sorry, no bacon, no croissant, no jam." It was mortifying to watch Léger, who had abided by his Communist principles when Jeanne was alive and lived in a small apartment in a working-class district, being exploited by this Stalinist. "Léger very great man: he need country house near Paris; he need Riviera villa; he need private projection room. . . . In Russia great artist have all this." Léger, who loathed all forms of privilege, seemed very depressed. For him, the whole point of films was going to the cinema and being together with *le peuple* and sharing their thrills and laughter and tears. He also said he preferred a sky with a lot of big white clouds, as in his native Normandy, to the monotonous blue heaven of the Riviera. Nevertheless, Nadia got her dacha, complete with projection room—in the valley of the Chevreuse, not far from the Duke and Duchess of Windsor—and a villa, the Mas Saint-André at Biot, where she would later memorialize her husband with a museum.

The mural on our staircase was a modified success. Douglas had chosen the subject from one of Léger's suite of 1950 lithographs, called *Le Cirque*. It represented a couple of acrobats suspended from trapezes above a net. The artist did a slightly different maquette, which he handed over to assistants to execute on canvas. As decoration, the mural was fine—striking, colorful fun—but the image was not powerful enough to "destroy" the wall, and the brushwork did not bear the idiosyncratic stamp of the artist's hand. How could it? Léger was seventy-four when it was painted and too heavy and shaky to clamber up ladders, which the size of the canvas (some thirteen by twelve feet) necessitated. His involvement seems to have been minimal. Shortly before he died, Léger came down to Castille to take a look. He strengthened some of the black lines, the net for instance, but this hardly entitled Douglas to claim, as he did when he sold the mural for a lot of money to the National Gallery of Australia in 1972, that it was a major late work by the artist's own hand. Twenty-three years later, when the gallery invited me to lecture in Canberra, I was questioned about the possibility of assistants' participation. The staff had gotten wise.

When Léger died in 1956, Douglas was extremely upset, not least at what he believed to be Nadia's high-handed behavior. Whether or not he had any justification, he claimed that this accomplished *pasticheur* of her husband's work had removed whatever painting was on his easel so that she could replace it with one of her own, a portrait of Mayakovsky, and pretend that at the end of his life Léger's heart went out to Mother Russia.

Douglas disliked most of the young recruits to the School of Paris, but there was one exception, a Russian giant who drove a large camper up to our gates one November afternoon in 1953 and sounded his horn. "I am Nicolas de Staël," he announced, "and I have an introduction from Denys Sutton [an English critic]." I let him in, a bit nervously. Although Douglas knew little about Staël, he was apt to dismiss him as just another of "those tedious *nouvelle vague* abstractionists." How would the two of them get on? I need not have worried. Staël had been elected to the Czar's College of Pages at the age of two, and his courtesy was more than a match for Douglas's truculence. What is more, Staël's charm turned out to be on the same scale as his frame—manic eagerness tempered with Russian melancholy.

Staël showed such understanding of the paintings on our walls, above all the Braques, that he won Douglas over in a matter of minutes. And then, far from being a hard-line abstractionist, Staël turned out to be in the process of making his way back to the figurative path. This ensured an instant entry into Douglas's good books. For his part, Staël, whose work had just begun to sell, was delighted to have found a new, famously discriminating fan. Over the next two and a half years he would give Douglas and me a fine, small group of his paintings and drawings. Pride of place went to a smashing landscape of *Agrigento* (1953)—vermilion roofs against a purple sky—which the artist had picked out specially for the *"château des cubistes."* Hung at the foot of the stairs, it vied with the Léger mural on the landing above.

Nicolas became a regular visitor. Douglas and I relished the prodigious way this giant ate and drank and laughed and groaned. He was extremely articulate, not only about painting but also about literature— Henry James in particular—and turned out to have a number of poet friends, among them the celebrated René Char. But Staël's principal passion was Braque. He regarded himself as Braque's disciple and had taken a studio around the corner from Braque's house on the rue du Douanier, so that he could have constant access to him. Just as well he did: one day Nicolas went up to Braque's top-floor studio and found the frail old painter in the throes of an emphysema attack. He summoned help and saved his life. The affection and respect were reciprocated. To my knowledge, Nicolas was the only young artist Braque spoke of with unqualified enthusiasm: he accepted him as a follower and occasionally subsidized him when money ran out. As for Picasso, Nicolas knew him and greatly admired him—but from afar. He liked to describe their first meeting at a Paris gallery toward the end of the war. Looking up at this giant towering over him, Picasso had felt like a baby. "Take me in your arms," he had said.

When Nicolas began frequenting Castille, I was writing the first of two books on Braque, and I profited greatly from his practical experience of Braque's theories of "tactile space" and the interrelationship of color and

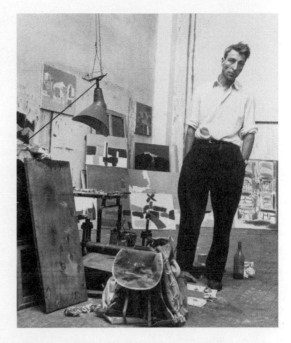

Nicolas de Staël in his Paris studio, 1954

texture. Nicolas's exploitation of impasto derived from Braque; so, less obviously, did the flat washes of color and infinite gamut of grays and blacks in his later work. More of a surprise was his obsession with the etchings of that rare and mysterious seventeenth-century Dutch artist, Hercules Seghers, whose prints were the inspiration for some marvelous drawings of boats that he gave us. After dinners at Castille, Nicolas would drive off into the night in the by-now-familiar camper, a kind of traveling studio, which he had filled up earlier that summer with his family and canvases and driven to Sicily—hence our Agrigento painting. On the way back to Ménerbes, he would stop by the roadside and make notes by moonlight. His attention had been caught by "the nothingness" of a particular stretch about two miles down the road from Castille. This was the inspiration for his minimal *Road to Uzès* landscapes: six irregular segments of thinnish paint in dullish blacks, greens, and grays is all they are, but these segments combine to form a vanishing point, toward which Nicolas, a maniacal driver, seems in my imagination to be forever heading.

In the winter of 1953–54, Douglas and I became regular visitors to Le Castellet, the fortified seventeenth-century house Nicolas had recently acquired at Ménerbes. It crowned one extremity of this hilltop village like the prow of a man-of-war, and in its imposing, fortresslike way it was eminently suited to this scion of the chivalrous Staël von Holsteins. Nicolas had done away with his predecessor's fustian decor and laid bare the medieval masonry of Le Castellet's vaulted rooms, which he furnished with a few bits of austere, Escorial-like furniture. "The only aristocrat since Delacroix who knows how to paint," Douglas said after visiting Le Castellet for the first time. And, true, the fastidiousness and cool Baudelairean dandyism of his style and the panache with which he attacked a canvas did have something aristocratic about it. Thank God for the Revolution, Douglas said. If Nicolas had inherited the family palace on the Nevski Prospect, he would never have been such a great painter.

Nicolas was one of the very few modern masters who had actually starved, not so much during his childhood as an orphaned refugee, but during the war, when he was in his late twenties and lived on next to nothing in Nice with a wife who was dying of tuberculosis. Like many another White Russian, Nicolas was too proud and fatalistic to hold his misfortunes against the world. Nevertheless, the scars went deep. As Douglas wrote, "He was a complex and in many ways contradictory character: autocratic, exacting, exuberant, morose, charming, witty and uncompromising. . . . He lived out his life between a series of violent extremes. . . . Pride would suddenly be replaced by humility, self-indulgence by asceticism, exaltation by gloom, uproarious laughter by withering scorn, supreme confidence by serious doubts, excessive work by deliberate idleness, great poverty by riches."

Marcelle Braque put Nicolas's dilemma in a nutshell: "Watch out," she told him, "you staved off poverty all right, but do you have the strength to stave off riches?" He did not. This Tolstoyan hero had always been beset by Dostoyevskyan demons, but after his sudden, huge success in America—a sharp-eyed friend of ours, Ed Bragaline, had been so impressed by his first New York show that he had bought several works for himself and persuaded his collector friends to follow suit—the demons got the upper hand. Money enabled Nicolas to indulge his Russian largesse to the full, but there was a certain desperation to his extravagance. One winter evening when he was on his own at Ménerbes, he invited Douglas and me to dinner. To start with, there was a great slab of foie gras. Then came a large turkey, which Nicolas had stuffed with a kilo of truffles. The three of us washed this down with most of a case of Cheval Blanc.

In the fall of 1954, Nicolas left Ménerbes. He had become infatuated with a young married woman called Jeanne—a protégée of the poet René Char. According to Nicolas, Jeanne was prepared to have an affair with him, but was not ready to leave her husband or show her lover much in the way of affection. When Nicolas dined with us on New Year's Eve, he described the hellishness of his situation. He adored his wife and family, but could not live with them; he resented his recalcitrant mistress, but could not live without her. Meanwhile, he had taken an apartment on the ramparts at Antibes, and was experimenting with a fresh, more figurative approach to a whole new range of subjects. Besides being tormented by *chagrin d'amour*, he was tormented by doubts about the new direction his work was taking.

Toward the end of February 1955, Douglas and I drove over to Antibes for lunch. Nicolas was in the depths of despair, and no wonder. The apartment looked across at Vauban's sullen-looking fort, which reminded him of the Fortress of St. Peter and St. Paul that his father had governed. It might have had a certain charm in summer, but on this dismal winter day the gray waves crashing onto gray rocks under a gray sky intensified the melancholy. "The noise of the waves is driving me mad," Nicolas groaned. And yet he had come up with some of the most exhilarating work of his career. Never had he laid on his color more luxuriantly and sensuously than in that mysterious paean to painting, *The Blue Studio*, which I would come to see as Nicolas's farewell to art and life. Subject and medium seem to fuse into each other, as in Braque's work. Douglas could not adapt himself to this sudden leap ahead, and this made him cross and critical. "It's all gone so soft," he said, evidently blind to the beauty and originality of the new paintings. Nicolas, who was in desperate need of reassurance, remonstrated with Douglas for his severity. I did my best to lower the tension by praising their symphonic sweep and orchestral color, but Douglas would not desist. I left them at it and went over to study a canvas that seemed the very essence of anguish: a vast, fearsome painting of seagulls flapping over tossing waves. On the

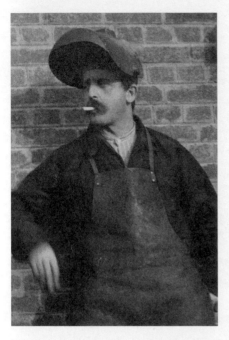

The sculptor César in his workshop, ca. 1955

same wall a window gave out onto an identical scene of gulls, grayness, and gloom. Just like the crows in van Gogh's ominous cornfield, I remember thinking. In retrospect, it is easy to see that this painting was a cry for help. Why didn't we respond to it?

Three weeks later, on the evening of March 18, Nicolas threw himself headfirst off his terrace, and landed just short of the rocks below. He died instantly. He was forty-two, and had barely begun to exploit his new-found lyricism. A few months before his suicide, he had sent me a bundle of collages to choose from: figures, still lifes, and a bullfight made of torn-up colored paper. I had not decided which ones to keep. Now that Nicolas was dead, Douglas suggested I hand all of them over to him "for safekeeping." Safekeeping indeed! I never got them back. After I left Castille, he used them to make swaps with dealers.

The only other young French artist to be included in Douglas's collection was the Marseille sculptor César Baldaccini, who preferred to be known simply as César. I had fallen for one of the welded scrap-metal pieces—a large *Fish*—in his first show in 1955 and had used up most of my savings to buy it. At first Douglas had been inclined to dismiss the *Fish* as too indebted to Germaine Richier. However, he came around to the power and originality of César's work after visiting the artist—a tiny tornado of a man with an enormous mustache and a quintessential Marseille accent—in his studio. On his way south a few months later, César stopped off for dinner at Castille. It must have been after a bullfight. Picasso was there, and given all that he had achieved with welded metal took a great shine to César as well as to my *Fish,* which had a place of honor in the hall. The following year, when César had a show at Vallauris, Picasso questioned him at length about his weld-

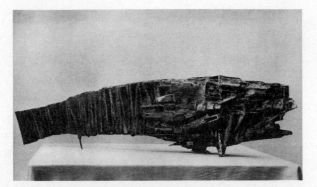

César, Fish, *welded metal, 1957; stolen from JR*

ing methods and nearly bought the iron *Turkey,* which Douglas later acquired. César was virtually the only young sculptor in whom Picasso took any interest.

César was proud of having grown up in direst poverty. To demonstrate how dire his early days had been, he took us on a visit to his father's shabby little bar in a section of Marseille so poor that cigarettes were sold individually rather than by the packet. And then, as a contrast, he took us on a short cruise off Marseille harbor on a rich friend's well-appointed yacht. The outing was intended to demonstrate to us, as well as to César himself, the conspicuous change he had wrought in his circumstances. It was done with irony and panache. People seemed to have more fun in the bar than on the boat.

This captivating bush baby of a man, with his dynamic energy and *joie de vivre* and ever more eye-catching style, soon became a major star of *le tout Paris.* In 1960 he had such a success with his *compressions*—automobiles crunched in a huge scrap-metal compressor—that chic Parisians lined up to have their Mercedeses and Alfa-Romeos transformed into pieces of sculpture that were rather more valuable. At almost exactly the same time, John Chamberlain, the New York sculptor, unwittingly started doing almost exactly the same thing. There is a subtle difference. The Frenchman's mechanical *compressions* are that and no more; the American's have a look of artistic contrivance. Douglas refused to let César crunch his Citroën; he had become too fond of it. In the mid-1950s, César took to using a pantograph, an instrument

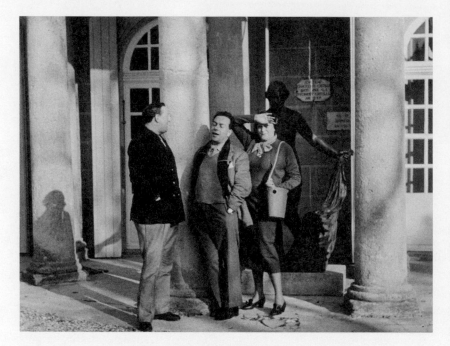

DC with Renato and Mimise Guttuso at Castille, 1954

that enables an artist to replicate his work on a larger scale. He would make a mold of his thumb or the breast of a go-go dancer and blow it up to monumental proportions. He also took to playing around with liquid polyurethane that sets in half a minute. He would throw a bucket of this new material down a flight of steps and the stuff would jell into instant "action" sculpture. Brilliant showmanship is about all one could say of these crowd-pleasing *expansions*.

César's *Fish* was one of the few possessions I succeeded in rescuing from Castille. Alas, I managed to lose it all over again. Shipping it back from Paris would have entailed so much expense and red tape that I left it on loan to a funny, feckless friend of mine, Jean Léger, the artist's great-nephew. When, a year or two later, I tried to get it back, Jean turned out to have contracted AIDS. He said he had grown so fond of my *Fish* that he wanted to keep it a little longer. In view of his illness, I refrained from pressing him, but after his death I tried to extract it from his estate, only to discover that his Haitian roommate had made off with it. César was also concerned, as he wanted to have the *Fish* cast in bronze for an edition he proposed to put on the market. He asked his lawyer to help, but the roommate turned out to have gone into hiding, and before we could take the necessary action, he, too, had died.

Another regular visitor to Castille was Renato Guttuso, then the most famous social realist of his day, now virtually forgotten outside his own country. Douglas worshiped this Sicilian maestro. He deluded himself that Renato was a modern Delacroix who had the virtuosity and ideology to breathe new life into the fustian genre of history painting and tackle such overexploited themes as the horrors of war in an eye-catching new way. Douglas maintained that Renato's verismo approach was more relevant to modern life than abstractionism, which he chose to see as "very old hat. . . . World War II had killed it off. Why ever resuscitate it?" It helped that Renato was handsome and magnetic, with fire in his eyes as well as his belly. Charisma had won him a seat on the Central

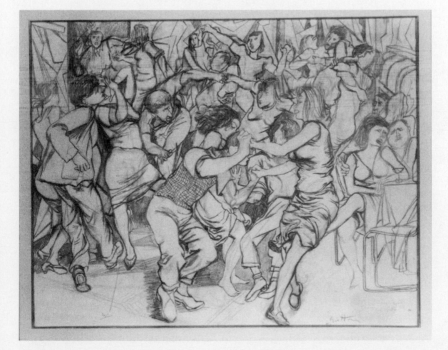

Renato Guttuso, Boogie-Woogie, *pencil, 1953*

Committee of the Communist Party, as well as the hand of the former beauty Contessa Mimise Bezzi-Scala, a delightful woman but a most inappropriate wife for a prominent Communist. Mimise was ineffably ladylike—always dressed as if she were about to launch a ship rather than take part in a political rally.

Apart from Edouard Pignon, Guttuso was the only one of the younger Communist painters with whom Picasso felt comfortable. Jacqueline and Mimise also got on well; boredom with Communism was a bond. Douglas and I used to join the Guttusos at La Californie, and sometimes return with them to Italy. In the fall we would stay in their villa near Varese. Mimise loved people who loved food and would serve us the best of all salads: porcini mushrooms or, better still, the orange ovoli, with shavings of Parmesan, white truffles, and some good olive oil. Winters we would visit the Guttusos in Rome, in their elegant apartment in the Palazzo del Grillo, hung floor-to-ceiling with a well-chosen collection of modern paintings and drawings, including several Picassos. Summers they would visit us. We would have a roll of drawing paper ready for Renato. After dinner he would ask what he could draw for us. "A disaster," Douglas would say. "The Black Hole of Calcutta, a fire in a lunatic asylum." Renato would usually come up with the same writhing figures—dynamic heroes and villains, not unlike himself, and a lot of big-bottomed women with spaghetti hair. Since I owned some fanciful, *verre églomisé* furniture that had been made for an eighteenth-century folly, the Villa Palagonia in Bagheria, near where Renato had grown up, he would also do drawings of the villa and its grotesque sculptures, which Prince Palagonia had commissioned in the hope of inducing a miscarriage in his wife.

Renato's after-dinner displays of virtuosity made one wonder whether his more serious work might not have been conceived in the same simplistic spirit. His sense of tragedy seemed as mechanical as a wind machine on a movie set. I had admired some of his earlier paintings, not so much the overwrought scenes of revolutionary fervor as the gutsy images of popular life—people in cafés, at dance halls, or at the beach. Renato gave me a fine drawing for his polemical set piece *Boogie-Woogie*—a denunciation of what was then called "cocacolonization," as well as a mockery of Mondrian—but the message comes across scrambled, and the image seems to promote what it purports to attack. I was not alone in finding most of his later work too hokey to take seriously. Before Mimise died, Renato had taken up with another ravaged contessa, but whereas Mimise was infinitely supportive, her successor turned out to be a voracious tigress, to judge by the references to her in his work. He sent this woman a drawing every day of her life. Toward the end, social realism gave way to tedious allegory, and prelates hovered. Renato's death left his reputation in limbo and his estate at the mercy of bickering heirs. Douglas had long since sold his extensive holdings of Renato's work. With them vanished any faith he had in the long-term prospects of social realism.

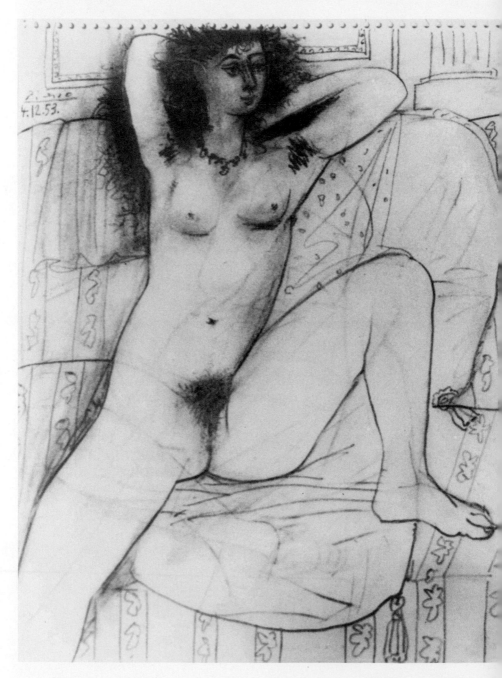

Picasso, Seated Nude, *pencil, 1953; given by the artist to DC and JR (one of the items stolen in the 1974 burglary of Castille)*

PICASSO AND DORA

On February 6, 1954—not quite halfway through my twelve years with Douglas—I turned thirty. Douglas planned a birthday celebration that would also serve as a belated housewarming. But on February 5, the arctic chill that had paralyzed much of Europe turned even fiercer, and for the first time in decades Castille was beautifully blanketed with a heavy fall of snow. Many of our neighbors, among them the Hugos, were marooned without electricity or water, so we put the party off until Easter, when Richard and Ann Wollheim were due to spend a week with us.

On Easter Sunday, Isaiah Berlin and his future wife, Aline Halban, who were staying at Avignon, arrived for lunch. In the afternoon some of us went to the bullfight, after which we had envisaged a quiet evening at home with the Berlins and Wollheims. However, in the course of the corrida, Picasso and Jacqueline announced that they and the rest of their group—sixteen in all, including Picasso's son, Paulo, and the Ramiés, the Tériades, and Jean Cocteau, plus entourage—would like to dine at Castille; he also announced that he had a present for us. The present turned out to be an Ingresque drawing that had obsessed me ever since I first saw it pinned on a wall at Le Fournas: an uncompromisingly frontal image of a naked girl, legs wide apart, seated like an odalisque on a pile of cushions. It had been heavily worked. To create highlights and smudge shadows, Picasso had used an eraser—a device he admitted borrowing from Matisse. The drawing was far more striking than any of the enormously popular "Verve" series—scenes in which Picasso caricatures himself as an elderly clown or a masked dwarf lusting after a young girl—which he did that same winter. I was surprised at his giving us something so personal until I realized that the gift must have been made at Jacqueline's behest. She would have had every reason to want this erotic image removed from the studio wall: it represented one of her rivals, Geneviève Laporte. Characteristically, Picasso brought the drawing in the box that had contained the Dior wrap we had given Jacqueline for Christmas. No less characteristically, he kept the box; he liked to incorporate *emballage* in his work. As Picasso handed over the drawing, he said, presciently, "When you two split up, you're going to have to cut it in half." After we broke up, Douglas simply kept it. Sadly, the drawing disappeared when Castille was burgled some years later. So far as I know, it's still in the hands of the Mafia.

Thanks to our store of truffles, Marie managed to transform slim pickings and cold cuts into the semblance of a feast. For Jacqueline, this was one of her first public appearances as Picasso's official mistress. She already radiated far more confidence than she had at Perpignan. At dinner Picasso watched sardonically as Cocteau launched into a display of conjuror's patter so dazzling one could only imagine he hoped to distract attention from its intrinsic triviality. The poet was in tauromachic mode, having made notes during the bullfight of Damaso Gomez's spectacular performance. These notes, which Cocteau would incorporate in his book *La Corrida du 1er Mai*, received their first airing in the course of dinner. Meanwhile Isaiah kept his attention on Picasso. He told us later that of all the great men he had known—scientists, historians, philosophers, politicians—Picasso struck him as the most impressive. Hence an unwonted shyness on his part. And then, when the artist readied himself to leave, Isaiah felt impelled to run after him and tell him a story that had amused us at lunch—a story about Lope de Vega on his deathbed. Am I sick? Spain's most illustrious playwright supposedly asked his doctor. Yes. Dying? Yes. Less than an hour to live? Yes. "Then I can finally confess that Dante bores me." With a look of terror, Picasso, who had no idea that Isaiah was one of the wisest men in England, jumped into the car and told his son to drive off. For his part, Isaiah had no idea that Picasso regarded any mention of death—above all the death of a great Spaniard—as tantamount to being subjected to the evil eye. When told about this, Isaiah was mortified.

Six weeks later, Picasso returned to Nîmes for the Whitsun bullfight—this time without Jacqueline. She must have been ill. Without a woman on his arm, he seemed a bit forlorn. However, over lunch at the

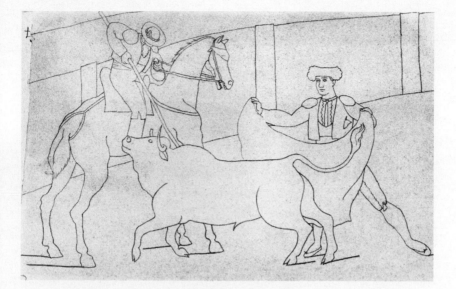

Picasso, Bullfight, *pencil, 1923; formerly in JR collection*

Hôtel du Cheval Blanc, across from the great Roman arena, he perked
up. The *novillada* was expected to be more exciting than usual, thanks to
the participation of a suicidally foolhardy Mexican torero. This new
young star gratified Picasso by dedicating a bull to him and proceeding
to defy death with such daring and elegance that when it was time for the
mise-à-mort, the entire arena seemed to hold its collective breath. Our
improvised dinner after the Easter bullfight must have pleased Picasso.
He asked us to do it again. However, there was a potential problem. A
week or two earlier, our neighbor Dora Maar—the mistress Picasso
abandoned for Françoise Gilot—had called to ask whether she and her
houseguest, James Lord, the young American writer who had attached
himself to her—could come and dine and stay that very same night.
James had formerly enjoyed Picasso's favor, but had recently incurred his
wrath. Douglas followed Picasso in blowing hot and cold where James
was concerned. However, a confrontation between Picasso, Dora, and
James was too good an opportunity for mischief to miss, so Douglas
agreed to their visit. Picasso turned out to be no less enthusiastic about
the encounter. *"Tant mieux,"* he said with conspiratorial relish, "I haven't
seen her in ages. Don't let her know I'm coming. It'll be a nice surprise."

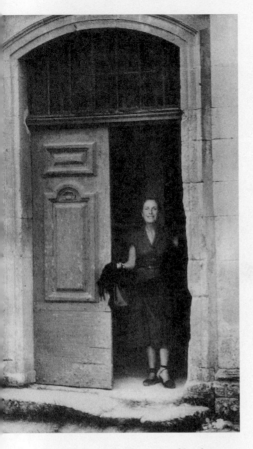

Dora Maar in the doorway of her house at Ménerbes, ca. 1954

On the evening in question, Picasso arrived first. With him were Paulo, who was acting as his driver, and Jean Leymarie (later director of the Musée National d'Art Moderne in Paris) and his wife. Jean was Picasso's foremost champion in the French museum world, and one of the few officials for whom he felt affection and respect. The only other guest was an old friend of mine, Richard Buckle, the British ballet critic. In the hour or so before Dora and James arrived, the artist reminisced about Dora—at first affectionately—how the steadfastness of her gaze reflected her intelligence, and how her outré sense of fashion had inspired the surrealistic hats trimmed with fish and fruit and sardine cans that figure in many of his portrayals of her— such a contrast, he said, to the tam-o'-shanter from Hermès that he gave her rival Marie-Thérèse. Hats differentiate the two rivals in his work. Did the craziness of Dora's hats, by Albouis or Schiaparelli, imply a certain craziness in the sitter? Yes, he thought it did. Despite her poise and sophistication, there was something about Dora that had terrified him. "I left her out of fear. Fear of her madness," Picasso said. "Dora was mad long before she actually went mad." True or not, this did not exonerate Picasso. If Dora terrified him, it was surely out of guilt; she held him responsible for her fate.

Picasso chose to blame the Surrealists—not least her previous lover, the erotomaniac Georges Bataille—for the breakdown Dora suffered after he left her. And as if to confirm the extent of her derangement when they first met, he recounted the story of watching her, all alone in the Café des Deux Magots, playing a kind of Russian roulette. After taking off her black gloves, Dora had placed her left hand on the café table, and proceeded to stab away with a penknife at the spaces between her out-stretched fingers. Every so often she missed and nicked a finger (the real object of the game, Picasso said) and began to bleed badly. According to Françoise Gilot, who wrote about this masochistic inci-dent in her memoirs, this is "what made up [Picasso's] mind to interest himself in her. He was fascinated." He asked Dora to give him the black gloves and kept them in a vitrine.

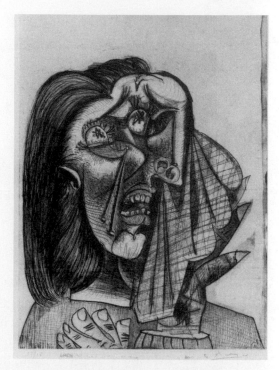

Picasso, Weeping Woman, *etching, aquatint, drypoint, 1937*

As for the religious mania that afflicted Dora after their breakup, Picasso told us that she had always had a mystical, occult streak—"at one point she had even taken up Buddhism"—but that until her breakdown she had had little or no sympathy for Catholicism. She associated it with the pious mother she loathed. According to Picasso, her rebirth as a manic Catholic in the course of her 1947 collapse had been the saving of Dora. After shock treatments had done more harm than good, Jacques Lacan, who had taken over her case at Picasso's request, apparently used her religious mania as a bridge back to sanity. Dora was now, to all intents and purposes, cured. To Picasso the transfor-mation of his *pleureuse* into a penitent Magdalene was only fitting.

What was Dora up to with James Lord, Picasso asked. Douglas was predictably scathing. The year before, he had been very favorably dis-posed toward James for setting up a committee to purchase Cézanne's studio at Aix-en-Provence, but he had, typically, turned against him

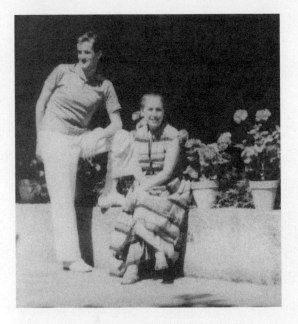

James Lord and Dora at the Mas Saint-Bernard, ca. 1952

when he brought this project to an extremely successful conclusion. Douglas was also jealous of James's burgeoning friendship with Dora; his friends had no right to prefer each other to him. For his part, Picasso claimed to be outraged at Dora's "romance" with James. Although ten years had passed since he abandoned her, the artist still regarded Dora as his property and was horrified that she should allow herself to be courted by someone else, above all someone who had courted him.

Gertrude Stein was indirectly responsible for his friendship with James, Picasso said. She maintained that the innocence and simplicity that had been the hallmark of the doughboys of World War I had been inherited by the GIs of World War II. Get to know one, she had told Picasso. And as if by magic, James had materialized and become something of a fixture. He had grown to like James, Picasso said, although he was anything but *une âme simple* as he had been led to expect. However, it was fun to have a human pet around, and he described how James would curl up in a corner of the room and go to sleep like a dog. When called, he would jump up and beg—not for a bone, but for an illustrated book or a drawing of himself. Wagging his tail at Dora was never going to work, Picasso said. She was too intelligent not to realize that he was using her as a proxy for him. Picasso did not believe for a moment that they were having an affair. "James doesn't like women, and the only man Dora really loves is God, *mais on verra . . .*" The noise of a car drawing up announced that Dora and James had arrived.

In his self-revelatory book, *Picasso and Dora,* James has given a riveting account of this evening based on his diaries. The evening was indeed memorable; it was the last time Picasso would see this woman who had been his tragic muse, the personification of *Guernica,* and the subject of his most anguished portraits—also the only one of his wives or mistresses whose temperament and imagination had been on the same mystical wavelength as his own. James's account tallies with notes I made at the time. The only difference, we were prepared for Picasso's onslaught, where-

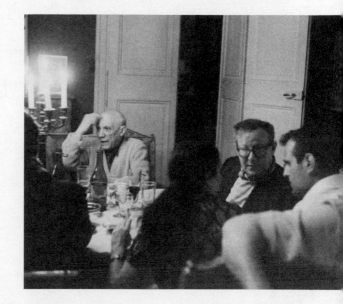

Dinner at Castille, ca. 1955: Picasso, DC, JR, Jacqueline

as poor James wasn't. Douglas did what he could to stir things up. I, on the other hand, sympathized with James's plight and did what I could to play things down. And then all of a sudden Picasso denounced James for daring to praise some genteel sketches he had seen by Boudin, though in reality for consorting with a woman who had the brand of his ownership upon her. This was my first, and I am glad to say my last, exposure to Picasso's icy wrath. Dora fared little better than James. It must have been torture for her to spend an evening with the man who had abandoned her and yet continued to treat her as if she belonged to him. I watched her as closely as politeness allowed and concluded that it was pride, bolstered probably by her newfound faith, that protected Dora throughout this unnerving evening—protected her not so much from Picasso's petulant barbs ("When are you two going to get married?") as from the mockingly affectionate looks he shot at her as if to reignite old ashes. It was pride, too, that prevented Dora from breaking

OVERLEAF: *Dinner at Castille: clockwise from left, Zette Leiris, unidentified woman, Lauretta Hugo, JR (behind candle), DC (at head of table), Picasso, Francine Weisweiller, Cocteau, Michel Leiris, unidentified woman, Jean Hugo (back to camera)*

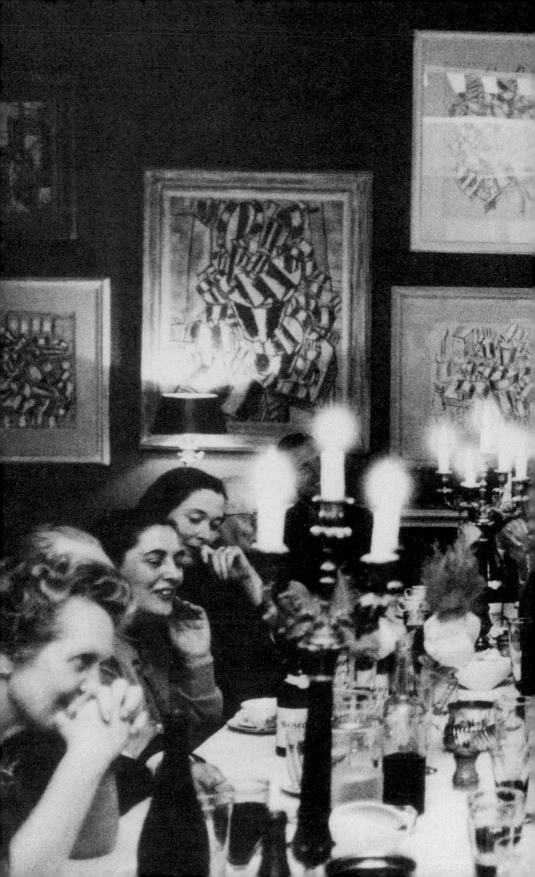

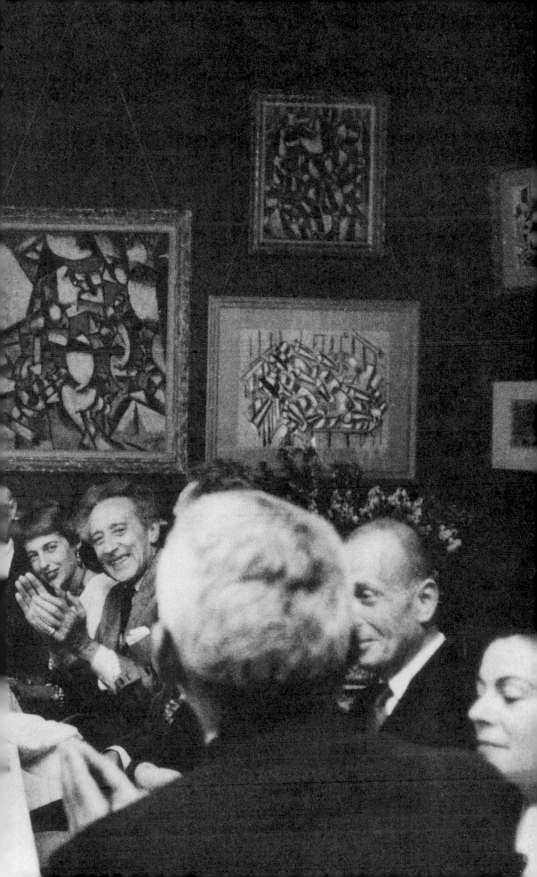

down and giving Picasso the *frisson* of seeing her once again as his weeping woman. And if Picasso's humiliation of James had not already done in their *amitié amoureuse,* her pride would see to that. After dinner, Picasso abruptly drove off, leaving Dora shattered and James's regard for his former hero reduced to umbrage.

Some three years later, James brought his relationship with Picasso to a dramatic conclusion. One morning early in November 1956, Picasso called Castille in a black rage. He told us he had just received a long letter from James, challenging him, as a key member of the Communist Party, to repudiate the party line and come out publicly against the Russian invasion of Hungary. "Can the painter of *Guernica* remain indifferent to the martyrdom of Hungary?" sets the tone of James's letter. If Picasso failed to do this, James threatened to turn his letter over to the press—"Very close to blackmail," as he admits in his book *Picasso and Dora,* "and not a course of which to be proud, but I felt then, and still feel, that both Picasso and the circumstances deserved strong medicine."

"How dare James set himself up as a man of principles?" Picasso asked. "Where has he been hiding them all this time? All he wants is his name in the papers, and to this end he will endanger the efforts that some of us in the party are making to draft a manifesto against Soviet repression." Would Douglas intervene and persuade James to withdraw his letter? I begged Douglas to act as a peacemaker rather than a warmonger, but he was not going to forgo the pleasure of acting as Picasso's enforcer. By calling up James and shrieking "You filthy little shit!" at him, he made things much, much worse. As James rightly said, Picasso "showed extraordinary lack of judgment in choosing this particular emissary. If he himself had called and asked me to desist, I would have found it impossible to refuse."

A week later, James's letter appeared in *Combat* and caused a small stir. Five days later, the document that Picasso had told us about— it called for a special congress at which the issues could be debated— was leaked to *Le Monde.* Although signed by Picasso and nine intellectuals, it was too equivocal to attract much attention, let alone have any impact on the situation. As he had expected, James was anathematized by Picasso, but he was upset to find himself scolded by his other hero, Giacometti, and dropped by his good friend Jean Cocteau for publishing this letter. I shared his horror at the Russian invasion of Hungary but felt that James had put himself in a very invidious position. He had rounded on Picasso, who had done so much for him, and played into the hands of the artist's reactionary detractors.

Before Christmas, we left for Paris. Douglas had to pick up a new

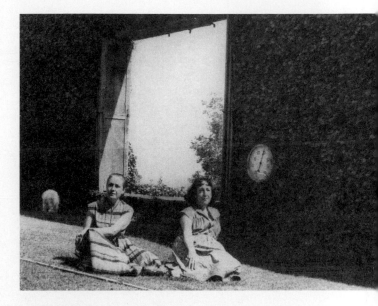

Dora and Marie-Laure at the Mas Saint-Bernard, ca. 1953

Citroën; I had to work on an interview with Braque. We saw a lot of Marie-Laure de Noailles, and had an occasional glimpse of her exquisitely courteous husband, the Vicomte Charles. Years before, the Chavchavadzes had taken me to see the Noailles' vast, treasure-filled *hôtel particulier* on the Place des États-Unis, which Marie-Laure had inherited from her immensely rich banker-industrialist father, Maurice Bischoffsheim, and I had been dazzled. Virtually every painting was of exceptional quality and interest. Besides Goya's incomparable portraits of his son and daughter-in-law, a Rubens sketch, a fine Bonington, and Géricault's delectable triple row of horses' rumps, the hexagonal downstairs library contained Picasso's big bland portrait drawing of Marie-Laure, which does little justice either to the sitter or the artist. Tables glittered with *objets de vertu* and gold boxes, most of which would later vanish in a burglary. Beyond this library were Marie-Laure's cozy, cluttered quarters, filled with a little girl's collection of "treasures": ex-votos, photographs of bullfighters, fetishes and miscellaneous mementos. In the entrance hall, mammoth narwhal tusks held up by tasseled ropes jutted out at the great staircase, which was hung with Picasso's monumental 1908 *Nude*, Juan Gris's cubist version of a portrait of

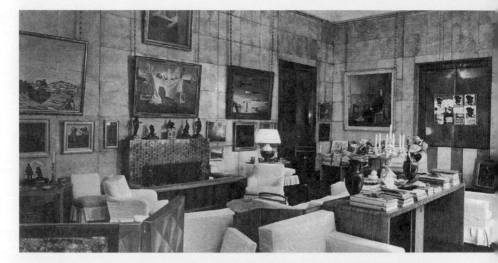

*The upstairs salon, decorated by Jean-Michel Franck, in the Noailles' Paris house.
Dalí's* The Old Age of William Tell *is over the fireplace.*

Madame Cézanne, one of Chirico's "metaphysical" still lifes, and a masterpiece by Burne-Jones—in those days considered the epitome of kitsch.
The large ballroom, all rococo gilt and mirrors, was still occasionally used
for concerts by musical boyfriends or fancy dress parties of utmost splendor and little mirth, whose only purpose was to give members of *le tout
Paris* a chance to preen in public and make epicene fools of one another
and themselves. The upstairs salon had been done over in the mid-thirties
by that influential decorator Jean-Michel Franck. The walls were covered
in great squares of creamy parchment, which resembled blocks of soft
masonry, and were hung with surrealist masterpieces—Dalís, Ernsts,
Mirós—and one or two daubs by ex-lovers. Tables were stacked with *édi-
tions de luxe* and musical scores. Dotted around were some of Balthus's
powerful little drawings for *Wuthering Heights.*

One evening Marie-Laure gave a dinner for Marcel Duchamp,
whose laid-back brilliance and wit and lack of pretension took me by surprise. Marie-Laure was in fine fettle. Earlier in the day, she had attended
the funeral of Jacques Fath, the flamboyant fashion designer, and she
regaled us with stories of a farcical mix-up over the flowers. Wreaths
intended for the bier of an old lady whose funeral was scheduled for the
same day had landed up on Fath's coffin, emblazoned with the words "À

notre tante adorée." The other dinner guests included Cocteau, Gia-cometti, and Dora Maar. Dora had turned back into the semblance of a worldly Parisienne. But there was no sign of James Lord. Marie-Laure told us that on the eve of his return to America, he had broken his ankle and spent two weeks in hospital. He was recuperating at Aix-en-Provence before taking a boat to New York. Dora, as Douglas had predicted, no longer saw him.

After dinner, Marie-Laure took us off to the opening of a Derain retrospective. For accepting an official invitation to visit Germany during the war, Derain had been denounced as a collaborator. However, he had recently died; hence this commemorative retrospective, the first official recognition of his work in years. One of his few champions was Giacometti, who vehemently defended him against charges of collaborationism. Giacometti had less success defending Derain's later work against Douglas's contention that this artist had sold out to a bourgeois public and had been cooking up saccharine confections, like his suburban pastry cook of a father, ever since. "Alberto, it's so *bad*." "Maybe that's why I like it," Giacometti said.

Meanwhile, Marie-Laure, who had consumed more champagne than usual, was stirring up trouble as only she knew how. Her *racé* Faubourg St.-Germain squawk got louder and louder. "Nothing but collaborators and denunciators here," she said as she positioned herself strategically next to the American-born Marquise de Polignac, who had been accused of fraternizing with the Germans. And then she started on people who claimed to have hidden parachutists and resistance workers in their attics. To believe her, they did so in expectation of a sexual quid pro quo. "You can be sure they would have denied shelter to a nice old Jew." Considering that Marie-Laure was a quarter Jewish and had had an affair with an Austrian officer, which would have made for terrible trouble if it had not been hushed up, she would have been wiser to keep her thoughts to herself.

Before returning to Castille, we went to see Dora, who told us that she had not been seeing James. She had not visited him in hospital; she had not replied to a long, reproachful letter that he later reprinted in his book about their relationship. Dora sent us a souvenir of

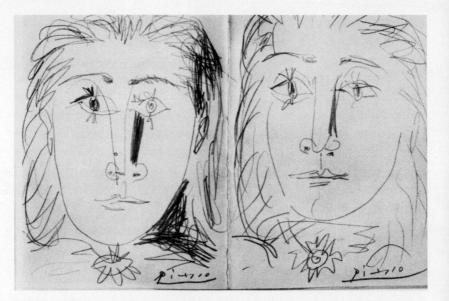

Picasso, Double Portrait of Dora Maar, *pencil, 1941. Given to DC and JR by Dora Maar; the left one was inscribed "pour Douglas" and the right one "pour John." DC kept both.*

her traumatic evening at Castille: a hand-painted Christmas card of a stump of a candle guttering with an eerie little flame. She also gave each of us a charming pencil drawing of herself by Picasso. Although she had inscribed the mount *Pour John* and *Pour Douglas,* this did not stop Douglas from keeping both of them. Dora also gave us several examples of her own recent work: sad, romantic views of the *garrigue,* slashed on with the palette knife. In return, Douglas wrote the foreword to an exhibition of them at Berggruen's gallery. Douglas was surprised to receive a letter from James, inviting himself to come and recuperate at Castille. He and his friend Bernard Minoret—a writer of singular erudition who is now an éminence grise in the intellectual and social life of Paris—went to stay at Aix-en-Provence instead.

In 1958, Picasso allowed Douglas to do a facsimile edition of a sketchbook belonging to Dora, one that dates from the summer of 1906, when he shut himself away with his first love, Fernande Olivier, at Gósol, high in the Pyrenees. *Le Carnet Catalan,* it is called, and the quality of it pleased the artist. "Let's do another one," he said. "Next time you go to

Paris, ask Dora to show you the *Facteur Cheval* sketchbook; it would be perfect—never reproduced." A few weeks later, Douglas and I were in Paris, so we called on Dora. She, too, had been delighted with the *Carnet Catalan,* but when we asked to see the *Facteur Cheval* sketchbook, she burst into tears. She couldn't possibly show it to us, she said; she refused to tell us why. Back in Cannes, a few days later, we reported to Picasso what had happened. He chuckled—"I suspected that might be her reaction"—and went and called Dora and, in a voice of ice, insisted that she show us the sketchbook.

Back we went to see Dora. She looked utterly humiliated. The handsome drawings in the sketchbook laid out on her worktable turned out to be bawdy but hardly offensive. They constituted what the Spaniards call an *Alleluja,* a kind of comic strip such as Picasso used to do as a child. The *carnet* told a story: the daily round of Ferdinand Cheval—the "Douanier Rousseau of architecture." This eccentric postman from Hauterives, a village in the Rhône Valley near Vienne, spent

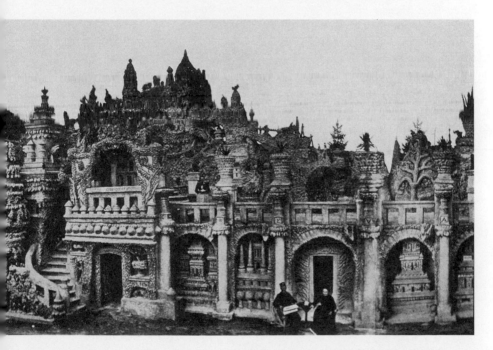

The Facteur Cheval and his wife in front of the Palais Idéal, his folly at Hauterives in the Rhône Valley

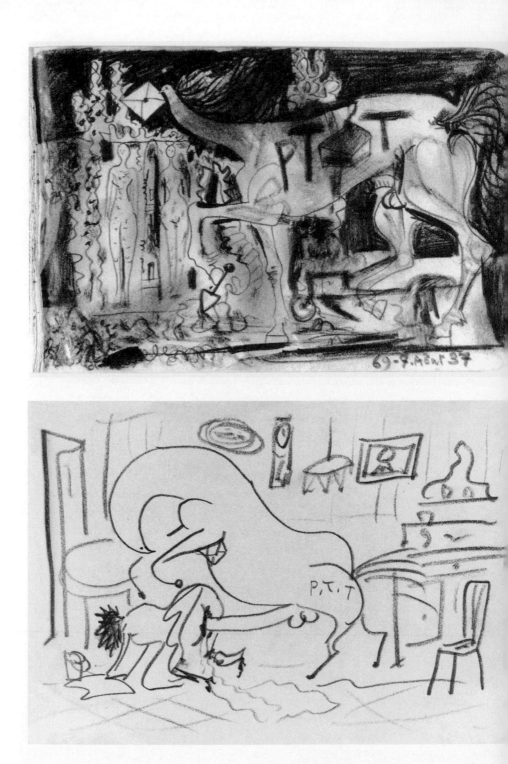

Picasso, two surviving pages from the Facteur Cheval *sketchbook, black chalk, 1937*

his spare time building a *naif* folly, the Palais Idéal, which was much admired by the Surrealists. In a pun on the postman's name, Picasso transforms Cheval into a centaur, with either the torso or the head of a man, or the head of a carrier pigeon grafted onto the body and legs of a horse. He wears a postman's képi, carries a mailbag, and has PTT (the initials of the French postal service) branded on his flanks. He also boasts a lengthy penis, with which he pleasures the housewives as he delivers their mail. If I remember rightly, the phallic joke extends to the finials on the postman's folly. The sketchbook is dated August 7, 1937. Picasso and Dora had recently visited the Palais Idéal with Paul Eluard.

As we went through the *carnet*, we could not help noticing that there was a very different set of drawings on the back of the pages, and that poor Dora was becoming more and more agitated at our seeing them. When we turned the sketchbook around to examine the verso, she started to sob—"the brute, how could he torture me like this?"—and she went on sobbing as we perused Picasso's exquisitely delicate views of her crotch, fore and aft, all too evidently done from life. There was no possibility, in those days at least, of publishing drawings as graphic as this. All Picasso wanted, in his sadistic way, was to assert his rights over Dora and turn her back into a tearful victim. "So she cried?" he said with a terrible predatoriness, when we described what had transpired. "Serve her right for being so *pudique*. She never used to be like that." I feared that Dora might have done away with the sketchbook. It did not figure in the posthumous sale of her effects in 1998. However, it eventually surfaced and was included in a subsequent sale. Many of the more explicit drawings are missing—presumably destroyed.

For the next forty years or so I remained in touch with Dora— often by telephone. Toward the end she shut herself away—out of vanity as much as reclusiveness. Osteoporosis had left her figure bowed and shrunken, and she, who had set so much store by her looks and appearance, did not want friends to see her so impaired. Besides, if she did see people she wanted to look presentable, and would spend hours maneuvering her old bones into a vintage Chanel suit. Another reason for discouraging visitors: she did not want anybody to see that, like Miss Havisham, she had allowed the once-handsome apartment Picasso had given her to become terribly neglected. The trompe l'oeil insects that Picasso had painted on the walls—Dora reminded him of an insect, he used to say—carried all the more conviction. Picasso had given Dora a great many portraits of herself, some of utmost importance, so she could well have afforded a maid or a nurse. However, even after selling virtually all the more tormented images—she kept back all the more flatteringly lyrical ones—Dora chose to live in self-inflicted penury. Might this have been a form of penance? As Dora aged, her perception of Picasso changed completely. She no longer saw him as the Antichrist who had victimized her, but as the saintly regenerator of modern art. There was an element of truth to both these perceptions.

One mystery I wish I had asked Dora about was the presence of *Mein Kampf* in the glass-fronted bookcase where she kept the illustrated books Picasso had given her. When I first glimpsed the book, I didn't attach much importance to it. Many of my antifascist friends owned copies of this loathsome manifesto on the principle that the more you know about your enemy, the better. That Picasso might have owned *Mein Kampf* would not have surprised me at all. Dora's possession of the book turned out to be less innocent than I had thought. After her death, a dealer whom I have every reason to trust told me how he had negotiated with her for months and finally persuaded her to sell him some of her own, as opposed to Picasso's, work. Before signing the agreement, Dora had looked up and asked if he was Jewish. He denied it—for the one and only time in his life, he said. Dora claimed to be very relieved to hear this; she told him she would not have signed the agreement had he been Jewish.

Since Dora had consistently sold her Picassos to Jewish dealers, notably Kahnweiler and Berggruen, I found her attitude extremely puzzling until I remembered that Jacques Lacan, the celebrated psychoanalyst Picasso had put in charge of her case, had seized on Dora's religious mania as a means to lead her back to sanity. This unorthodox therapy seems to have worked, but it may have opened the door to ideological perversions that were in direct opposition to the ideas and values by which she claimed to live. For instance, in the course of her bizarre journey back to a measure of sanity, Dora may have taken against the Jews for crucifying her Savior. Alternatively, her attitude may have had something to do with the fact that she was often said to be Jewish. When I asked Dora about this, she insisted that in Yugoslavia her father's name, Markovic, was sometimes but not always Jewish, certainly not in the case of *her* family. The most probable explanation is that these Hitlerite sympathies were a symptom of Dora's psychosis. In this respect she reminded me of a great American poet who was periodically institutionalized for manic-depression. In early stages of his attacks, he would carry *Mein Kampf* around concealed in a dust jacket of Baudelaire's *Fleurs du Mal.* This was all the odder, given that in his saner moments this poet was antifascist and proud of having some Jewish blood. Dora may have suffered from a similar syndrome.

I will never forget the last time I visited Dora, a year or two before she died: the long wait while she shuffled to the door and struggled with the bolts, and the shock of looking down and seeing her mauvish wig askew and her body so bent and shrunken; and then the relief, when she looked up, that those radiant eyes still seemed to send forth the rays that Picasso had endowed them with at the time of their first love. Mentally, Dora was lucid, so long as one stayed away from religion. On this occasion, Dora told me that she was leaving everything she had to a monastery in Paris where the monks had been her spiritual advisers. She gave me the names of her lawyers and assured me that her will was in order: since she had no survivors there would be no problems. Poor Dora appears to have been under a delusion. The only will that was found after her death proved to be invalid. As a result genealogists had to be called in. They came up with two very distant cousins, one in France and one in Yugoslavia. In October 1998 and May 1999, Dora's possessions—a mass of works by Picasso, Balthus, and Wifredo Lam, as well as all her own paintings and photographs, books and papers—were auctioned off. What was left after the state had taken over half the proceeds was shared by the heirs Dora never knew and the genealogists who tracked them down, not to mention the lawyers—just what she would most have dreaded.

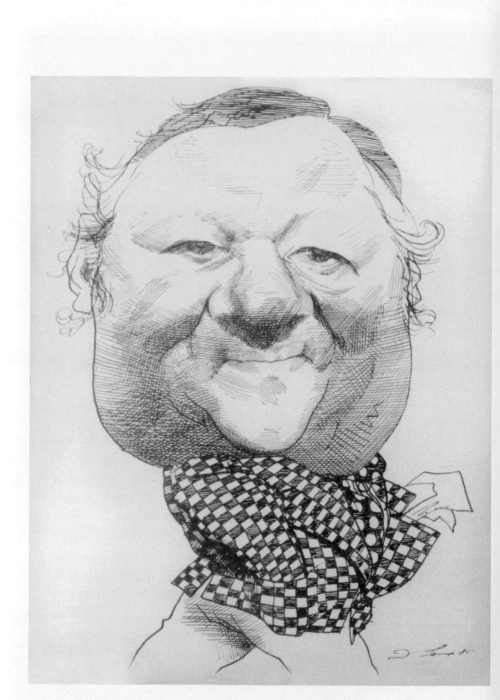

David Levine, Caricature of Douglas Cooper, *pen and ink, 1989*

COLLECTORS

After an article on Castille—"Le Château des Cubistes"—appeared in *L'Oeil* magazine, collectors and dealers and curiosity-seekers, mostly American, descended on us in droves. Douglas enjoyed this. He liked showing his collection to people who knew what they were looking at, or to students who wanted to learn. But what gave him the greatest satisfaction was having his brain picked by collectors, dealers, and museum directors. He had come to see himself as the Berenson of cubism. When pilgrims arrived, he would preen with pleasure, flattered by their attentions into being infinitely helpful: "Don't make an offer on that drawing until I've asked Pablo about it." But woe betide me if I dared to interject a view of my own, or, as I was sometimes tempted to do, correct Douglas, who was a bit vague about technical procedures. He would give me an "Aren't we getting above ourselves?" look and suggest I see if someone needed a drink.

A few of these visitors—notably Victor and Sally Ganz, who struck both of us as far and away the most perceptive and courageous of the new generation of American collectors—would become close friends. Others, and by no means the least interesting ones, would turn out to be unscrupulous operators who sucked up to Douglas for the free advice and studio gossip that he dispensed. The most persistent of these was a zircon in the rough from Pittsburgh called Dave Thompson, who looked like the very successful scrap-iron dealer he had formerly been, and who fancied himself, with some justice, as a latter-day Dr. Albert Barnes, the Philadelphia collector who outdid all others in rapacity and beastliness. As with Barnes, Dave's passion for collecting was born of resentment— resentment of stuffy Pittsburgh society, which had supposedly scorned him. (Not entirely justified, a Pittsburgh friend told me. It was Dave's aggressiveness and bragging, not his humble origins, that made him persona non grata. Before anyone could snub him, he would have snubbed them.) To get back at the old guard, Dave set about trouncing them in the field of modern art—the one field where the old guard would not have noticed or cared whether they had been trounced or not.

Like many a new collector, Dave had started off in the relatively easy area of Americana, where he is said to have done very well. But he soon abandoned Americana for modernism, and in this infinitely tricky area he applied the same ruthlessness and canniness that had enabled him to make a fortune in scrap iron during World War II to making a fortune in Picassos and Klees and Giacomettis after the war was over. Dave called it "collecting"; most other people would have called it "dealing." Some of his victims might even have called it "fleecing." (A Danish doctor who told Dave that his Klee meant so much to him he would never sell it, but only give it away, was horrified when Dave said thank you and walked off with it.) By the early 1950s, prices for modern art were already on the rise but still astonishingly low, and a goodish Picasso or Matisse could still be acquired for around $20,000. In the absence of much aesthetic discernment, a flair for the market stood Dave in good stead; so did his personal schlepper, a fat little German woman who scoured European dealers and auction houses for him. Dave used many of the same brash, bullying methods that had made Barnes so loathed, notably bulk-buying. "What isn't selling? Late Klee, maybe? Okay, I'll take everything." Beyeler, the formidable Swiss dealer who remembers Dave saying this, rates him as a "truly vicious" buyer. Nevertheless, it was Beyeler who ultimately benefited from Dave's depredations, for it was he who sold his 100 Klees *en bloc* to the Düsseldorf Museum, and his 70 Giacomettis—the biggest privately owned group of the artist's work—to a consortium of Swiss museums. And it was Beyeler who handled a great many of the 340 works remaining in what was, albeit briefly, the largest collection of modern masters in the world.

Dave's eye was far from dependable, so he would usually call Douglas before making an acquisition. Everything about a painting had to be "right": the period, the provenance, the condition, the subject, the size, and above all the price. More than once, Douglas saved Dave from making a costly mistake; and since Dave was far from generous, Douglas was sometimes obliged to insinuate himself into a deal so that he, too, could make some money. Otherwise compensation took the form of Countess Mara ties—"Unwearable and, worse, ungiveawayable," Douglas would shudder—and overelaborate dinners in three-star tourist traps. Since Dave enjoyed being the center of attention, he liked each course—on one occasion even the soup—to be flambé. People at neighboring tables would titter as blue flames would erupt yet again from our vicinity, and Dave would pyromaniacally urge the waiters to keep the sea bass or the crêpes suzette ablaze. Later we would have to go back to his hotel to inspect some new acquisition. On one of these occasions he started making snarling noises and tearing the bed apart the moment he entered his room.

"What on earth are you doing?" Douglas asked.

"Getting back at the French for having such filthy minds," Dave said. "Didn't you see the sheets were turned down on *both* sides of the bed? Well, that filthy-minded maid is going to have to make it up again properly."

Dave, it appeared, suffered from blue-collar prudery and could not forgive the implication that he was sharing a bed with the woman he would eventually marry. That Helen had the room next door was clearly anything but a fiction. "You've got to stop being such a hick," Douglas said. To cover his embarrassment, Dave showed us a Miró he had bought that morning. "What is more," Douglas went on, "you've got to stop being such a sucker. That Miró's not a Miró."

Much as Dr. Barnes had liked to raise and then dash hopes, Dave entered into negotiations with his local museum, the Carnegie Museum of Art, regarding its possible acquisition of his collection. He even took the director and his wife on trips to Europe, only in the end to renege on what would have been a great coup for Pittsburgh. Why, Dave said, should the city that had snubbed him get his treasures? Far more kudos would accrue from donating a painting to the Museum of Modern Art. By giving his great 1906 Picasso, *Two Nudes,* to MoMA "in honor of Alfred Barr," Dave won himself a prestigious place in New York's art establishment.

And then one morning we got a frantic call from Dave. Thieves had broken into his suburban house (Stone's Throw, it was called), ripped some of his best paintings from their stretchers, and made off with them. Dave had received a ransom note asking for a largish sum of money to be paid into a numbered Swiss bank account, but when he asked his bank to wire the money, he met with a rebuff.

"Buying more pictures?" the bank manager had asked.

"No, ransoming some back," Dave replied.

"In that case we cannot act for you." Banks are not allowed knowingly to sanction payments to criminals, the manager explained. The matter had to be referred to the FBI. In due course, the paintings mysteriously returned to Dave's walls. How did this come about? A friend in the FBI called Joe Chapman eventually filled me in.

Dave was too volatile to be allowed any role in the negotiations, so Joe had to install himself in a New York hotel and assume Dave's identity. Easy, he said: all he did was throw his weight around and behave "like a prick." The thieves lost no time in contacting him. They instructed the man they thought was Dave to leave a message in the pages of a telephone directory at the New York Public Library. FBI operatives had the place staked out, and when someone picked up the message, they followed him back to Philadelphia and easily identified the rest of the gang. One of them had been newly released from prison as well as newly wed. Persuading him to rat on his accomplices was easy, though he may have been killed for doing so. The FBI rounded up the crooks and retrieved the paintings. They were even able to identify the man who had masterminded the theft, but were unable for some reason to bring him to justice. Who was he? I asked Joe. A very respected member of the art world. Did I know him? Probably, Joe said, but that was all he would divulge.

Sheer luck and a little amateur sleuthing enabled me years later to identify the mastermind. I was having the kitchen of my New York apartment painted by a young pop artist, whose subject matter was so outrageous that he sold very little and lived by painting houses by day and hustling by night. Beau was a spotty decorator but an enthralling raconteur. "I bet you know some of my art world clients," he said. And he went on to regale me with stories about a heavily married art historian of utmost respectability, who had a taste for young hoods. "The badder, the better," Beau said, "but I find him kids who are reasonably safe—don't want any trouble." I did indeed know the art historian in question: a very reputable man, whom I knew to have been badly used by Dave and in need of money. Everything fitted: I realized that he must have planned the theft.

Next time Joe and I had lunch, I brought the subject around to Dave. Was the mastermind married? I asked. Joe thought as much. It was so-and-so, wasn't it? Joe pulled out his diary and erased the entry that recorded our meeting. This lunch never took place, he said as he hurried out.

Back, however, to Douglas's relationship with Dave. They were too alike in certain respects, too combustible for safety. A flare-up was inevitable. Dave was always pushing Douglas to sell him a work from his collection, so when Douglas needed money to finance some deal or other, what more natural than that he should turn to Dave? The only important painting he could bear to part with was a handsome, rather decorative still life by Juan Gris, which Dave had often admired. After much haggling, the two of them finally agreed on a price. And since Dave was in a hurry for the painting, and Douglas was in a hurry for the money, he shipped it off to Pittsburgh by express. A mistake. The promised check failed to materialize. When Douglas expostulated, Dave claimed that he would never have bought the painting if he had known Douglas was so hard up. That rankled, more especially since Douglas knew that if he fired off one of his wounding salvos, the check would take even longer to materialize. Henceforth he would resent yet respect Dave rather more than before.

When Douglas arranged for Dave to buy *Feuerwerke,* the little Klee he had given me, things went more smoothly, except that Dave would ultimately emerge from the transaction as even more of a crook than I had thought. Next time I saw *Feuerwerke,* it had grown to almost twice its original size. Dave had had a "restorer" enlarge the brown night-sky background by several inches. (I am glad to say the addition has now been removed.) How many other works, I wondered, had had their value increased in this way? And how ironic this enlargement was. When the paintings that the thieves had cut from their stretchers were returned to Dave, they were quite a bit *smaller* than before.

Another American collector for whom Douglas had a very special regard was a Chicagoan called Morton Neumann. Picasso, who introduced us to him, described Morton as *"un vrai numéro,"* who had made a fortune out of a product that straightened kinky hair. He was much

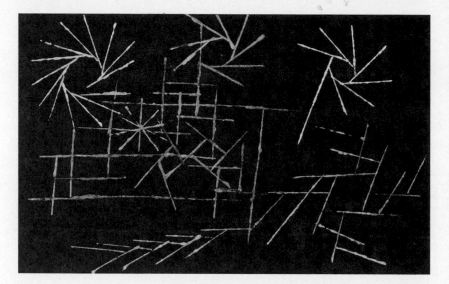

Paul Klee, Feuerwerke, *mixed media, 1930*

more interesting, Picasso said, than most of Alfred Barr's flock of obedient sheep, who all looked the same, sounded the same, and wanted to buy the same thing. "Neumann is his own man." He certainly was.

The Neumanns had won Picasso's heart by giving him half a dozen cheap watches, with the twelve letters of the artist's name in place of numerals. Picasso was tickled. At a bullfight we attended a few weeks later, he presented one of the Neumann watches to a torero who had dedicated a bull to him. (Not to be outdone, Cocteau tore off his gold Rolex, while his companion, Francine Weisweiller, threw her emerald earrings in the direction of the bullfighter. Surprisingly, she got them back.) And then the artist had been much amused when he offered Rose Neumann a cigarette. She said she wouldn't let something he had given her go up in smoke; he had to sign it. When Picasso heard that Rose kept the signed Gauloise on a little red velvet cushion under a glass cloche in the middle of her Picasso-filled living room, he liked the Neumanns even more.

In the course of a luncheon to which Picasso had asked the Neumanns and Douglas and me, I discovered a further reason for this friendship. Picasso was convinced that Morton was taken in by his mimicry of English. Although the artist knew next to no English, he could improvise gibberish that sounded extraordinarily like the real thing (thanks to his first wife, Olga Khokhlova, Picasso could do the same in Russian). "Morton is convinced we understand each other's English," he said. And sure enough, by modulating his voice and expression and raising or lowering his voice at the end of a sentence or shrugging his shoulders, Picasso seemed able to manipulate his Chicago friend into answering "yeah," or "sure," or "hell no," to his quasi-English mumbling. But the more I listened, the more I realized that, far from being taken in, Morton was fooling Picasso into believing that he, Morton, was the one being fooled.

When I visited Chicago a year or two later, I was amazed at the extent of the Neumanns' collection. Besides acquiring a roomful of Picassos, Morton had made friends with Tristan Tzara and Man Ray, and they had helped him put together a group of Dada and surrealist treasures. The collection also included seventeen mostly major Mirós, several superb Giacomettis, rather too many Dubuffets for my taste, key paintings by Gris, Léger, Mondrian, Chirico, and much, much more. On subsequent visits, I was amazed to find Morton always ahead of the game. He was a pioneer collector of virtually every avant-garde movement of the sixties, seventies, and eighties: op art, pop art, photorealism, neo-Dadaism, and so on. New acquisitions (including some fifty Malcolm Morleys) overflowed closets, hung on doors, dangled from ceilings, leaned against windows, accumulated on chairs. On our way to dinner at the Standard Club, I was unnerved by a sinister-looking rubber bag in the back of Morton's car. It gurgled and smelled funny. One never knew with Morton—was it perhaps some new form of art? No, it was the cadaver of a cat, on which the Neumanns' medical student son had been honing his skills.

After visiting Picasso at Cannes, we would often drive on to Roquebrune to see a fascinating couple, Emery and Wendy Reves. Born in Hungary, Emery had made a fortune brokering the memoirs of Churchill, Eisenhower, Montgomery, and other wartime leaders to

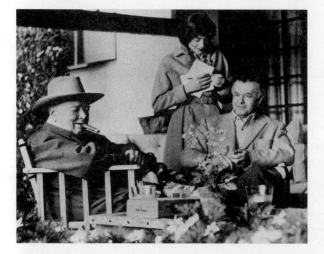

Winston Churchill, his daughter Sarah, and Emery Reves at the Villa La Pausa, 1957

newspaper and magazine publishers all over the world. In doing so he had become their close friend and adviser, as an impressive display of memorabilia confirmed. Emery was a perfectionist, but much more relaxed than most. Likewise Wendy, who was—indeed still is— a fragile blond beauty with a taste for pale pastel colors and a fund of down-to-earth Texan wit. Their small collection of impressionist and post-impressionist paintings—Manet, Cézanne, Degas, Monet, Bonnard—was of the most rarefied quality. And the life they led at La Pausa—the white marble villa the Duke of Westminster had built for Chanel—was as idyllic as anybody could possibly want. Wonderfully comfortable rooms gave onto a central courtyard, in the middle of which stood a large white marble figure by Rodin. The setting was no less idyllic: a grove of ancient olive trees amid row upon row of immaculately trimmed lavender bushes. All La Pausa lacked, Douglas said, was something ugly—the glimpse of a billboard or a gas station—to exorcise the too-good-to-be-true look.

At the end of his long life, Churchill was so besotted by the delights of La Pausa and the charms of the *maîtresse de maison* that he settled into the house for weeks and sometimes months at a time. Emery knew just how to indulge this exceedingly spoiled, increasingly babyish eighty-something-year-old. He would engage a star chef from the Château de Madrid and lay on the lashings of brandy, champagne, and cigars to which his eminent guest was addicted. But what Churchill liked best was to sit under an umbrella in the beautiful garden with the adorable Wendy at his side and daub away in the sunlight. The great man's pet budgerigar, Winnie, would twitter away—"Winnie, Winnie, Winnie"—

and sometimes, it was said, nest in Wendy's pale blond hair. On one occasion the bird was left behind in London, and, unbeknownst to British taxpayers, Churchill's official plane had to fly back to retrieve it. Lady Churchill told my old friend June Churchill (second wife of Winston's son Randolph) that she did not approve of her husband's crush on "Windy," as she chose to call her. Insofar as she could, Lady Churchill kept away from La Pausa. Churchill did not seem to mind.

One summer morning, Douglas and I drove over to La Pausa to look at a painting that Emery was thinking of buying. He introduced us to the great man, who was taking his ease on a terrace with Wendy and Winnie. I was worried that Douglas might be obstreperous, but for once he behaved like a starstruck little boy.

"Why don't you both stay for lunch?" Emery asked Douglas. "You'll amuse Winston, and he'll enthrall you."

"Sorry, Emery, we're lunching with Picasso." Douglas could not resist raising his voice in the hope that Churchill would hear. And back we drove to Cannes, Douglas agog to tell the artist that we had turned Churchill down for him. "I should hope so," Picasso said. "Didn't we have a date? Maybe you should have brought him along. After all his *conneries* about my painting, he should hear what I think of his."

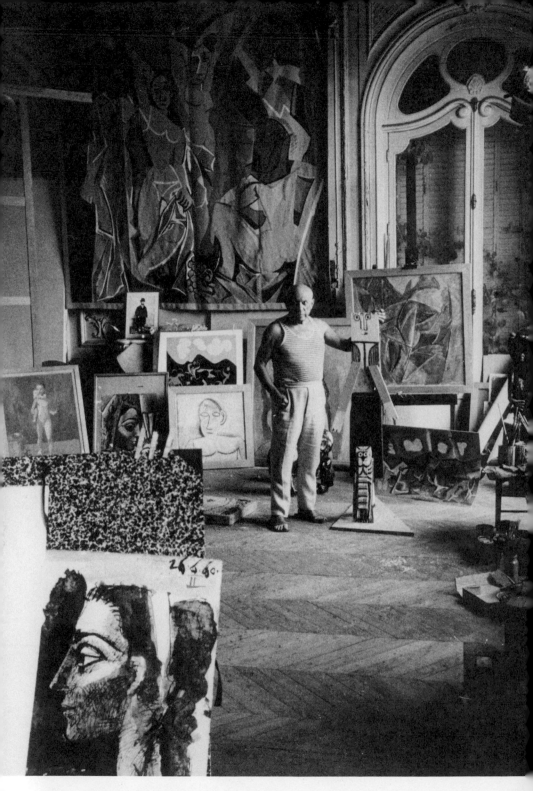

Picasso in his studio at La Californie, 1960

PICASSO
AND JACQUELINE

Meanwhile, what of Jacqueline Roque, whom we had last heard of in Perpignan in September 1954? After her season in hell at the Lazermes, she and Picasso had returned to her Villa Le Ziquet (hence Jacqueline's temporary code name, Madame Z.), at Golfe-Juan, but it proved too small for them, so they moved to Paris. And there, in his studio on the rue des Grands Augustins, Picasso embarked on a series of variations after Delacroix's *Women of Algiers*, which had been inspired by Jacqueline's striking resemblance to the squatting odalisque on the right of the composition. The day after Picasso brought this series to an end, his wife, Olga—they had been estranged for twenty years—died after a long illness at Cannes. (Even in death she had a raw deal: buried by mistake in the Protestant rather than the Orthodox cemetery.) Jacqueline maintained, not very convincingly, that the news prompted each of the ex-mistresses to call up and propose marriage to him, now that he was free. To get away from these supposedly importunate women, Picasso and Jacqueline fled back to Cannes, where they bought the imposing villa La Californie—"partly for its Orientalist air." Picasso said he had put so much thought into the *Women of Algiers* paintings that he had ended up with a house that, as it were, "matched."

The changes in the pattern of Picasso's life resulting from the change of mistresses took place just as Dora Maar had predicted. As well as moving from the poky Vallauris house to a grand new villa—a move that inspired a number of decorative paintings of his attractive new mistress in his attractive new quarters—he took on Jean Cocteau as his new poet laureate, a post that had been vacant since Paul Eluard's unexpected death in 1952. Cocteau, who had been out of favor for some time, was delighted to be back in the position he had held some forty years earlier. And just as he had done in the past, Cocteau would add some of his friends to Picasso's circle: his rich protectress, Francine Weisweiller, her daughter Carole, and his lover and adopted son, Doudou, plus Doudou's sister, Emilienne.

Besides Douglas and myself, Picasso's new *tertulia* would include Pierre Daix, the most assiduous of his chroniclers; David Douglas Duncan, the American photographer; Lucien Clergue, the French photographer; Paco Mounios, the bullfight impresario; Sapone, the Italian tailor who would make the artist's eye-catching trousers; Eugenio Arias, the Spanish barber who would come and cut his hair before a bullfight; the Guttusos; Luis Miguel Dominguín, the torero, and his movie-star wife, Lucia Bose; Gustau Gili, the Barcelona publisher of the classic bullfighting manual *Pepe Illo* (one of Picasso's greatest illustrated books); the Crommelynck brothers, who would supervise the printing of most of the artist's later engravings; Alberti, the Spanish poet, with his daughter and her husband, Roberto Otero; Heinz Berggruen, the Paris dealer; Siegfried Rosengart, the Lucerne dealer, and his daughter Angela; Gérald Cramer, the Geneva dealer, with his wife, Inez; Lionel Prejger, the metalworker who did so well making Picasso's cutouts that he became a dealer; and many, many more, some of them—like Manuel Pallarès from Barcelona, who had been at art school with Picasso, Clive Bell, Josette Gris, Marie Cuttoli—revenants from much earlier periods. Mention should also be made of Picasso's old friend and Douglas's old rival, the biographer Roland Penrose. A past master at dividing and ruling, Picasso enjoyed playing these two admirers off against each other and putting their devotion to the test. He would keep Roland, who had come specially from England, waiting for days at a time in Cannes, saying that he was busy with Douglas. Next time, Douglas would be reduced to begging Jacqueline to arrange an audience with the master. Whoever was the victim of these teases would usually be rewarded with a drawing. Picasso would play similar tricks on his dealer, Kahnweiler. No less important were the animals: a dalmatian called Perro and a dachshund called Lump (a present from Dave Duncan), a goat called Esmeralda, which also had the run of the house, and any number of songbirds.

When Picasso was working, the atmosphere of La Californie would be tense; when he was idling, the atmosphere would be relatively calm. Every month or so, Douglas and I would drive over for lunch. Sometimes we would be summoned upstairs to Picasso's bedroom for a Chaplinesque parody of a royal levée. The artist would sound an imaginary fanfare before putting on his shirt; mimic a minuet before donning a sweater; Which of the countless pairs of peculiar trousers made by Sapone would he wear? The ones with horizontal stripes? Would these go with the multicolored socks knitted by Clive Bell's girlfriend, Barbara Bagenal, or the jersey borrowed from Jacqueline? And so the farce would continue. On closer acquaintance, he would dispense with these charades. They were a strategy to disguise his shyness, and make it easier for him to communicate with visitors who were tongue-tied with awe or had no language in common with him. Downstairs, visitors would be waiting, a bit nervously, much as they had been on my first visit to Picasso's Paris studio, clutching odd-shaped presents. They came to life when Picasso and Jacqueline made their entrance.

First, the gifts would have to be unwrapped: exotic clothes, a deerstalker from Scotland, a knitted mask from Peru, magnums of champagne, a bunch of wildflowers, an elephant's-foot wastepaper basket, a potted pineapple plant, a chocolate eel from Barcelona, whoopee cushions, boomerangs, comic objects from joke shops on Forty-second Street. Picasso liked the jokes. When I gave him a roll of lavatory paper printed to look like dollar bills, he was delighted. "I have often wanted," he said, "to have some printed with Pascal's more boring *Pensées.*" Picasso would behave like a savage seeing new objects for the first time. Things would be tried on, tasted, jammed in vases ("No need to put flowers in water," he said. "They are going to die anyway"), or carefully set aside to become part of the enormous accumulation that made magpie nests of his studios. He seldom threw anything away, even old envelopes, so his hoard was constantly growing and threatening to engulf room after room in house after house. Many of the things were valueless, but for Picasso they were talismans.

Everything had its allotted place. I remember an unopened bottle of Guerlain cologne inscribed "*Bonne Année, 1937*"; a framed letter from Victor Hugo to a mistress; masks of all kinds, from eighteenth-century Venetian ones to modern monstrosities in rubber; a Daumier

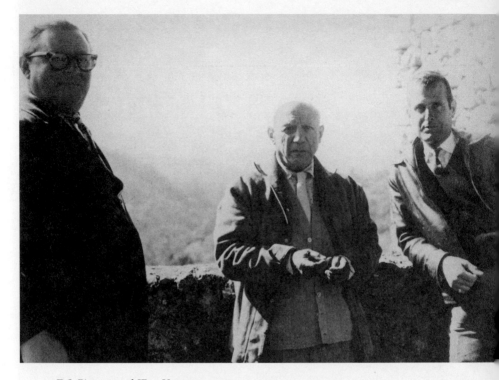

DC, Picasso, and JR at Vauvenargues, ca. 1959

bronze; a model of Barcelona's Christopher Columbus monument in
marzipan; a set of Hepplewhite chairs bought by Picasso's father from an
English wine merchant in Málaga, an ancient panettone that had been
nibbled away by mice and resembled a model of the Colosseum, a pile of
good, bad, and indifferent tribal sculpture, a distorting mirror from a
fairground, photographs (the best of them by Jacqueline) of bullfights
and friends, hats by the hundred, and piles of letters, many of them
marked with a cabalistic sign—the word *ojo* (Spanish for "eye") drawn
like two eyes and a nose, meaning "Attention." Nesting in the clutter
would be a number of Picassos: among them the bronze cat he used as a
stool, precarious stacks of ceramics, lithographs and linocuts pinned to
boards, paintings and drawings of all periods, framed and unframed, in
all states of completion. But it was typical of Picasso's sardonic humor
that the work which dominated the studio at La Californie was a huge,

garish tapestry, a travesty of the *Demoiselles d'Avignon.* "Much more shocking than the original," Picasso would say when he wanted to tease earnest art historians.

If there were a lot of guests, Picasso would take them to a restaurant; if there were only a few—family members or close friends—he usually preferred to eat in the studio. With the help of a maid called Garance, Jacqueline would prepare the food. Sometimes she would devise surprising Chinese or Indian dishes, but more often meals would consist of simple, basic fare enhanced by such house presents as canned rattlesnake, foie gras, ancient Chinese eggs, brandied peaches, kippers, caviar. Picasso's favorite food of the moment might be served: *brandade de morue* (a purée of stockfish), eels, brains, Stilton, or preserved ginger. Though he was very curious about food, Picasso ate little and drank less. But he enjoyed the ceremonial role of host. Meals seemed to activate his sense of improvisation. He would carve a very thin slice of tongue, hold it up, and announce that he had done a portrait of Vollard. True enough, the fleshy part of the tongue was the exact shape of Vollard's domed head, the scrunched-up bit underneath the image of his blunt features. Or you would be eating frogs' legs when a frog would start croaking in the middle of the table; Picasso had simulated the croak by drawing the edge of a serrated knife along the side of a plate. To amuse children or to gratify adults on the lookout for giveaways, Picasso would sometimes contrive heads, birds, or people out of torn paper napkins, corks, burnt matches, flower petals—anything that was to hand, even the food. Occasionally there would be lapses in his ironically courteous manners. Once, I remember him helping himself to a small fried octopus with his fingers and wiping his hand in what was left of his hair. "Beast," Jacqueline said, "just because you've so little sense of smell doesn't mean that everybody else is the same." Picasso thought the oil might make his hair grow. "In Barcelona we used to make hair tonic from oil that lavender had been fried in—so why not the oil from fried octopus?" And then there was the time he took to rubbing mutton fat onto his bronzes to improve the patina. Jacqueline complained that not only the bronzes but also Picasso, the dogs, and the whole studio had begun to stink. "Monseigneur [I found her use of this fanciful honorific embarrassing; Picasso seemed to enjoy it], of course, had been unaware of it." Such things did not bother him, Monseigneur said. Had the patina improved? No.

After lunch, especially in the summer, admirers would wait outside in the hope of an audience. The concierge would appear with a message from a photographer recommended by Cocteau—"Let him in," Picasso would say regally; from a Swiss journalist wanting an interview—"Certainly not"; from a boring old friend—"Why not?"; from a deputation of German students with a laurel wreath, or a South American nun with an illuminated address, or tittering starlets in bikinis—"KEEP THEM OUT!" One day I was there when two Scandinavian girls asked to be admitted. They had won a prize in a television contest called "Your Life's Dream Gratified." Their dream was to meet Picasso. "I'm not going to be the first prize in anybody's TV contest," Picasso said, and insisted they go back to where they came from. I sympathized with him. From the mid-1950s onward, he was increasingly pestered by inquisitive tourists, rapacious fans, unscrupulous journalists, lunatics, and, once, a murderer. Concierges had strict orders not to admit unauthorized people to his houses. Picasso was delighted when the papers reported, wrongly, that he had bought a castle near Rome. He told his concierge to tell journalists: "Monsieur Picasso is not here. If you read the newspapers you would know he has moved to Italy."

On another occasion, an unknown woman forced her way past the concierge into the studio on "important business": she was determined that Picasso should listen to her revolutionary new concept of *Don Quixote.* After half an hour or so, his eyes glazed over and a waxbill in one of the birdcages on the wall behind him fell dead from its perch. Such was Picasso's fear of death that Jacqueline smuggled the cage out to the kitchen and had the driver fetch a replacement from a pet shop in Cannes. On the woman droned; Picasso was too deaf and sleepy to hear the driver return and replace the cage with a new bird in it. However, he was not deceived. A few weeks later I watched him entice a couple of birds, which had been flying about the room, back into their cage. "My birds are immortal, at least that's what Jacqueline would have me believe."

What Douglas and I enjoyed most about our visits to Picasso was the opportunity to study the recent work with the artist. He turned out to enjoy these sessions as much as we did: they provided the feedback he craved. Not that he set much store by his friends' comments. What

Picasso needed even more than their understanding was their fealty and a shot of their energy. And he knew how to extort it. On one of our earliest visits, he had shown us a series of drawings and discussed them with us at some length. When, shyly and hesitantly, I tried to explain what struck me about one particular drawing, he was surprisingly responsive. Back in the studio two or three months later, I was thunderstruck to

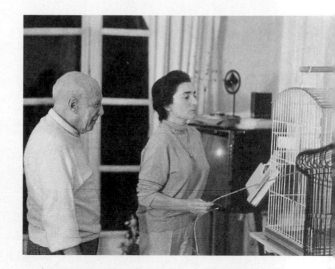

Picasso and Jacqueline in the studio at La Californie

find that he had taken this particular drawing out of its portfolio so that we could have another look at it. That Picasso should care enough to remember, let alone care, was astonishing. Tears welled up in my eyes. The third time he played this trick, I realized it was not my opinions he valued, it was the tears he squeezed out of me—palpable evidence that his magic still worked. Once I cottoned on to this, I would watch with fascination as he manipulated anyone who seemed vulnerable into an emotional response to him and his work. He would switch on the magnetism and let his ego feed on whatever critical understanding, starstruck admiration, or devotion could be extracted from those around him. At the end of the day, Picasso would have made off with everyone's energy; it would fuel a night of work in his studio. No wonder we guests would be left in a state of nervous exhaustion. No wonder Jacqueline took to the bottle.

Clouds soon gathered over La Californie. A seventy-fifth birthday was most unwelcome. Around the same time, the Hungarian revolution soured Picasso on the USSR, though not enough to undermine his faith in Communism. Meanwhile, Jacqueline was recurrently ill. Far from feeling compassion, Picasso resented these lapses. "Whenever women are ill, it's their fault," he once announced in front of his ailing mistress.

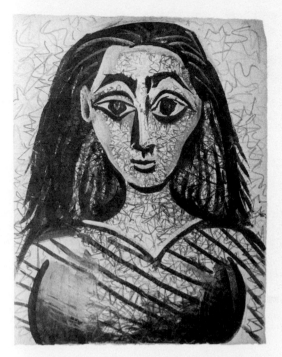

Picasso, Portrait of Jacqueline, *colored chalks, India inks, gouache; Valentine's Day, 1957*

And just as he had improved upon Jacqueline's circumstances in some of his earlier portraits of her by giving her a long neck and other attributes she lacked, he was no less capable of doing the reverse. By adjusting her image, he could humiliate or test Jacqueline, indicate love or anger or desire, and even, on occasion, predict or ordain a bout of illness. Prediction might take the form of a drawing, such as the one he did on Saint Valentine's Day, 1957, in which her triste features are superimposed on a fever-chart network of zigzag pink lines. A day or two later, when Jacqueline obligingly ran a temperature, Picasso said to me, not entirely in jest, "You see, I'm a prophet." Another time, he showed me a no less pained portrait of Jacqueline, and said rather proudly that a good doctor should be able to base a diagnosis on it.

One evening, when Picasso and Jacqueline arrived for dinner at Castille, she looked as if she was about to collapse. Sure enough, she did. "I seem to have a corpse on my hands," Picasso said as he handed her over to me, hiding his concern, as was his Spanish way, under a show of heartlessness. I managed to get Jacqueline up to my room and lay her on my bed, and then did what I could to persuade her to have the operation which was long overdue. "I can't," Jacqueline said. "Pablo doesn't want to live with a eunuch." Nothing could shake her out of this ridiculous notion. She was like a saint intent on martyrdom. Years later, Jacqueline provided a partial explanation. She told me the all-important secret that Picasso told only to the women in his life—the secret of his childhood

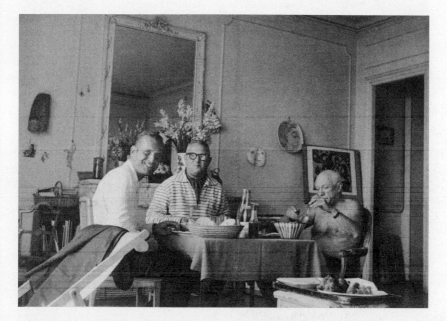

JR, DC, and Picasso, photographed by Jacqueline from her bed at La Californie

vow to God. When his younger sister Conchita was dying of diphtheria, he made a vow that he would never paint again if his sister's life was spared. He *did* paint again, and her life was not spared. This explained Picasso's identification with the Minotaur, to whom women had to be sacrificed, it also explained Jacqueline's dutiful acceptance of the role of sacrificial victim.

Not long after this, Jacqueline suffered a total collapse and had to be rushed off to a hospital and operated upon. Picasso was so undone by her absence and so elated by her return home that there were no recriminations. While Jacqueline was recuperating, Douglas and I drove over and had lunch in her bedroom—an occasion she commemorated by photographing us from her bed. Picasso was in a mischievous mood. Cocteau had apparently wanted to join us for lunch, but had been told to come in afterwards for coffee. "Don't, for God's sake, let him embrace you," Picasso said. "He's suffering from a nasty skin disease—something he caught from the Germans during the war." Picasso loved Cocteau, and relied on his services as a court jester, but could seldom resist a

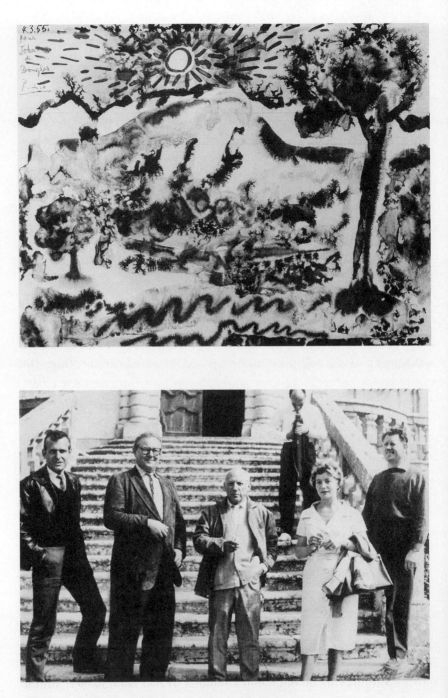

TOP: *Picasso,* Montagne Sainte-Victoire, *ink wash, 1955*
ABOVE: *JR, DC, Picasso, unidentified woman, and Jeannot, Picasso's driver, on the steps of Vauvenargues, 1958*

derisory crack. Jacqueline soon recovered her strength; however, years of trauma would leave her psyche in a very fragile state. She became more and more unpredictable.

By the end of 1957, high-rise buildings and paparazzi were encroaching on the privacy of La Californie. It was time to move away from tourist-ridden Cannes. Picasso made another bid to buy Castille from Douglas, but there was no way we were going to move so soon after restoring the place. And so, when we heard in 1958 that Vauvenargues, the seventeenth-century château dramatically set on the slopes of Cézanne's Montagne Sainte-Victoire was for sale, we told Picasso about it. He drove over and bought it, and gave us a drawing done three years earlier that, he said, was prophetic of his new abode. As soon as they had moved in some furniture—including the hideous Victorian Gothic dresser that figures in several paintings—and Picasso had frescoed the bathroom with playful fauns, they had us over. He was going to live there like a country gentleman, he said; he had even brought an expensive-looking gun along with him and proposed to go rabbit shooting. He boasted, jokingly, of being a very good shot—the winner of many a fair-ground prize. Jacqueline enjoyed being *châtelaine* as much as he enjoyed being *châtelain*. On one or two of his mock state-portraits of Jacqueline he wrote in large letters, as if he were a seventeenth-century portraitist, "*Jacqueline de Vauvenargues.*"

In March 1961, Picasso, who would be eighty later in the year, finally got around to marrying Jacqueline. I suspect that this was an alternative to making a will—something he had no intention of doing. "I know that I would die the next day," he said. Under French law, his wife would share the estate with his one legitimate son. Nothing would go to his three illegitimate children unless he recognized them. In June the Picassos shut up La Californie, leaving it full of stuff, and moved a few miles away to an attractive, well-protected villa on a terraced hillside near Mougins. They would regret not buying the land below the villa; they would soon find themselves hemmed in by an unsightly develop-ment. A former *mas*, the house had been transformed before the war into a luxurious villa by Benjamin Guinness. It had been named after a neighboring pilgrimage chapel, Notre-Dame-de-Vie, and this no doubt commended it to an eighty-year-old whose greatest fear was death. The

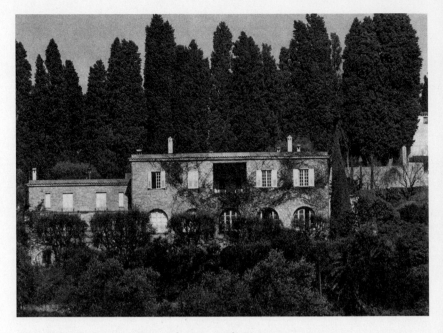

Picasso's last house, Notre-Dame-de-Vie, outside Mougins

house lived up to its auspicious name. Picasso spent the last twelve years of his life there, working on what amounted to a whole new oeuvre.

A few months after the Picassos moved in, I drove over and found the rooms already overflowing with the artist's habitual clutter. Like any newly married couple, they were touchingly house-proud, and angry that a journalist had described their grandiose villa as a "bungalow." Beyond the sitting room were three studios, one full of Picasso's current work, one filled with earlier canvases, and the third stacked with his magnificent variations on Manet's *Déjeuner sur l'Herbe*. Picasso claimed that the feeling of the new house was already reflected in his work, "but go and see for yourself," he said, and left me in the studio, alone except for a parrot.

Almost at once he was back to give me a tour of the house. Upstairs he showed me a secluded balcony for sunbathing, then the Picassos' large bedroom, furnished with nothing but a huge bed, piles of newspapers and books, and a lamp made out of a jeroboam champagne bottle. Next door was a sumptuous bathroom. "There are nothing but bathrooms in this house," Picasso complained, showing us several, but even he got confused, opening door after door and muttering: "Here's another bathroom—no, I'm wrong, it's a bedroom," or vice versa. Many of these rooms had not as yet been slept in; they were used for storage—mostly ceramics from Vallauris.

As usual, everybody but Picasso was flagging, so we returned to the sitting room—camomile for the host, whisky for me. I asked to go back to the *Déjeuners sur l'Herbe,* but hardly had time to look at them before there was a shout from Jacqueline: Monseigneur had decreed that we were going to a film. Back in Cannes, we finally found the place where *L'Année Dernière à Marienbad* was on, but it had already started and the old shrew at the box office—"like one of those frightful women at the post office," Picasso said—wouldn't let us in.

We went to *La Dame aux Camélias* instead. I was worried that the tearful story, with its deathbed climax, would irritate Picasso, but he enjoyed every minute. The old procuress reminded him of Misia Sert, and he found Garbo's performance as Marguerite Gautier very moving, except she didn't cough enough. Even after we came out, Marguerite remained a reality for Picasso, and he kept bringing her into the conversation—"It was just as well she didn't cough more, or she might have infected us with her disease."

"Now let's go to the other film," he suddenly announced. "Are you mad?" said Jacqueline. "All I want is to go home." She spoke for all of us. "Very well, back to Notre-Dame-de-Vie—see you the same time, same place tomorrow." Picasso took his leave. He looked so full of energy, I wasn't surprised to hear later that he had worked into the early hours.

Over the last twelve years of his life, Picasso's children would come to see Jacqueline, with some justice, as a Kali-like figure. She courted Paulo, the one legitimate child, but saw to it that the three illegitimate children had no access to their father or his fortune. This inexcusable behavior would result in prolonged litigation after his death. In a very literal sense, however, Jacqueline became Picasso's Notre-Dame-de-Vie. It was her solicitude, patience, and sacrificial ardor that sustained the artist in the face of declining health and his great enemy death and enabled him to be more productive than ever before and go on working into his ninety-second year.

After Picasso's death on April 8, 1973, I would go and stay with Jacqueline every year or so. These visits were apt to be exceedingly painful. We would sit in a darkened room listening to recordings of Rostropovich playing Bach's doleful cello sonatas. She would clutch not so much my hand as a single finger with the desperation of a lost child and sob and sob. Every so often she would disappear to the kitchen to sneak a drink, and return more tearful than ever. Finally, I would have to carry her to bed and hold her in my arms until she fell asleep. Each time she passed the huge blowup of Picasso in the hall, Jacqueline would look up at it and greet "Monseigneur" and ask him how he was in a woebegone voice. Crises became more and more frequent. Jacqueline's faithful Kikuyu maid, Doris, was always having to summon the doctor, who would administer massive shots of tranquilizers.

When Jacqueline flew to New York in 1980 for the great retrospective at the Museum of Modern Art, she seemed much better. At first, all went well. Carolyn Lanchner, Jacqueline's friend at MoMA, and I went to meet her and her confidante Kitty Lillaz at the airport, and although she balked at going to the White House, she seemed to enjoy being feted at the various ceremonies that her visit to the exhibit involved. She even wore the Dior scarf I had bought her thirty years earlier. On the last night, I made the mistake of taking Jacqueline to a small party given by Connie Mellon, an ex-wife of the director of the National Gallery in Washington. Nothing to fear, I assured her—no press, no dealers, no pushy people. I was wrong. Hardly had we arrived than an officious woman ajangle in homemade jewelry came up and, in Jacqueline's hearing, assured me that she knew the real Madame Picasso and that this one was an imposter. I shooed her away. A few minutes later she was back, to apologize and make matters even worse. So silly of me, she said, of course you are the real Madame Picasso; and she went on to explain that she was a painter of hands and was anxious to paint Jacqueline's beautiful hands. In fact, Jacqueline's hands were anything but beautiful, as Picasso frequently emphasized in his paintings of them. She looked down at her stubby fingers and up at me with a look of utter panic. I got her out of there as quickly as I could.

The last time I stayed at Notre-Dame-de-Vie—1984 or 1985— Jacqueline seemed more tormented than ever, as fraught as any of

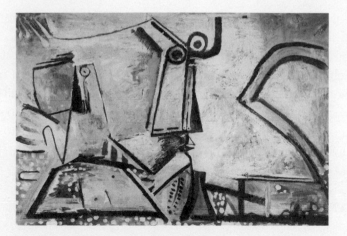

Picasso, Reclining Nude and Head, *oil on canvas, 1972*

Picasso's terrifying late images of her. "Pablo is not dead," she kept reiterating. I finally calmed her down by questioning her about Picasso's early life for the first volume of my biography, which she wanted to be as accurate and definitive as possible. She let me have keys to the studios, and seemed to derive a measure of consolation from going through the stacks of paintings with me. At one point, she came upon a loose drawing, which she asked me about and then gave me. We spent a long time studying Picasso's penultimate painting, *Reclining Nude and Head*—a barely figurative evocation of himself and Jacqueline in a miasma of white paint, with a mysterious configuration with a cross on it along the bottom of the canvas—which he had worked and reworked for months on end. It was an attempt to come to terms with death, hers as well as his. What does it represent? I asked Jacqueline, although I already knew the answer. "A coffin," she said. "Pablo knew he was going to die; I too know I'm going to die." Stacked next to it was an equally large canvas that was blank except for a signature—Picasso's way of leaving his work open-ended.

One morning I was combing through a pile of rubbish in a corner of one of the Notre-Dame-de-Vie studios when I came upon some crumpled drawings by Picasso and a pile of letters to him from Max Jacob, his first poet laureate. I called Jacqueline over to take a look. As

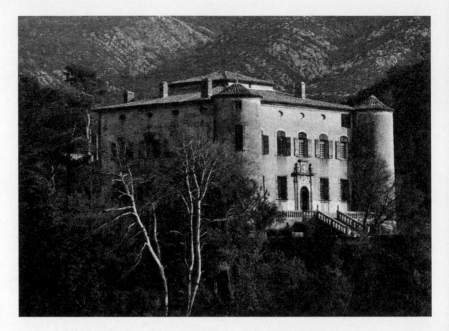

Château de Vauvenargues, where Picasso and Jacqueline are buried

she ran toward me, she suddenly collapsed, sobbing incoherently. Doris telephoned for the doctor to come and give her a shot. The two of us planned to fly to Paris together that afternoon, but the doctor had her consigned to a clinic. I never saw her again.

A year or so later, I heard that Jacqueline was better. She had gone to a hairdresser, had the living room repainted, and even been to a bullfight for the first time since Picasso died. These were in fact ominous signs. Jacqueline had been in the habit of going to Vauvenargues on the eighth of every month to sit by Picasso's tomb and commune with him. She told me he wanted her to join him. She was now ready to do so. On October 15, 1986, ten days before what would have been Picasso's 105th birthday, she shot herself. She was fifty-nine years old.

I flew over from New York for Jacqueline's funeral, a macabre affair. Fortunately Dominique Bozo, the sharp-eyed scholar who was in the process of setting up the Musée Picasso, and Michel Guy, the Minister of Culture who had rescinded Douglas's right to take his collection out of France, were on the same plane to Marseille. They gave me a lift to Vauvenargues in a Citroën driven, as ministerial cars usually are, at topmost speed. The fate of the enormous quantity of Picasso's work that would now belong to Jacqueline's daughter Cathy was much on their minds. Jacqueline had wanted Vauvenargues to be *her* Picasso Museum; Bozo and Guy thought this a bad idea: better get whatever they could for *their* museum. When we arrived at Vauvenargues, it was a shock to see Picasso's grave gaping open and the *Woman with a Vase* sculpture that stood over the grave pushed to one side. A young priest presided over the minimal rites that the Catholic Church accords to people who have died by their own hand. Although spacious, the guardroom, where the ceremony took place, was unseasonably hot and airless, and crammed with flowers. Four hefty grave diggers stood ready to lift up the coffin. Beside them, holding the aspergillum, the holy water sprinkler, was Cathy, who must have been in her late thirties but looked forlorn and freckled as a child. All of a sudden there was a crash: Hubert Landais, the elderly head of the Musées Nationaux, had collapsed. Whereupon the grave diggers hoisted him up and carried him, instead of the coffin, from the room, followed by Cathy, splashing his deathly white, backward-hanging head with holy water. And then they returned for Jacqueline's coffin—a very fancy one in the Empire style, which Picasso would have appreciated for its inappropriateness. Cathy, wearing three rings—her mother's, Picasso's, and a ring for the child they never had—followed, as did the rest of us, down to the grave. And there Jacqueline was reunited with Picasso, her sacrifice finally consummated in this belated ritual of suttee. As we left, the grave diggers were already re-cementing the grave, but I could not forget Jacqueline's cry that Picasso wasn't dead. She was right: the old shaman's shadow, not to mention his vast legacy, continue to bedevil the lives of his descendants.

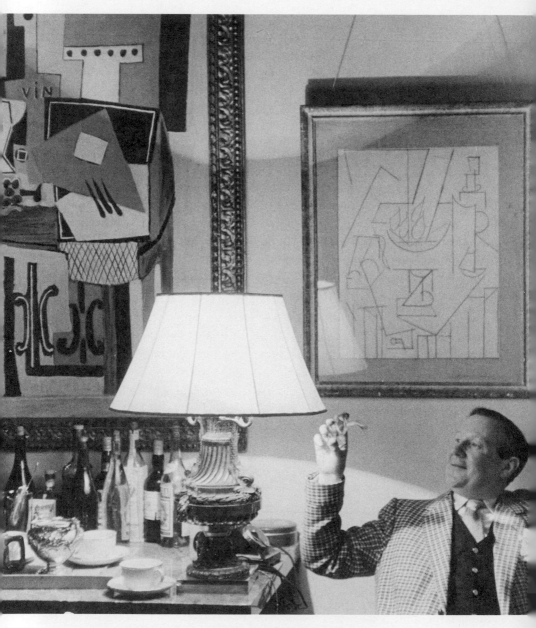

DC in the living room at Castille, in front of two of his Picassos

THE SORCERER'S
APPRENTICE

When Douglas and I were on our own at Castille, the arrival of the mail was usually the most momentous event of the day. Occasionally it could cause anguish. If Douglas was in a dour mood, he would keep the mail to himself. Or he would use whatever might be in it to stir up trouble: "I see you have a letter from so-and-so—let's hope he's not inviting himself to stay." If Douglas was in a good mood—as much of the time he was—we would go through the letters, catalogues, magazines, and so forth together. Collectors, curators, dealers from all over the world, would send in photographs with demands for information or authentication; there would also be requests to see the collection—requests to which Douglas, who was excessively proud of his treasures, would usually accede.

One day our friend Henry McIlhenny, the Philadelphia collector, wrote that he was sending Douglas "a nice young homonym: the Swedenborgian Douglas Cooper"—Swedenborgian in that he had married a daughter of the Reverend Theodore Pitcairn, the sect's rich and powerful leader. Pitcairn owned one of the world's most celebrated Monets, *The Terrace at Sainte-Addresse* (a painting I would arrange for Christie's to sell, some years later, for a record sum), as well as a number of mostly dud El Grecos. The Swedenborgian Douglas Cooper turned out to be personable if a bit cocky. He was the proprietor of a large Philadelphia jewelry store, and he used photographs of himself clutching the world's largest star sapphire or other such bauble to advertise his wares in the national press. The Castillian Douglas Cooper was thrilled with him. Late that night the colonnaded balcony that extended around three sides of Castille, enabling guests to nip surreptitiously from bedroom to bedroom via the windows, saw more action than usual. After a spell in his homonym's bed, the Swedenborgian Douglas Cooper tapped on my shutters and, half an hour later, went on to service another guest. When I saw him a few years later in Philadelphia, he was so revved up on booze and speed and the horsepower of his overchromed Harley-Davidson as to be in a state of terminal meltdown. I declined the offer of a ride on his buddy-seat. That pleasure was better left to a skeleton wielding a scythe. Sure enough, the Swedenborgian Douglas Cooper died young.

Another day—a fateful day for me—a letter arrived from our Pittsburgh friend, Dave Thompson, enclosing photographs of two *Contrastes de Formes,* supposedly by Léger, which he contemplated buying. After living with the world's largest collection of these works, I had developed a sharp eye for their qualities, and so was full of curiosity. The harder I looked at the photographs of Dave's paintings, the less I liked them. They had none of the energy of Douglas's versions, and there was no contrast to the forms; they had to be fakes. "Poor Dave," I announced, stupidly assuming that Douglas would be impressed by his pupil's expertise; "How could he have been taken in by such inert daubs?" There was a terrible silence, during which Douglas's pink face turned the color of a summer pudding. "What a little expert we've become." And then came a shriek like calico ripping—comical but also alarming. "How *dare* you pontificate to *me* about Léger!" he yelled. *"Those paintings are absolutely authentic.* Get out, get out. . . ." And then he took another look at the photographs, and I realized that he realized that I was right and he was wrong. Things would never be the same again. I had become the sorcerer's apprentice. In my head I could hear Dukas's maddeningly catchy *l'Apprenti Sorcier* scherzo and I could see myself as Mickey Mouse in a red robe and a wizard's hat as in Disney's visualization of it, but this time it was not the meddlesome apprentice who had screwed up; it was the silly old sorcerer. The apprentice had turned into a detestable rival—the more detestable for doubling as a lover. This row had a seismic effect on our relationship. Aftershocks rumbled on for weeks. Douglas's letters to friends recounting our joined-at-the-hip activities ceased mentioning me. Henceforth it would always be "I" and not "we" who did things. Consciously or not, Douglas was trying to write me out of his life.

I half hoped that I would turn out to have been wrong about the Légers. Kahnweiler, who had been the artist's dealer at the time of the *Contrastes de Formes*, had asked for the two paintings to be shipped to his gallery for examination, and for Douglas and me to be present when this took place. The canny old dealer—by now the very image of an oriental sage—went on scrutinizing the paintings long after he had clearly come to a conclusion. In his excellent English he finally murmured, "They are fakes—no question about it." I was careful not to show that I felt vindicated. Douglas was equally careful not to show that he had ever thought otherwise. "I knew they were wrong," he said, "but didn't want to commit myself until I had seen the originals." Kahnweiler, who knew Douglas of old, gave him a quick, sly glance. Somehow or other he had divined the truth. Five years later, when the Dortmund Museum decided to put on a Juan Gris retrospective, he arranged for me, rather than Douglas, to organize it. He could not have administered a more painful rebuke.

This incident put me in mind of Francis Bacon's terrible remark about the merits of Douglas's eye: "She's only got one, so it better be good." Douglas's good eye was as good as anyone's in his particular field, but it was an academic's eye. He had a theoretical knowledge of technical processes, but he himself had never applied paint to canvas or used a pen or pencil to delineate form. To this extent I had the advantage of him, having started life as a painter, albeit a bad one. I knew more than he did about the problems the métier involved. I could usually spot when an artist was fudging or repeating himself or taking an easy way out, having done a lot of that myself in my student days. The seven years or so I had spent helping Douglas take care of his pictures, as well as discussing them with the artists who had painted them, had not been wasted. Douglas would ask Picasso or Braque questions a cataloguer would ask—dates, provenance, and so forth. I would ask them questions an art student would ask: the nature of the additives—ashes, tobacco, coffee grounds—they had used in cubist paintings; whether I was correct in thinking that certain canvases had been worked on upside down as well as the right way up and so forth. The answers to my questions would enable me, decades later, to publish an article begging restorers to respect these artists' wishes and *never* varnish the surface of their paintings, as virtually every collector, dealer, and museum director, not to mention Douglas, had been in the habit of doing. Matte surfaces for Cubist paintings are now mandatory.

Douglas was always banging on moralistically about the venality and trickery of dealers and so-called experts. However, as the prices of modern art—particularly the sort he collected—started to soar in the late 1950s, he, too, began to lapse into venality and trickery. Around the time I broke with Douglas, there would be another unfortunate episode involving early Légers. This time the habitually scrupulous Kahnweiler was for once at fault. After Léger's death, Kahnweiler had acquired, supposedly "from an impeccable source," a cache of hitherto unknown *Contrastes de Formes:* smallish ones executed in gouache and watercolor. They were so attractive that collectors and dealers gobbled them up, but I was suspicious—they looked too good to be true. Whoever was responsible had opted for half-tones (salmon pink, pistachio green, lavender), instead of the primary colors that Léger favored, and he had also indulged in a lot of flimsy, translucent faceting. But who was I to gainsay Kahnweiler? Nor, given my previous experience, did I want to tangle with Douglas, who was off in America when the matter arose, lecturing and advising collectors to invest in these very Légers, among other things. The commissions that his advice generated enabled Douglas to acquire one of them for himself. It turned out that I was not alone in doubting these pretty-pretty works. Kahnweiler continued to maintain they were authentic, but in the face of complaints from some of his more valued clients, he consented in certain cases to refund the money. Our enterprising friend Heinz Berggruen was one of the first to reach a settlement. After abruptly switching from adulating Kahnweiler's little gems to denigrating them, Douglas followed suit and got his money back.

Had Douglas always been such a humbug? I don't think so. The trouble was, the market for modern art had skyrocketed. The Goldschmidt sale at Sotheby's in 1958 had set new records (£220,000 for Cézanne's *Boy in a Red Waistcoat,* and £132,000 for van Gogh's *Jardin Public à Arles*) for impressionist and post-impressionist paintings. Prices for twentieth-century art, for fauvism and cubism in particular, followed suit. Douglas's collection, which had been worth six figures when we first met, was worth seven figures by the mid-fifties, and eight figures by the

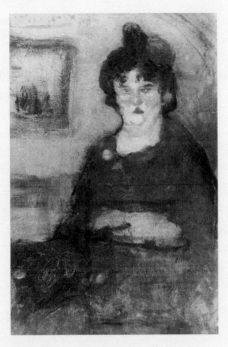

Picasso, Seated Woman, *oil on canvas,*
1900

time I left him. At today's valuations it would be worth well into nine figures. Meanwhile, the income from Douglas's securities had not kept up
with the postwar rise in the cost of living or with the ever-increasing
expense of life at Castille. To make up the difference, he took to exploiting his expertise and would sometimes do things that were foolish and
unethical. Years later an acquaintance told me that he had gone to hear
Douglas lecture somewhere in the United States in order to show him
an unpublished Picasso drawing he had inherited. He wanted to have it
authenticated. Douglas could not have been more helpful—at first. "It's
absolutely right," Douglas said, and confirmed the date and other
details. What is more, he would like to buy it, and he offered the owner a
derisory sum. No, the owner wanted to keep it. At this, Douglas declared
that he was not so sure that the drawing was right after all—just as well it
wasn't for sale. In the past, this was the kind of sharp practice that Douglas had loved to expose and denounce. He continued to do so.

After being deceived by Douglas and vindicated by Kahnweiler over the fake Légers, I thought it safer to absent myself from Castille for a month or two. I had always longed to visit America, but had never had the means. All of a sudden I was able to do so. Some months earlier I had bought a small early Picasso painting of a Barcelona prostitute for around $2,000 off a refugee from the Hungarian revolution; and I was reasonably hopeful of selling it for enough money to cover the expenses of my trip to New York. I was assured of somewhere to stay. John Hohns-been had moved in with the architect Philip Johnson, and providently offered me his apartment. An added inducement: my friend Lil was going to be there at the same time. And then a Provençal neighbor, Paul Hanbury, turned out to have made reservations for himself and some friends on the *Queen Elizabeth* early in December—why didn't I join them? I agreed to do so.

Douglas proceeded to do everything possible to stop me from going—cajoling, threatening, will-rattling—to what he called "that bar-barian bedlam and jazz palace." But the more insistent his reproaches, or, for that matter, his endearments, the more adamant I felt about get-ting away. If I was ever to do my own thing, I had to regain my freedom. The Léger incident had opened my eyes to an earlier abuse on Douglas's part. In 1957 the two of us had collaborated on a Monet retrospective for Britain's Arts Council, to be held at the Edinburgh Festival and then at the Tate. Douglas had written a preface; I had done a chronology and most of the research; both of us had worked on the notes. Douglas could not get away, so I went to Edinburgh on my own, only to discover that Douglas had managed to take virtually all the credit for the show which we had supposedly done together. All the Arts Council's fault, he said. At the time I had believed him. Now I could no longer do so. This greatly strengthened my resolve to try my luck in America. Ten days before Christmas, 1958, I sailed off with Douglas's abusive farewells ringing in my ears. Threats that I would never again darken the door of Castille set me thinking that this might not be such a bad idea.

New York turned out to be the promised land. Life in a walkup apartment was far more stimulating and liberating than life amid the colonnades of Castille. And what a revelation the Museum of Modern Art proved to be! That so many of the collectors, curators, and dealers had visited Castille opened a lot of doors. That first Christmas, Philip

Johnson had me to stay in the guest house of his Glass House. Besides John Hohnsbeen, the guests included Alfred Barr, the founder of the Museum of Modern Art, and his acerbic wife, Marga; Barr's assistant Dorothy Miller; and Picasso's old friend, the sculptor Meric Callery. Philip introduced me to the work of the young artists of the New York School—artists whom Douglas had done his best to turn me against. In the course of bird-watching walks in the snow, Alfred questioned me about Picasso's latest work. I was as yet unaware of the Byzantine intrigue and divisiveness of the New York art world, and did not realize how fortunate I was to have an easy entrée to it. In the course of the next two months I visited most of New York's modernist collections. The quality and quantity amazed me, as did the uniformity—a measure of the power that Alfred Barr exercised over his flock of collectors.

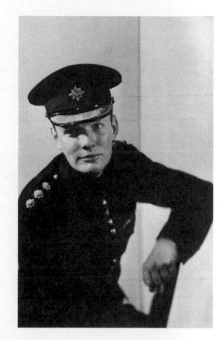

Patrick O'Higgins in Irish Guards uniform, 1946

The seal of his approval did not extend beyond certain periods of certain artists' work. There was nothing wrong with these parameters, except that they made for collections that reflected Alfred's ideas rather than the owner's predilections.

Another thing that struck me about these collectors was the contradiction between their enlightened patronage of modern art and their anything-but-enlightened views on political, social, and moral issues. This dawned on me one afternoon while having tea with a Park Avenue matron whose attitude to everything but art was redolent of a nineteenth-century Sunday school teacher. "Don't you love our Miró?" she said. "We have keyed the color of the room to it, because our little girl likes it so much." Did this woman realize, I wondered, that the pink balloon the male figure brandished was a penis and the black starfish was a vagina, and the configuration in the corner represented a Catalan peasant taking a shit? I would recount these stories to the couple I had come to regard as far and away the most perceptive collectors of modern art in

the United States, Victor and Sally Ganz. They were in no need of guid-
ance and knew exactly what the sexual puns in their Picassos implied.
Although their resources were limited, the Ganzes ended up with the
world's greatest collection of Picasso's later periods. To my delight, they
would become close friends.

A chance meeting in the street with an old friend from childhood,
tall, witty, red-haired Patrick O'Higgins, would prove a great piece of
luck—for him as well as me. This half-Irish, half-French journalist was
the right-hand man of the cosmetics tycoon Helena Rubinstein, about
whom he would later write a funny, surprisingly touching book called
Madame. Back at Patrick's apartment, I was surprised to find a marvelous cubist collage by Juan Gris on the floor. "It's nothing," Patrick
said; "a fake that Madame [as Rubinstein was known in the cosmetics
business] threw out. One of my friends has taken a shine to it, and I'm
giving it to him for Christmas." The friend must be very astute, I told
Patrick. Far from being a fake, it's absolutely okay and probably worth
around $20,000 (more than $500,000 today). Why didn't I sell it for him?

Sure enough, I did; and sure enough, when Patrick took me to
meet Madame, I found several more "fakes" relegated to a closet, among
them a series of large Juan Gris still lifes on paper, done at a time when
he was unable to afford canvas. Some idiot had told her they were fake
Marcoussis. Instead of offering Madame a pittance for her "fakes"—a
pittance she would probably have accepted—I arranged for Knoedler's
to pay a fair price for them and cut Patrick and me in on the deal.
Henceforth, this mistrustful old woman would deal only with me. I had
another small hold over Madame. After years of coercion, she had finally
persuaded Picasso to do some drawings of her, but he had refused to
show her the results. He had, however, shown them to me. What are
they like? she kept asking. Brilliant, I said quite truthfully. I did not dare
tell Madame that many of the drawings were studies of her jeweled wat-
tles and ring-covered claws, and that the ones of her head made her look
as bald and rapacious as an eagle. "Picasso has ennobled you," I told her.
"He has made you his eagle."

Whenever I was able to raise some money, I would go around to
Madame's enormous triplex apartment, wave bundles of fifty-dollar bills
at her, raise my eyebrows quizzically, and point to one of the Picasso
drawings, which her first husband, a Greenwich Village intellectual

called Horace Titus, had acquired in Paris in the 1920s. Madame could not resist the fresh green smell of newly minted banknotes. Far from being offended by my pushiness, she would go to the wall as if in a trance, and remove the drawing off its hook. Then the haggling would start. Counting the money would take even longer. Madame liked to use her bedroom as an office. We would sit side by side on her unmade Lucite bed with a pile of dollar bills between us. Sometimes we would have to recount them as many as six times before the figures would tally. Madame counted slowly out loud, and every time she reached a hundred, she would puff out her lips and make a raspberry noise. Patrick, whose job it was to smuggle the dollars out of the country into Switzerland wearing a money belt so capacious he looked pregnant, told me this meant Madame was happy.

Madame preferred to be addressed as Princess Gourielli, having married a self-styled prince of that name; and she chose to surround herself with others of the same ilk: overdressed, overjeweled, over-made-up women from Eastern Europe, whose titles carried as much conviction as their gems. There was a fat Russian one called Princess Mdvani, and a Baroness Kuffner, who embodied the lurid Nazi allure of Hitler's favorite singer, Zara Leander. I can see her still, in a fur shako and a floor-length lynx coat that had once been white, towering over her hostess like a borzoi over a Fabergé frog. "Go visit Tamara's studio," Madame told me. "Tamara is famous modern painter." What sort of thing do you paint? I asked. "My art transcends all schools." The baroness narrowed her eyes and drew herself up. "Tamara has done it all: symbolism, cubism, futurism, purism, surrealism, realism, you name it. Tamara is always Tamara. Since you are a friend of Madame's, I invite you to take a look for yourself." The vampish opulence of Baroness Kuffner's studio surprised me less than the vacuous competence of her hard-edge abstractions. Painted in Esperanto, I remember thinking. Who on earth was this Baroness Kuffner? Some years later, when art deco returned to fashion, and stylized portraits of fascist femmes fatales in flying helmets and their sleek male counterparts became a camp cult, I realized that the leading exponent of this style, Tamara de Lempicka, was one and the same as the Baroness Kuffner. It figured.

I felt reborn in New York. Then as now, the city opened itself up to outsiders. I felt like a child let loose in a huge store, free to switch from department to department, floor to floor. The art world was only one of a great many options. Thanks to my friend Lil, I had access to almost too much social life. After a particularly star-studded event—a traditional New Year's bash given by the theater producer Gilbert Miller and his witty, walleyed wife, Kitty—I took Lil, who had drunk almost as much as I had, back to the elegant *dix-huitième* house she had been lent. We sat down on a delicate little settee, and I tried to maneuver Lil, who was as tall as I was, onto my knee. In my cups, I ended up on her knee. Where-upon the little settee gave an ominous creak. There was nothing to do but laugh. After this episode, we kept our relationship on a platonic basis.

Hitherto, I had been in the habit of sleeping for eight hours a night. In New York the excitement and pressure were such that I made do with three or four hours at most. After the uptown festivities were over, I would race back home and change from a black tie into a T-shirt and go out on the town. A wild, new, permissive spirit was already in the air, and I proceeded to explore all facets of it. Patrick O'Higgins took me to spectacular drag balls in Harlem, where I was amazed at the elabo-rateness of the boys' beaded gowns. Truman Capote—an old friend of Douglas's—took me to a lesbian bikers' hangout, which we had to leave in a hurry: Truman said he was frightened of getting raped. And a gifted albeit unsuccessful painter friend of mine, Onni Saari, introduced me to some amazing downtown bars—a great improvement on London's gay clubs, where an old thing at a white piano would play versions of Cole Porter—"You stepped out of a drain"—and a lot of shy young men in three-piece suits waving cigarette holders would eye each other ner-vously and bridle or pout. New York's downtown bars had a macho, west-ern allure. The experience in Wystan Auden's garden ten years before became a matter of course. How was I going to settle down again at Castille? Douglas's nasty, nagging letters merely made me want to stay on longer and longer in New York. Hearing that he had moved a former lover into Castille and taken him over to see Picasso did not encourage me to return, let alone curtail my own newfound freedom.

After a month in New York, I left on a tour of museums and private collections: Boston, Baltimore, Washington, Pittsburgh, Cleveland, Detroit, Chicago, and St. Louis. After a week back in New York, I flew off to Paris, where Douglas awaited me. He was touchingly careful to show me only his best—brightest, funniest, sweetest—side. When I returned to Castille, I found Marie so relieved to have me back, the cherry orchards in bloom, the colonnades golden in the sunlight, and the collection much finer than anything comparable in private hands in America. Wasn't this where I belonged? Miró was coming to dinner the evening after our return, the Hugh Trevor-Ropers the following weekend. Then we had the Easter bullfights with Picasso to look forward to. Wonderful, but I couldn't get New York out of my mind.

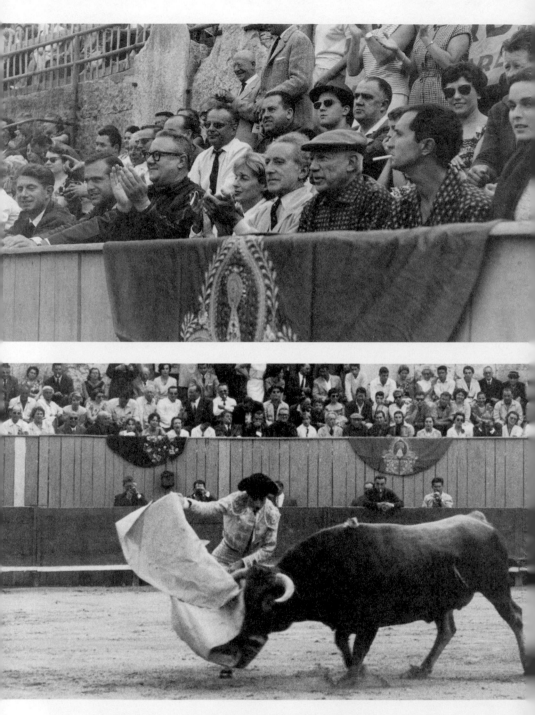

TOP, *Paulo Picasso, JR, DC, Francine Weisweiller, Cocteau, Picasso, Luis Miguel Domin- guín, and his wife, Lucia Bose, watching Antonio Ordóñez* (ABOVE) *in the arena at Arles, summer 1959*

THE BEGINNING
OF THE END

After my return from America, Douglas was at pains to make life at Castille as pleasant as possible. Much as he discouraged my attempts to become financially independent, he refrained from kicking up a fuss when I returned to New York for ten days to do some more business with Helena Rubinstein. Meanwhile, more visitors descended on us than ever before; and our dinners for Picasso after the bullfights were becoming increasingly frequent. Picasso and Cocteau rarely traveled without an entourage, so these parties had to be infinitely elastic. Marie, the cook, would set up an alfresco banquet in the *magnaneraie*, the old silkworm barn, whose walls Picasso would later decorate.

That summer (1959), the two most celebrated toreros in Spain, Luis Miguel Domínguin and his brother-in-law, Antonio Ordóñez, had embarked on a series of *mano a mano* appearances (bullfights in which two toreros, instead of the usual three, take on the traditional six bulls). These appearances had caused tremendous excitement in bullfighting circles, as had the news that Ernest Hemingway, who was a fan of Ordóñez, was covering the series for *Life* magazine. For their appearance in the Nîmes arena, Douglas and I had our usual seats alongside Picasso and Jacqueline. Immediately below us, behind the barrier in the bullring, was Hemingway, playing the role of aficionado to the hilt—something that Picasso could not abide. As the band struck up the "Marseillaise," we all stood. Suddenly Picasso laughed and pointed down at Hemingway. The author of *Death in the Afternoon* was standing rigidly to attention, his right hand up to his peaked cap in a military salute. When Hemingway looked around and saw that nobody else was saluting—the official presiding over the bullfight was picking his nose—he

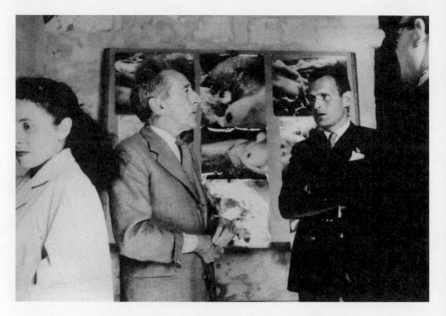

*Jean Cocteau, JR, and DC at the opening of Lucien Clergue's photography show at Arles,
ca. 1958*

withdrew his hand and ever so slowly repositioned it in his pocket.
Picasso watched this episode intently with what I can only describe as a
delighted "gotcha" look in his huge eyes. Never again have I been able to
read Hemingway. Even the early stories, which I used to admire so
much, seem spurious.

After the bullfight, we raced back to Castille to welcome Picasso
and Jacqueline in a black Citroën driven by a new driver called Jeannot,
followed by a *défilé* of three or four vehicles. These included Picasso's
son Paulo with his new wife, Christine, and a drinking companion called
Baudouin; his painter-nephew Xavier Vilató; his disagreeable secretary,
Sabartés; the Leirises (the great writer Michel and his wife, Zette, who
was Kahnweiler's stepdaughter and partner); Edouard and Hélène
Pignon; David Douglas Duncan, who was keeping a photographic
record of Picasso's life; a printer who was working with the artist at
the time, as well as the toreros with their camp followers. Cocteau
and Francine Weisweiller arrived with their dependents—Cocteau's
adopted son Doudou, Doudou's sister Emilienne and Francine's daughter Carole—in two gleaming black Bentleys. Carole and Emilienne were

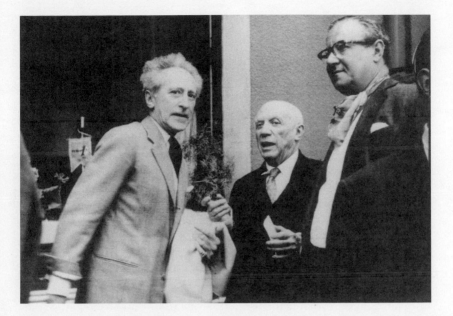

Cocteau, Picasso, and DC, Arles, 1957

still at school, and, as Carole relates in her touching memoir of Cocteau, they were thrilled to tag along on these outings under the poet's auspices.

Said to be a budding painter, Doudou was the son of a Triestino iron miner who had settled in France. Spectacular Mediterranean looks and considerable sweetness of nature, rather than any talent as a *peintre naif,* had propelled Doudou from the mines of eastern France into Cocteau's glamorous life—first as a gardener, then as a driver, ultimately as a lover and son. Francine doted on him, and when this exquisitely dressed, excessively spoiled little beauty appointed herself Cocteau's muse, she installed Doudou as well as his adoptive father in her luxurious little hideaway, the Villa Santo-Sospir at Cap Ferrat. And there for the next twelve years or so the three of them would spend their summers bound together as much by mutual admiration—a sort of collective narcissism—as by opium. Doudou, who liked to sleep until four in the afternoon, trailed languor behind him like a gauzy cloak. Cocteau was very proud of his son, whose silence and air of aloofness were a perfect foil for the poet's conversational sparkle.

Dinners at Castille brought out the best in Douglas. Fussing over the festivities, he would be as rubicund and bonhomous as Mr. Pickwick at Dingley Dell. Cocteau would assume the role of master of ceremonies. Now that he was a member of the Académie, he would repeatedly point out that although he took precedence over everyone except a cardinal, he was always prepared to cede his place of honor to Picasso. Waving his long-fingered hands in the air, Cocteau would stand in for the fireworks that had failed to materialize. Usually he would have a glittering conversational set piece all prepared. On this particular evening he gave us a vivid description of his recent visit to Rome: how a group of American ladies at a papal audience had kissed Pope John's hands so passionately that his white gloves turned red from their lipstick, and how the new Pope's decree that trains should be cut short had irritated a frivolous old cardinal so much that he had sewn the bits off the other cardinals' trains onto his own. And Cocteau mimicked the old prelate at his sewing machine, botching the job so that the train jiggled and wiggled all the way up the aisle of St. Peter's. The fascination of Cocteau's conversation lay not so much in the actual incidents as in his theatrical gestures and mimicry, and the emphasis on a single droll detail like the cardinal at his sewing machine. I have never heard a raconteur to equal him. Meanwhile, our bull-breeder friend from the Camargue, Jean Lafont, to whom Jacqueline had taken a great fancy, had laid on a group of Gypsy dancers from Les Saintes-Maries-de-la-Mer, their pilgrimage place. Cocteau was fascinated by them: he had recently based his frescoes in the church at Villefranche on Lucien Clergue's photographs of some Brueghelesque Gypsies horsing obscenely around. Picasso, too, enjoyed the Gypsies—the meaner and more thieving the better. He would get up and dance flamenco with them and laugh and clap his hands as they ground their heels in the glasses they had smashed and fought over things that glittered.

In her recent memoir Carole Weisweiller describes one of these evenings—a candlelit dinner in our garden in honor of Cocteau and Ordóñez. Luis Miguel Dominguín had brought along a dwarf in his *cuadrilla*. As our guitarist started to play, "the dwarf got up and did a handkerchief dance round and round a woman three times bigger than him. . . . So fascinated were we by this baroque spectacle that we stopped talking and laughing. . . . The nobility of this dwarf, who was out to seduce this giantess at any cost, amazed me. . . . Unable to take my eyes off this strange pantomime, I forgot all about his smallness and ugliness. As he warmed up, the *cante jondo* became more and more intense, the other singers and dancers crowded around him."

In the middle of June, Douglas and I left for Florence, where we stayed with Henry Clifford, curator of painting at the Philadelphia Museum of Art, and his bluestocking wife, Esther. The Cliffords owned the medieval Villa Caponi, which was celebrated for its terraced gardens. Sunk deep into one of the terraces was a *giardino segreto*, which you could not enter; you could only look down into it over a balustrade. Gardeners had access through an underground passage. After a few days in this sumptuous house, I began to see the secret garden as a metaphor for the private life of our host, who devoted a lot of time to doing flower arrangements with his friendly Italian butler. Life in Florence was unremittingly grand. Harold Acton asked us to lunch. The front door of his magnificent villa was opened by a flunky in gold-braided livery and mud-covered shoes. When I saw the flunky in a pair of shorts, digging away in the garden, I understood about the shoes. I found Harold totally beguiling, and wished I had had more time with him. The Cliffords spent a great deal of time gossiping. Henry maintained that Harold Acton's father, an antique dealer who had married a Chicago heiress, was the son of the last of the Neapolitan Rothschilds and his cook. The other main topic of conversation was Bernard Berenson. One of the American contessas whom Henry took us to see filled us in on B.B.'s quarrels with his colleagues and his business deals, and then became sanctimonious. "B.B. may have done some bad things in the name of Mammon," she said, "but [he did] many very good things in the name of art."

Douglas was determined to pay B.B. a last visit. Although the ninety-four-year-old scholar was on his last legs—mobility, sight, hearing, and speech all going or gone—curiosity got the better of him, and for all that he was reputed to dislike Douglas, he granted us an audience in a smallish, darkish, library-like room at I Tatti. A brawny young nurse hovered briefly over her fragile charge, adjusting his rugs and shawls, and then vanished. We were left alone with this withered wraith, the embodiment of sanctified wisdom—or so I had always been told. Even Douglas was awed into behaving respectfully. B.B.'s intelligence was unimpaired, but the filament through which its light once shone had lost

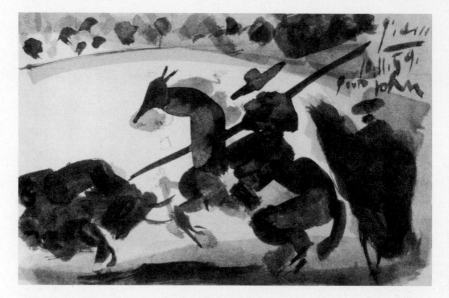

Picasso, Bullfight, *India and colored ink wash, 1959*

its incandescence. The flickering of his mind gave an added poignancy to his complaints, for instance, that he no longer derived any pleasure from music; even the finest recordings or the finest music sounded faint and cracked and tinny to his failing ears. B.B. told us this in a voice that sounded no less faint and cracked. "So sad," Douglas said as we left I Tatti. "As a young man, he must have had one of the most protean minds of his generation; he was simply too materialistic, too greedy for pomp and circumstance, to live up to it. Besides the caterwauling of bereaved acolytes, what will he leave behind? A fine house filled with fine things, a magnificent library, a formidable body of pioneer work, but one that will be forever tainted by dealers' commissions." This most sacred of sacred monsters died a few months later.

Over the next few weeks, Douglas would often revert to the subject of B.B., criticizing him for the way he had conned the world into perceiving him as the world's most revered art historian, while he "was never off the blower to the marketplace." Knowing Douglas, I realized that his censoriousness was a form of approval, and that he had resolved to follow Berenson's example and put his incomparable knowledge of the modern field on the market. And indeed, from this point on, commissions and profit-sharing projects would ensure that Douglas never had to worry about his diminishing trust fund again. If only he had had more of Berenson's finesse and guile.

Venice, our next stop after Florence, was more relaxed. We stayed with the Sutherlands. They had been lent a dark, overdecorated house on a back canal and, more to the point, a magnificently appointed gondola and two dashing, horribly spoiled gondoliers, by their rich friend Arthur Jeffress. The former backer of London's Hanover Gallery, Arthur was the subject of one of Graham's less successful portraits. The gondoliers would be the indirect cause of Arthur's death. At a grand Venetian dinner party, the Duchess of Windsor asked Arthur whether he would take her home in his gondola. Of course, said Arthur, only to find that his horribly spoiled gondoliers had once again gone off carousing. This time he fired them and sold the gondola, whereupon they denounced him to the police, who were trying to purge Venice of homosexuals. Heartbroken at being exiled from his beloved Venice, Arthur, who was rumored to wear a ring containing cyanide, fled to Paris, where he killed himself. He had always loved sailors, and left much of his considerable fortune to a home for old salts.

Over the years, Douglas and I had frequently discussed the future of Castille, its collection and library. Since the strength of the collection resided in its historical completeness and consistent quality, there could be no question of breaking it up. How could it best be kept together? As Douglas had recently published a catalogue of the Courtauld collection of impressionist and post-impressionist masterpieces and frequently lectured at the Courtauld Institute, he decided that the château and its contents should become a center for modern French studies under the auspices of the University of London (of which the Courtauld Institute was a part). In the event of Douglas's death, I was to take over as curator and have my own apartment on the as-yet-empty top floor of the château. Originally, I had been thrilled with the idea; it seemed to give my career a sense of purpose. Since my trip to America,

OVERLEAF: *On the way to the bullfight, Paulo Picasso, Picasso, Jacqueline, Christine Picasso, JR, Cocteau, and DC in the streets of Arles, 1957*

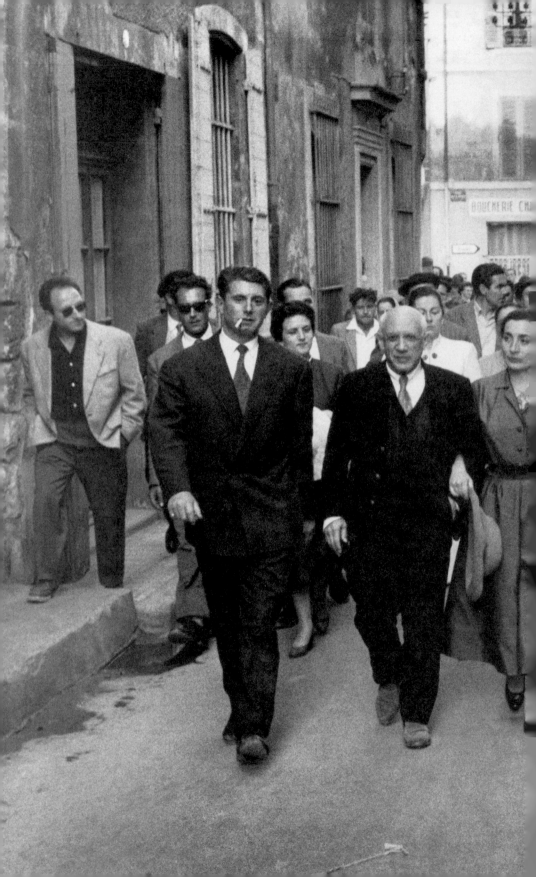

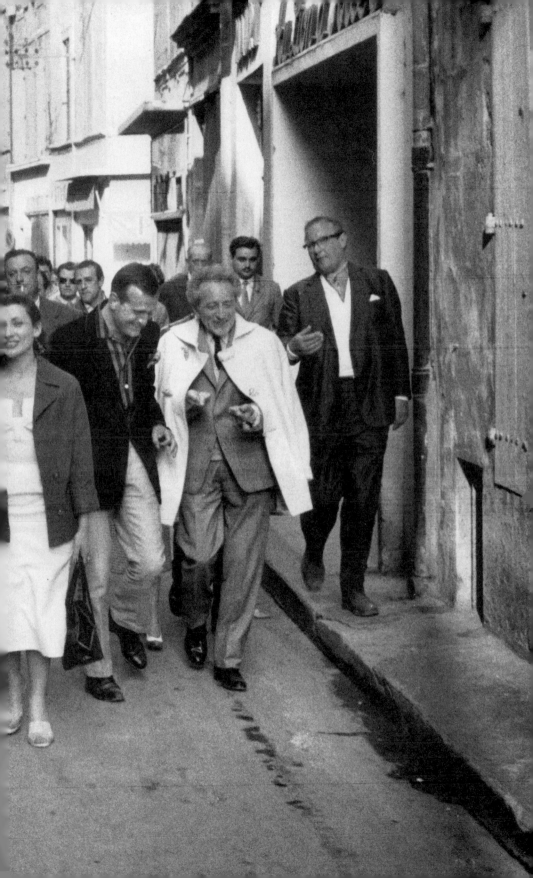

however, I had begun to have second thoughts. I had been twenty-five when I first met Douglas; I was now thirty-five, and the prospect of spending most of the rest of my life as a resentful apprentice to a capricious sorcerer had little appeal for me.

The more I thought about it, the more I realized that if I were to go on living at Castille, it would have to be on a part-time basis. My affection for Douglas was no longer strong enough to withstand the strain to which it was constantly subjected. When I told him that I intended to return to New York for a couple of months at the end of the year, he turned back into a monster. There were horrible rows. These often ended in humiliating fights, which I always lost: Douglas knew just how to use his weight; he would fall on top of me and pin me to the ground. "Have a heart," I would yell. "Have a heart? How could I possibly have a heart?" he would say. "Have you ever looked at me?"

Nevertheless, we continued to drive around France (race around France would be more accurate—Douglas's cruising speed was never less than ninety miles an hour). In July we went to Bordeaux and Biarritz, where I very nearly drowned bodysurfing in the treacherous undertow. In August we went to music festivals at Menton and Aix-en-Provence. In September, Cocteau invited us to Les Baux to watch him make his film *Le Testament d'Orphée,* on the day that the Picassos and the Dominguíns were due to appear in it. Serge Lifar and his Swedish countess were also there—"purely by chance," Lifar said, but in fact by design. Jacqueline told us that this portly dancer would do anything to resurrect the reputation that his wartime collaboration had wrecked. Picasso turned out to be thrilled at appearing in a film and rolled his eyes at the camera as if he were the villain in a silent movie. Getting him to relax and play himself required several takes, which he found boring. As a distraction, the artist did drawings of Francine and colored them with juice from the petals of wildflowers. The finished film struck me as symbolist claptrap of the most vacuous kind; but then I could never take Cocteau's self-mythologizing seriously. Paradoxically, the stills taken by our friend Lucien Clergue have far more depth and mystery than the actual film.

And then in October we went to stay with one of the last of the old-time Riviera hostesses, Florence Gould, in her lavish villa at Cannes. Born to a French father in San Francisco, Florence had started life as an

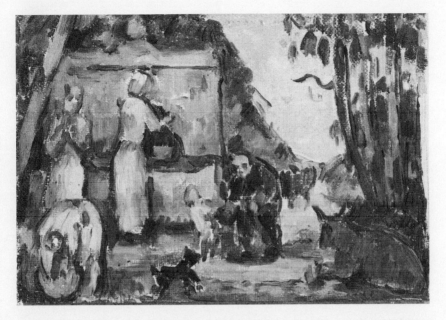

Cézanne, The Fountain, *oil on canvas, 1876–77; sold by JR to Florence Gould, Cannes*

opera singer. In the course of a concert tour in the early 1920s, she had met Frank Jay Gould, son of a famously rich robber baron. To avoid U.S. taxes, the Goulds settled in France, where they became major real estate developers. They bought a vast tract of land to the east of Cannes, on which they built hotels, restaurants, and a casino. This became a summer, as opposed to a winter, resort, and was called Juan-les-Pins. Florence, who was *sportive,* is said to have introduced waterskiing to the Riviera. During the war she had stayed on in Paris, where her vast reserves of champagne made her exceedingly popular. By the time I knew her, Florence had put on a bit of weight (which she carried remarkably well) and taken to drink and literary patronage and the company of aging playboys who looked as over-restored and mahoganized as the stuff in their chic antique shops. After wasting a lot of money on Bernard Buffets, she had graduated to buying Bonnards from the Wildensteins. Douglas planned to rescue her from them and turn her into a serious collector. On this occasion he persuaded her to buy a beautiful little unpublished Cézanne painting (unpublished, because its fastidious former owner, Charles Loeser, hated having his treasures catalogued), which I had managed to pick up earlier in the year for a song at Sotheby's. Florence paid a good price, but extracting the money from Douglas required as much skill as landing a salmon.

By the time we went in to dinner Florence was quite drunk, but nevertheless in control of her numerous guests. Halfway through dinner she asked if we would like to see her celebrated collection of pearls. Of course we would. Asked to bring down an assortment from the safe, her two security men returned bearing a number of large round tins—the sort that used to contain plum cakes from Dundee—stacked one on top of another. These tins were filled with birdseed, in which nestled the biggest and best-matched pearls I had ever seen. Why the birdseed? Instead of paying an oily-skinned pearl feeder to sit in a bank vault nurturing her pearls, Florence said it was simpler and cheaper to keep them in linseed (or was it caraway seed?). "Just look at the sheen." And she proceeded to pass them down the table, telling us about the celebrated people—Marie Antoinette, the Tsarina, Tipu Sahib—who may or may not have owned them. Florence seemed instinctively to know which of her pearl necklaces—pink, gray, black, white—was in whose hands. "Chuck, dear, could you pass the pink ones back?" Despite all the security, most of the jewelry—$750,000's worth—was stolen by masked robbers in 1978. I was relieved when the pearls were restored to their tins, relieved to leave this over-upholstered bank vault of a house the following morning, and to have lunch with Cocteau in the Villa Santo-Sospir.

Cocteau was alone, and as so often when he was alone, at his very best—overflowing with the charm and brilliance engendered by his infinite desire to please. Cocteau's anecdotes about Picasso were enthralling, but his comments on the work—"The only difference between me and Picasso is that I always use one continuous contour, whereas Picasso breaks things up"—did not inspire much confidence in his judgment. As he talked—with the cuffs of his jacket turned back to set off his hands—I noticed that he had covered over his bald spot with strokes of gray crayon. While Cocteau sparkled away like a fountain, the rest of the house seemed drenched in eerie drowsiness. The heady scent of massed tuberoses masked the smell of opium ("that most intelligent of smells," as Picasso once said), but the campy allegorical frescoes with which Cocteau proudly claimed to have "tattooed" every wall of the house underscored the artificiality of Francine's little paradise. This paradise turned out to be on the verge of dissolution. Francine had recently met a more macho, less obtrusive writer, Henri Viard, and would soon install him in the house. Within a year Cocteau and Doudou would be expelled from their Garden of Eden. Cocteau never fully recovered from the shock. After his death in 1963, Francine would summon Doudou back to the Villa Santo-Sospir. He returned—this time with a wife.

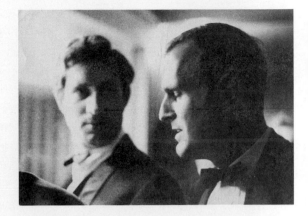

Robert Rushmore and JR, ca. 1962

On January 12, 1960, I flew from Marseille back to New York and arrived in a snowstorm. Friends had arranged for me to stay in an apartment overlooking the East River that belonged to George Plimpton. George was famously hospitable to stray writers. As usual in those days, a party was in progress. Somebody gave me a joint (my first), and this, combined with booze and jetlag, set my libido free—rather too free. After the guests had left, I tore off my clothes and tried to force myself on a lady novelist from the South who was sleeping in the next room. She was horrified. To recover from this rebuff, I went off to a downtown bar and ended up making friends with a young writer and lieder-singer called Robert Rushmore. We got on much too well, and I moved in with him a few days later. As I wanted to explore America, Robert suggested that we answer an ad in the *New York Times* and drive somebody's car to San Francisco. We took twice as long as we should have done. Having just read *Lolita*—greatest of all American travel books—I was ready for the unfamiliar joys of motel life: the thrill of traveling through dry states with bottles of bourbon and tequila in my suitcase and drinking the evening away on one of those mechanically activated beds, watching old movies on TV, and the breakfasts of hush-puppies and grits. And then back on those endless highways, straight as the canals on Mars, speeding toward the Grand Canyon, the Painted Desert, or the Carlsbad Caverns. It was all so different from the art-historical pilgrimages organized by Douglas. I felt free as the tumbleweed I was seeing for the first time.

Douglas must have heard about this adventure. He had flown over from France and was waiting for me when I got back to New York. He was in such a pitiful state that I agreed to return with him to France on the S.S. *United States,* but not before I had arranged to organize a major Picasso show in New York, which would necessitate my return at the end of the year. On the boat, we ate and drank too much, and as a result were liverish and quarrelsome. Back at Castille, I broached the idea of spending six months there and six months in New York so that I could follow up the contacts I had made and finally—I had just turned thirty-six—earn some money. Douglas was adamantly against any such arrangement: he said he would never be able to adapt himself to any solution which involved my appearing at Castille as an occasional guest. Having made his point, he insisted that I stay on with him.

For the rest of 1960, I used Castille as a base. Robert came over to spend the summer in England. I would join him for weekends, with an old friend of mine, Alfreda Urquhart—wife of the secretary-general of the United Nations—who had a cottage in Sussex and would later fall in love with Robert and marry him. Friends who realized that my relationship with Douglas was unraveling felt that I was foolish to "burn my boats." Picasso and Jacqueline, whom I continued to see on my own, were of a similar opinion: "For God's sake, don't walk out on Douglas," Jacqueline said. "Castille is so gloomy when you're not there." After flying back to Nice after one of these sorties, I looked in on the Picassos at Mougins. They asked me to drive with them to Vauvenargues, spend a night there, and go on to join Douglas at the Nîmes bullfight. As a present I had brought Picasso a set of scraperboards—cards coated with white clay, which an artist can ink over, then scrape with a *burin.* Picasso told me he had not used one of these since his student days. He proceeded to do a black-and-white version of a favorite painting of mine (the 1956 *Woman in Front of a Mirror*), which he gave me. The thoughtfulness and generosity of this gesture enabled me to feel that by now my rapport with Picasso was independent of Douglas. I had already started working on a study of Picasso's portraits; however, after I went through hundreds of photographs with him and he pointed out the iconographical complexities involved—how certain images represented not only Dora Maar but also her predecessor, Marie-Thérèse, as well as

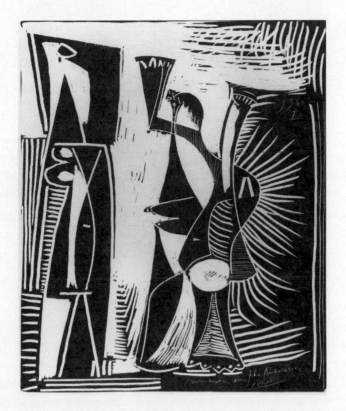

Picasso, Woman in Front of a Mirror, *scraperboard, 1960*

Lee Miller and Inez, the maid—I began to realize that the subject called for biographical treatment. Thirty years later, the first volume of my Picasso biography would appear.

After the September bullfight, the tension began to build up again at Castille. Douglas's parents arrived for a week, which always put him in a terrible mood. When we dropped them off at Avignon station, Mabel managed to smash her husband's fingers in the car door, so back they came. "Good for Mama," Douglas said. "That was no accident; she meant it." There was a disturbing precedent for this. Francis Watson told me that when he and Douglas were in their twenties, Artie Cooper had come to see them off at a railway station. A row had ensued, in the course of which Douglas had managed to slam the door of the railway carriage on his father's hand. "That'll teach the little bastard," Douglas had said as the train moved out of the station. And now it seemed that the mother was adopting her son's methods. I began to feel sorry for the much-put-upon Artie.

To escape the traumas at Castille, I left for Barcelona to dig up portrait material for my book. Before leaving, I checked in with Picasso. He asked for my diary so that he could write down the name and address of Carlota Valdivia, a walleyed procuress who had sat for his finest blue-period portrait, *La Celestina*. "She'll find you anything you want," he said. "Of course, by now she would be about a hundred and fifty years old." On my return, I went to Paris to spend a couple of weeks with Virginia Chambers, a gutsy, almost blind American woman with a passion for modern art, who had become a very close friend. She and her husband, an international lawyer, lived in a beautiful half-timbered house *entre cour et jardin* on the rue Monsieur that had previously belonged to Cole Porter. The property included an *immeuble* where Ginny put up an assortment of brilliant young friends, including her godson Peter Duchin, Robert Silvers, and George Plimpton. They doted on her. She was tremendous fun; she also served some of the best food in Paris. One after the other, Ginny's chefs were bribed away from her, but this did not faze her. "I loathe complicated dishes," she said. "So I replace them with sous-chefs from the Rothschilds' nurseries." Ginny's furniture was in keeping with the food. At a time when the overblown Beistegui look was all the rage, she went in for very simple Louis XVI furniture—preferably by Cannabas—pared down to the point of minimalism.

In the 1960s and 1970s, Ginny and I would often go on vacations together. She made light of her ever increasing blindness. I once left her on her own in the Rome airport while I attended to our reservations. As usual there was nowhere to sit down, but Ginny spotted a leather armchair into which she sank, only to discover that she had sat on a gigantic black soldier. Fortunately he took a shine to her. On another occasion in Paris, I was desperately trying to get Ginny a cab, when she suddenly said she had found one and started frantically waving at a hearse. To my horror, it stopped. "Hop in, you fool. It's started to rain." Ginny was a wise old bird, good-hearted, hard-drinking, down to earth. She did not mince words. "Get the hell out of Castille before it's too late," she said, "and while you're about it, get that other guy out of your life. See you in New York."

In a last desperate attempt to dissuade me from going off again to America, Douglas took me on successive visits to the Picassos—once in October, once in November, and twice in December—in the hope of changing my mind. After lunch in the studio on December 14, Picasso showed us a series of large ink-wash drawings of Jacqueline that he had just completed. As usual, he asked each of us which we thought was *"le plus fort."* Douglas picked out the most ornate. My choice was a much starker image, which seemed to distill the same anxiety and tortured love that the artist had evoked in his portraits of Dora Maar. After telling me I had chosen the drawing he would have chosen, Picasso gave me one of his complicit Andalusian glances and told Douglas exactly the same thing. He then announced that these were our Christmas presents.

As if on cue—the cue for Picasso to turn into a manipulative tease—the New York dealer Sam Kootz and his wife were ushered into the studio. "Look what I've given Douglas and John," Picasso said, much to the Kootzes' annoyance. "The only problem, Douglas prefers drawings that look important—you know, expensive—so you must wait while I do a bit more to it." And for no better reason than to irritate the Kootzes, who had hoped to wheedle some pictures out of him, the artist proceeded to add color and otherwise embellish the already overworked image. How he dawdled over it! Mrs. Kootz looked more and more impatient. Finally she caught her husband's eye, grimaced at her watch, and pointed at her hair. No way she was going to miss her hairdresser's appointment. Picasso, who had been watching this charade out of the corner of his eye, jumped up full of apologies and ushered them out with a ceremonious show of courtesy. So sorry to have held them up; of course Madame Kootz's coiffure took precedence over other considerations. Would they please let him know the next time they came to Europe? After they left, Picasso gave a prodigious shrug and asked Douglas to leave the enhanced drawing with him. "I've fucked it up," he said, "but don't worry, I'll rescue it!" And then, with a sardonic grin of satisfaction, he added, "Poor Mrs. Kootz. Kootz must be ready to kill her."

After a gruesome Christmas at Castille, I left Nice for New York on December 30, 1960, to start a new life in the United States. Ginny and my other great friend, Lil, did their best to ensure that I set off on the right foot. They would open all the right doors; I would race through them and more often than not come a cropper.

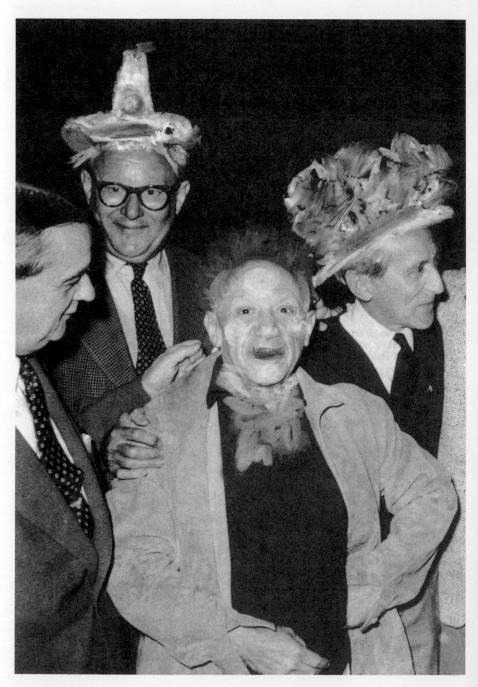

Georges Auric, DC, Picasso, and Cocteau at the Cannes Film Festival, 1957; detail of press photograph heightened by Picasso with gouache

THE END

Ten months after leaving Castille for good, I returned to the south of France to celebrate Picasso's eightieth birthday, which fell on October 25, 1961. I had asked Jacqueline what I should give him. "The thing that would please him best would be a reconciliation between you and Douglas," she said. "It would also raise Douglas's spirits." Jacqueline was clearly putting words into Picasso's mouth; he would no more have expressed such a trite thought than he would have made a reconciliation with Douglas the price of my attending the birthday party he claimed to dread. I too dreaded it, above all the confrontation with Douglas it would involve. His recent letters had been full of threats, at least one of which, a denunciation to the immigration department, he said he had carried out.

For the occasion I was putting up at La Fiorentina, the famously fashionable villa at the tip of Cap Ferrat, which belonged to two of Douglas's least favorite relatives, Rory Cameron and his mother, Enid, Countess of Kenmare, the dazzling Australian adventuress who had married and supposedly murdered Mabel Cooper's first cousin "Caviar" Cavendish. Mabel said it was unlike Enid to have done him in before he became Lord Waterpark. Information about my hostess's three other epicurean husbands came from a glamorous cousin of mine, Tony Pawson, who happened to be staying in the house. Enid's first husband, Rory's father, had apparently been a nice, rich, elderly American; he died after only a year of marriage. When an attempt to ensnare the Duke of Westminster came to nothing, Enid chose as her third husband the shipping-line owner Lord Furness—by far the richest and longest-lasting of her four spouses. Marmaduke, he was called, and he died mysteriously after seven years of marriage, in 1940. There was a certain irony in Furness's death: he had been suspected of drowning his first wife in the course of a pleasure trip to Monte Carlo on his yacht. Although Enid's last husband, the Earl of Kenmare, had disgraced the nobility by becoming "the first gentleman gossip columnist," he represented a step up for Enid. Marriage to this overweight fop, who died less than a year later, enabled her to upgrade the coronets on her silver and linen from a viscount's to an earl's. Why else marry this raffish old bounder?

Although over sixty, Enid was still an uncannily beautiful woman. Her beauty owed less to cosmetic surgery than to a lifelong addiction to Coca-Cola and an allergy to liquor. Enid had another addiction, heroin, on which she also seemingly thrived. She had even taken the radical step of registering herself as an addict with the British Home Office; this entitled her to obtain drugs legally. Drugs explained Enid's eerie cool: the impression she gave of being an alien from some other planet—a witch of a woman, like the protagonist of Rider Haggard's *She,* whose eternal youth depended on magical baths of fire. Drugs likewise explained the erratic workings of her biological clock. Enid was on time only by accident. Hence Daisy Fellowes's devastating comment apropos an endless wait for lunch: "Enid must be very busy with her needle."

One never knew whether Enid would keep to her room or make a belated entrance set off by a dozen or more scruffy little poodles. On her shoulders would be a bush baby, or a hyrax called Ticki, or a parrot that she had trained to mimic her. In her jeweled hand a casually picked flower or two suggested that she might have been gardening. After lunch she would wander off to a pavilion that she herself had frescoed in a gay, *dix-huitième* manner, and play cards with a group of golden oldies, among them Somerset Maugham—a neighbor Enid doted on, although, as she well knew, he could never resist telling his guests why she was known as "Lady Killmore."

When I saw Enid again a few years later, her addiction had caught up with her. I had gone to stay with her son Rory's best friend, Henry McIlhenny, at his castle in County Donegal. I remember coming back covered in mud from a day's deer stalking, to find three new guests emerging from a large car: an elderly man who turned out to be a doctor, an elderly woman who turned out to be Enid's sister from Sydney, and the bent-double object of their attention, Enid. As I looked down, she looked up. The beautiful-as-ever face with the unflinching extra-terrestrial eyes moved toward me at knee level, as if she had turned into a sphinx. Osteoporosis or, according to some, injections into her spinal column had left her back as curved as a question mark.

Back, however, to 1961. Rory's niceness to me, now that I had broken with his cantankerous cousin, would get him into trouble. In due course Douglas would avenge himself on Rory for having me to stay by panning his book on the Riviera as cruelly as he could. Douglas ended with a personal attack on Rory, calling him "an expatriate playboy and a dilettante" for whom writing was no more than a means of "maintaining his would-be high-hatted social status."

In fact, Rory was a big, bland, soft-looking bachelor of ineffable geniality and charm. He had made a name for himself as a paragon of taste—the high priest of decor. He had Palladianized the outside of La Fiorentina and Indianized the inside in the manner of the British Raj, with eighteenth-century topographical paintings, botanical watercolors, and collections of rare shells. The result was most impressive, as witness recent rumors of a possible sale at a figure of more than $50 million. Handsome Indian retainers in cockaded turbans enhanced the decor. Rory had also created a magnificent garden with a huge pool that sloshed over into the Mediterranean and, to a swimmer's eye, seemingly merged with the horizon. For anyone who was not inured to the high-octane atmosphere of café society, visits to the Fiorentina could be dangerously pleasurable, but it was not a house to dally in. Grand luxe can be addictive, and for an outsider like myself the return to real life could involve a bad case of the bends.

A day or two before Picasso's birthday, I was soaking away in a bath, wondering how to sidestep a confrontation with Douglas, when Rory bang-bang-banged on the door and announced, anything but regretfully, that he had just heard on the news that Douglas had been knifed by an Algerian and was fighting for his life in the Nîmes hospital. I told Rory that I had to get to him. But how? It was eight o'clock in the evening. I did not have a car, and Rory was unable to lend me one of his until the following morning. As so often in France, trains and buses were on strike. I called friends in Nîmes and pieced together the following story.

Late the previous evening, Douglas had driven into Nîmes to mail

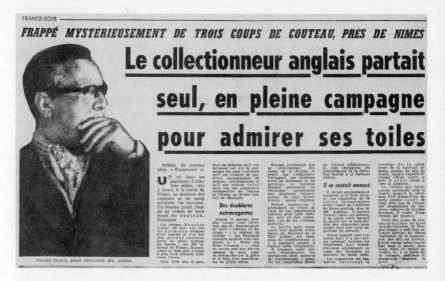

The newspaper account of the attack on DC

an article about Picasso's forthcoming birthday to one of the London papers. Feeling lonely and horny, he had cruised a louche area near the barracks and picked up a young Algerian fellagha—a detainee in a nearby "open" prison camp. In his almost total inexperience of rough trade, Douglas had rashly given the fellagha a lift and driven him to a *terrain vague* in the hills above the city. The fellagha had promptly drawn a knife and demanded his money or his life. Like many people in France at that time, Douglas carried two wallets: one for everyday expenses, the other full of thousand-franc bills for major transactions that had to be settled in cash. He handed over the first wallet, but not the second one. Suspecting that Douglas was holding out on him, the thief demanded more money, also his watch. Foolhardily, Douglas refused, whereupon the fellagha lunged at his large belly with a sharp knife, slashing him once vertically, twice horizontally, cicatrizing him with an emblematic Croix de Lorraine. *"Faute de mieux,* I've become a *Gauliste,"* Douglas would say when he was able to make light of the experience.

Douglas's courage and toughness, not to speak of his training as an ambulance driver, saved his life. Holding his guts in place, he managed to stagger and crawl toward a distant patch of light and shout for help. In that none-too-friendly area, nighttime cries were seldom heeded. He was lucky. The black concierge of a rural school heard him and took him in. Trust Douglas to tell her very firmly what to do and what not to do: "And now race to the nearest telephone and call an ambulance." The police were sent for. They caught the culprit, who claimed that he had been defending his virtue, and fetched Marie from Castille. Faithful woman that she was, she settled into a deck chair by Douglas's hospital bed and looked after him until I was able to take over.

The prognosis was bad. Douglas had lost a lot of blood, and his guts had been so badly perforated that he was in danger of dying of septicemia. According to the doctors who had sewn him up, everything depended on the efficacy of the antibiotics. Since there was a shortage of nurses, I took Marie's place by Douglas's bedside and, insofar as I could, monitored his treatment. Basil was unable to absent himself from his duties, but I sent him regular bulletins. I also kept the Picassos informed. Meanwhile, our best friend in Nîmes, Suzanne Barnier, took care of the practical problems. I had to keep the press at bay—the English press especially—and play things down. After a week, Douglas's fever began to subside, and he appeared to be out of danger. I badgered him to do something for the woman who had saved his life. He gave me some money for her, but it was so little, I had to shame him into doubling it. It was still insufficient. The woman tried in vain to hide her disappointment.

And then one morning Douglas, who had hitherto been a model of gentleness and patience, awoke with a demonic glint in his eye and a shrill, keening note in his voice: "Tell me, my dear, why did you hire that assassin?" The devil had taken over from the angel; I was too traumatized by fury and lack of sleep to reply. Instead, I folded up the deck chair, packed up my suitcase, and prepared to leave. "Good-bye," I said with exasperated finality, and drove back to Castille to collect some of the possessions I had left there and make plans to return to New York. No sooner was I back at the château than the telephone rang. It was Douglas, in tears, claiming that the attack on his life had affected his sanity. "Did I do something to offend you? If so, forgive me. I'm still suffering from shock and delusions and don't know what I'm saying. Johnny, come back, come back, I beg you. I need you so badly."

Like an idiot, I returned to the hospital. For an hour or two Douglas maintained his composure, but Dr. Jekyll soon turned back into Mr.

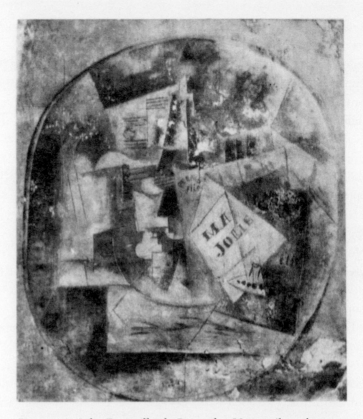

Picasso, Ma Jolie/Bouteille de Pernod et Verre, *oil on plaster, 1912, before it came to grief*

Hyde. "Why did 'Filth' [his name for Robert Rushmore] hire that assassin?" By now all I could do was give a weary shrug, an even wearier sigh, and make arrangements to get away from this madman before I, too, went mad. I checked into a hotel and got drunk. By the following morning I had cooled down enough to accompany Douglas back to Castille. The Picassos had said they would drive over from Cannes to see how Douglas was, and tell us about the celebration we had missed.

Picasso had another reason for making this two-and-a-half-hour trip so soon after his eightieth birthday. He was anxious to see a cubist painting that Douglas had acquired shortly before the stabbing: a large oval still life that included the title of a popular song, "Ma Jolie" (a tribute to his then mistress, Eva Gouel). Picasso had painted this love-token directly onto the whitewashed wall of the little villa at Sorgues (near Avignon) where he and Eva had set up house in the summer of 1912. This "fresco" had meant much to Picasso. After leaving Sorgues, he had asked Braque, who also had a house there, to remove it from the wall and have it shipped to his dealer in Paris. *Ma Jolie* had then been acquired by Eugenia Errazuriz, a rich Chilean woman of great discrimination who had fallen in love with Picasso and supplanted Gertrude Stein as his principal patron. Eugenia had given the fresco to her nephew, Marie-Laure's friend Tony Gandarillas. And it was at his house—on the Noailles' property—that I had first seen *Ma Jolie* and been so worried by its condition that I had advised a friend against buying it. The plaster had been coated with varnish, which had sunk in and given *Ma Jolie* an ugly, grubby sheen; there had also been some damage and clumsy restoration. A large packing case, which had been delivered to Castille while Douglas was in the hospital, turned out to contain this dilapidated icon. Douglas had given some major items from his collection in exchange for it. Of all people, he should have known better.

The Picassos' arrival recharged Douglas's spirits. They had brought some caviar with them. My drawings have become so valuable, Picasso said, that caviar works out cheaper. After lunch, Douglas had the gardener bring in the packing case containing *Ma Jolie*. From within came an ominous rattling sound, as if a gigantic jigsaw puzzle had been emptied into it. We waited nervously for the lid to be pried open. Eventually a wooden chassis materialized, but the plaster had come away from its support and disintegrated into hundreds of minute fragments and a great deal of dust. "*Hélas,*" Picasso said, "*il ne reste plus rien de moi.*" Douglas turned white, as if he had been stabbed all over again. Picasso, too, looked stricken, and hurried Jacqueline away. He had a superstitious terror of bad luck, especially the serial kind to which Douglas seemed to have become prone.

This was not the end of the story. Some years later, when I was working as Christie's U.S. representative, I was summoned to London to inspect a group of "modern masterpieces" with which a certain Baron X. proposed to purchase a share in the auction house. When the paintings were produced, I could not believe my eyes. *Ma Jolie* had been resurrected from the dust. What had happened? Douglas turned out to have acted as Baron X.'s adviser, and to have persuaded him that a major cubist still life by Picasso, preferably a 1912 *Ma Jolie* one, should head his list of requirements. *Ma Jolies* were very rare, but Douglas thought he might be able to come up with one. Sure enough, he did. After getting a dubious restorer to reconstitute the debris into a convincing facsimile of the original, he found a dubious dealer to handle the sale of it to the collector he had been paid to advise.

I suppose I should have blown the whistle on Douglas, but could not bring myself to do so. Picasso would never have forgiven him, and I would never have forgiven myself. There was another reason. When Douglas had heard about my Christie's appointment, he had sent each of the directors one of his poisonous letters, accusing me of faults more redolent of his conduct than of mine. Once again Douglas's malice proved counterproductive, and his injurious letters might have been glowing references for all the damage they did. Any action that I might have taken against him would have been interpreted as a vengeful tit-for-tat.

A day or two after Picasso's visit, I left Castille for what I assumed would be the last time. I was enormously relieved but also sad: sad at leaving Marie; sad at leaving this beautiful house, with its beautiful paintings; sad, too, at leaving Douglas, after trying so hard and failing so dismally to transform him from a toad into a prince. That he was even more corroded with resentment, envy, and rage than he had been when I first met him twelve years before was no cause for pride. Before departing, I told Douglas that I wanted to have my things shipped to New York. If there were specific bits of my furniture he needed, he could have them on loan, but I insisted on taking my personal papers, clothes, silver, as well as the books and drawings I had accumulated while living with him. Douglas was anything but cooperative. "Why bother? Everything in this house is left to you," he said. Again and again I pointed out that I wanted *my* things, not his. And whether he liked it or not, there was one thing I was taking with me: the Juan Gris (one of the still lifes I had discovered at Helena Rubinstein's), which constituted my only negotiable nest egg. Take it, he said, then claimed he could not find it, then finally handed it over. "You would never have spotted this if it hadn't been for me," he said. I could only agree. Heaven knows he had taught me almost everything I knew.

After I left, Douglas lit a bonfire in the park and ceremoniously burned all my clothes, papers, photographs, and other personal effects.

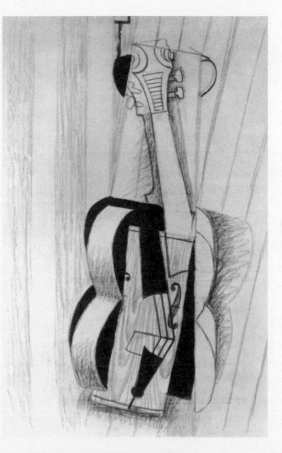

Juan Gris, Guitar, *India ink and colored crayon, 1913*

What upset me most was the loss of my father's ivory hairbrushes—the only memento of him that I owned. No less upsetting was the feeling that Douglas had incinerated my past. I did not care about the clothes, except insofar as I had promised them, as Douglas well knew, to Marie's son. As for things of value—furniture and silver, as well as the gifts I had received from Picasso, Braque, Staël, and Sutherland—Douglas effectively stole them. Over the next three years I made repeated requests for their return—to no avail. Finally, I decided to steal them back.

In 1965, Kahnweiler arranged for me to organize a Juan Gris retrospective at the Museum Am Ostwall in Dortmund. Douglas, who regarded this artist as his private preserve, was outraged, and I had to make repeated trips to Europe to counter his sabotage. After visiting Dortmund in March to make final preparations for the show's opening in October, my friend Jimmy de Vries and I drove on to Switzerland and ended up in Cannes. I had not seen the Picassos in more than a year, and wanted to spend some time with them at nearby Mougins before descending on Castille.

At the age of eighty-four, Picasso was as vigorous and focused on his work as ever. He showed me what he had been doing—mostly paintings and drawings of Jacqueline, including the amazing image of Jacqueline pissing on the beach. There seemed to be a lot of rage and disgust in his work—and with reason. Françoise Gilot's book about their life together had appeared the year before in English, and was about to appear in French. Picasso was doing everything to block it. I was reviewing the book for the *New York Review of Books,* and was therefore anxious to check certain points. But apart from complaining that he did not know the meaning of some of the words Françoise had put into his mouth—"architectonic," for instance—Picasso was too angry to discuss the matter. Jacqueline, on the other hand, was only too ready to fill me in on his objections. Much of what she said was too scurrilous to print, but it certainly colored my review. Looking back, I think I was overcensorious. I still feel that Françoise overstates her claim to have been an innocent girl betrayed by a manipulative old man, but her analysis of Picasso's character and working methods is enormously valuable. If only the publication of this book had not blown the artist's family apart. Picasso used it as a pretext for never again seeing the children, Claude and Paloma, he had hitherto adored. They became hostages to his resentment of their mother.

Picasso was intrigued by a tattoo I had recently had done on my arm in New York. He recalled how Braque had wanted him to tattoo his back and chest when they were staying at Le Havre in 1912. "Imagine what he would have looked like with a cubist still life—a guitar and the words *Ma Jolie*—on his chest." He offered to tattoo me "with a needle and some ink like they do in jail," if I could face it, saying I could exhibit myself in a frame at Knoedler's and sell my skin to a collector. He was also intrigued by Douglas's jealousy. He compared it to Diaghilev's. He told me that when he was working for the Russian Ballet, the great impresario had fallen in love with his star dancer Massine. Massine was heterosexual but ambitious, and he slept with Diaghilev to further his career. ("It was rather like going to bed with a nice fat old lady," the dancer told one of his mistresses.) The only problem was Diaghilev's jealousy; he tried to persuade Picasso to spy on Massine and his current girlfriend. The artist described farcical chases in and out of bedrooms, up and down staircases and elevators in the Hôtel Continental, where the stars stayed; also an attempt to break up a clandestine rendezvous, which resulted in Diaghilev and Picasso driving round and round the Arc de Triomphe for most of one night. Did Douglas go to such maniacal lengths? Picasso asked. I told him I was on my way to a showdown at Castille, and would let him know what happened. Picasso, who enjoyed manipulating his friends' relationships—bringing them together, breaking them apart—wished me luck. Jimmy and I then drove on to stay at the Hôtel du Pont du Gard so that I could have a confrontation with Douglas.

Jimmy dropped me off at Castille. The gates were open, so I walked in—to the kitchen, not the salon. Marie was welcoming and tearful. Poor thing, she had been sacked; or rather she had given notice in a moment of pique, and was very upset that Douglas, whom she had served faithfully for thirteen years, intended to take her up on it. As soon as Douglas heard I was there, he materialized like Mephistopheles and insisted I stay for dinner: "But, my dear, why didn't you announce your arrival instead of breaking in?" The dîner à quatre—Raoul Lévy, the movie director, and a girlfriend were the other guests—was sticky. Finally we were alone. When I told Douglas I had come to take my things away, he said, "I've burned all your clothes and papers. As for your pictures, you took them last time you were here." Only one, I said, and pointed to some drawings on the wall. Douglas allowed that they were mine, but claimed that he could not hand them over for at least three days; the shock of seeing me had been too demoralizing. "Anyway, I can't think why you fuss about your things; you should return here to live. You know perfectly well that everything in this house is yours"—and much else in this vein. And then the wine started to take its toll. Douglas's bitterness reduced me to tears of frustration. "Don't waste your tears on me, my dear, you can't have forgotten that in place of a heart I have a large empty hole." The thought that this might indeed be true started him, too, making glottal, sobbing noises. Finally he drove me back to the Pont du Gard.

I was not prepared to hang around for days in the vain hope of getting my belongings back, so I decided to take the law into my own hands and, with Jimmy's help, raid the château. At six o'clock the following morning, we drove to Castille. I climbed a wall at the back of the house to encouraging shouts of "*Au vol*" from the local farm workers on their way to the vineyards. After Marie unlocked the gates so that Jimmy could drive into the courtyard, I sent her to the top of the house to look for a suitcase I knew she would never find, and then set about gathering together some of my valuables. These included two Roman portrait busts, the aforementioned *Fish* by César, some gouaches by Braque, and numerous items by Picasso, which were mostly inscribed to me. While we were stashing this stuff in the car, Marie reappeared, crying because she felt she had to wake Douglas; also because we had been through so much together and this seemed like the final act. Off Jimmy and I drove to Nîmes. As we did so, a gardener, who was new to me, took down the license number of our car.

The road from Castille to Nîmes passes through the gorge that Clouzot had used, a few years earlier, for Yves Montand's fatal crash at the end of that thrilling film *The Wages of Fear.* Memories of this dramatic scene, coupled with the threat of pursuit by Douglas or the local police, made the drive all the more fraught. Once we arrived in Nîmes, poor Jimmy raced to the nearest café to steady his nerves with slug after slug of scotch. He said he knew how Bonnie and Clyde must have felt. Meanwhile I called my lawyer friend Paul Carcassonne, who told me to come and see him immediately. Under French law, I had committed a criminal act. "But I only took things that are demonstrably mine," I told Paul. "That's beside the point," he said. "You have put yourself in the wrong by breaking and entering. You better call Douglas before he calls the police and has you arrested, as is his right. You know what a fiend he can be."

And indeed Douglas turned out to be reveling at the prospect of mayhem. "I've just given details of your car and license number to Interpol as well as the local police," he said. "If you don't bring back the things you took from my house you are going to be arrested. You and your accomplice will go to jail for a very long time." Paul told me to do as Douglas said, but as a precaution to have a *huissier* present (a bailiff who records incidents or accidents that might entail legal action). With some difficulty we located one and arranged for him to drive over to Castille the following morning. Douglas was ever so friendly, but when the *huissier* materialized, he became hysterical. "Send that awful little man away. This is a private matter, which we are going to settle amicably, between ourselves, *aren't we, my dear?*"—the last phrase said with a menacing smirk. I was foolish enough to let the *huissier* go.

To my surprise, we did manage to settle things amicably. In all but one case, Douglas admitted my ownership. The exception was one of several drawings that Picasso had inscribed *"pour Douglas et John."*

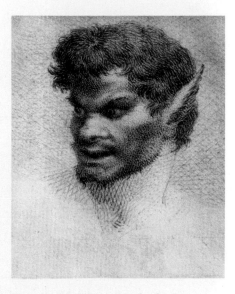

Pierre-Paul Prud'hon, Head of a Faun, *sepia ink*

"There are at least five; it's only fair that I should have one of them," I told him. "No, my dear, *our* drawings have to remain in *our* house," he said. "Besides, they are a token of Pablo's affection for us both, and they remind me of you." I remarked that most of my things, including a favorite bull chair, could hardly fail to remind Douglas of me, but that seemed no reason for him to keep them. When I asked about some of my other possessions, including the *Firebird* painting I had bought from Braque, Douglas claimed to be unable to find them. Maybe next time, he said. In the interests of future rapport, I left behind my little Prud'hon drawing as a *gage d'amitié*—a token of friendship.

Douglas pressed us to stay for lunch, during which he paid court to Jimmy and tried to persuade him to stay on at Castille. After showing us the huge murals after Picasso drawings, which the Norwegian sculptor Carl Nesjar (inventor of a process called *bétograve*) had sandblasted onto the walls of the *magnaneraie*—a monumental waste of money, I felt—Douglas waved us off in his most avuncular way. "Come back soon, both of you," he said. Our sighs of relief proved premature. As I unlocked the door of my London flat two days later, the telephone was ringing. It was Heinz Berggruen, sounding very concerned. Douglas had

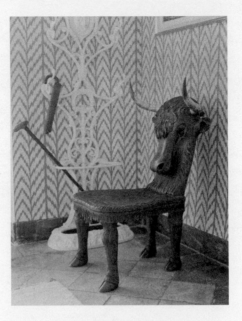

JR's bull chair, which Picasso coveted

called to tell him that I had broken into Castille with an accomplice, had stolen a number of *his* paintings, had been arrested by Interpol, and was facing a long jail sentence. Heinz was not altogether surprised when I explained that the only thefts involved had been committed by Douglas. Over the next few days Jacqueline Picasso and other mutual friends rang to say that they had had similar calls. Anyone who continued to be friends with John, Douglas had informed one and all, "ceases to be a friend of mine." And he proceeded to make an example of the saintly Basil, who had courageously defied Douglas and insisted that I continue to see him whenever I was in London. Basil was so upset at being shut out of Douglas's life for defying him that I was obliged to cut myself off from Egerton Terrace. So much for the Prud'hon drawing as a token of friendship.

As usual, Douglas's ukase proved counterproductive. Friends rallied to my side as never before. The only ones who went along with his sanction were a predictable little crew: a vapid society woman fearful of being struck off the Castille guest list, various young men who hoped to take my place, small-time dealers anxious to get a foot in the door, and, not surprisingly, a couple whose friendship had always been a matter of strategy rather than affection—the Graham Sutherlands. One afternoon a few weeks after my last brush with Douglas, I was walking along Bond Street when I spotted the Sutherlands advancing toward me, very dolled up. I was about to greet them when they saw me and attempted evasive action. Graham tried to pull Kathy across to the other side of the street, but it was too late: a number 25 bus was coming, and Kathy, as so often the worse for champagne, stepped back unsteadily and got her high heel stuck in a gutter grating. When I described the scene and the reason for it to Francis Bacon, he gave a delighted gasp. "Didn't I warn you that she was a thoroughly treacherous woman?" It took me a minute to realize that Francis was talking about Douglas.

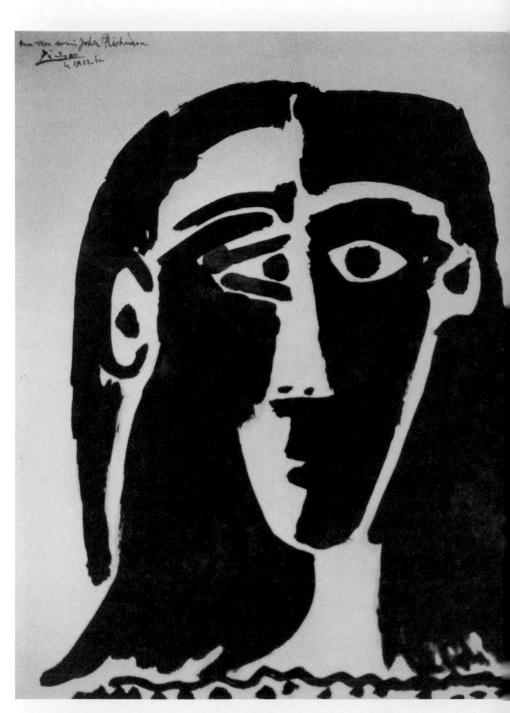

Picasso, Portrait of Jacqueline, *ink wash, 1960; given to JR by the artist*

EPILOGUE

For the next sixteen years I saw nothing of Douglas, but that did not stop him from campaigning against me. When the widow of the Canadian tycoon Sir James Dunn (soon to be the wife of another tycoon from New Brunswick, Lord Beaverbrook) put me in charge of the Dunn International Exhibition of Contemporary Art—a mini-biennial that opened at the Beaverbrook Museum in Fredericton and ended up at the Tate in London in 1962—Douglas wheedled his way onto the organizing committee and proceeded to harass me at every turn. As a cat's-paw Douglas settled on an ambitious young porter who had prevailed upon a friend of ours at the Birmingham Art Gallery to recommend him for a job at Sotheby's. Bruce Chatwin, he was called, and at Douglas's behest he would appear in my office with a supercilious smirk on his pretty face and proceed to relay insultingly officious messages. A call to Peter Wilson, Sotheby's chairman, who used Bruce to soften up special clients, put an end to this little game. When Bruce subsequently reinvented himself as a writer we became friends—sort of.

Ten years later, Douglas was still up to the same tricks. When he heard that Artemis, the international art fund, might appoint me managing director, he wrote to the chairman, Baron Léon Lambert, "You are not going to add luster to the shield of Artemis by employing him." Léon promptly hired me. He also gave me the libelous letter. Friends advised me to sue Douglas, but given the beneficial effects of his intervention, I could hardly claim to have been damaged. Besides, a lawsuit would have given Douglas too much pleasure.

Back at Castille, Douglas was foolish enough to let Marie, the devoted housekeeper, leave. She had looked after the place ever since

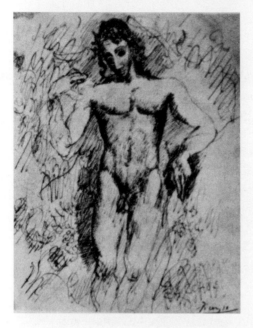

Picasso, The Young Bacchus, *pen and ink, 1906; one of the many Picassos stolen from Castille in 1974*

we moved in, and had grown accustomed to Douglas's moods and manipulative ways. She knew when to mollify him and when to stand up to him. None of her successors could tolerate his meanness of spirit and purse for long. Resentful servants were thought to have organized the theft of many of the smaller paintings and drawings in the ground-floor rooms that took place in 1974. Douglas was convinced that this was an inside job, convinced that both he and the watchdog had been drugged and that the servants had let in the local Mafia. How else could he and the dog have slept through it? Nothing was ever proved, and Douglas was obliged to retain the servants in his employ. Since there were no burglar alarms and no proper bolts on the shutters, the theft would have been an easy job. To make matters worse, the collection had become so valuable that Douglas had long ceased to insure it. In due course he received a ransom note, supposedly for a million dollars, but refused to buy back his own property. He also received death threats. Since a million dollars was a fraction of the pictures' true value, Douglas soon changed his mind and tried, repeatedly and unsuccessfully, to contact the robbers. Among the stolen Picassos was the wonderful nude drawing of Geneviève Laporte that the artist had given the two of us.

The burglary terrified Douglas—terrified him into leaving Castille. He had some difficulty finding a buyer; there was so little land, so little protection. The château was finally bought by a Greek couple from Marseille. They proceeded to decorate the château in a piss-elegant orientalist manner, to judge by photographs in *Architectural Digest.* "When the present owners acquired the property," the magazine claimed, "they found little more than vacant rooms and a few pieces of furniture with lugubrious echoes of provincial France." So much for the monumental Picasso wall that Douglas had hated to leave behind.

In the interest of security, Douglas moved into three small apartments in an ultra-safe, bunkerlike building in Monte Carlo, which had been erected on land reclaimed from the sea. The rooms were poky and low-ceilinged, so some of the more important paintings had to be sold. When I eventually saw what remained of the collection, and how diminished it looked in its elegant if cramped new quarters, I was saddened. The decor turned out to be the handiwork of Billy McCarty—an attractive decorator who had replaced the men's haberdasher, Mr. Fish, in Douglas's life. "I've adopted him," Douglas told me with paternal pride when we met again in Monte Carlo in 1981. He explained that he did not want his "ghastly family" laying claim to his estate. "That's why I had the adoption done in France and not England. Under the *code Napoléon*, everything I have goes to my son. There's nothing, absolutely nothing, my family can do about it—besides, it's fun having a son."

I had gone to Monte Carlo to write an article about the place and on the very first night had come face-to-face with my nemesis in the bar of the Hôtel de Paris. In the course of the next week we kept each other company. Douglas had lost much of his menace, which enabled us to be affable with each other; otherwise he had not aged well. While his body, not to speak of his self-esteem, had ballooned, his intellect—as happens in Monte Carlo—had done the reverse. Occasionally a flash of wit or *méchanceté* would shine through the querulousness, but there was little trace of the passionate mentor who had opened up the world of modern art to me and so many others—little trace, either, of the mercurial manipulator who had been the source of so much laughter and so much mischief. The narcissistic cement that had once held the components of Douglas's character had crumbled.

Douglas's *dégringolade* stemmed partly from drink, partly from ill health (his feet had given out), and partly from a terminal row he had had with Picasso shortly before the latter's death. Jacqueline told me what had happened. One evening, circa 1970, Douglas appeared unannounced at Notre-Dame-de-Vie and insisted on being allowed into the studio where Picasso was working. Let him in, the artist said, on one condition: he must not talk. But Douglas did talk. He told Picasso it was time he recognized his illegitimate children—a subject the artist adamantly refused to face, because it presupposed the eventuality of his death. At first Picasso, who was a bit deaf, could not understand what Douglas was driving at. When he did, he exploded in rage and threw his old friend out of the studio. Jacqueline described how Douglas had gone down on his knees to her and tearfully begged her to intercede with Picasso—to no avail. Thereafter Douglas, who had served with such honor as Picasso's Falstaff, turned fiercely against his former hero. A few months after the artist's death in 1973, he published a letter in *Connaissance des Arts* criticizing the magazine's praise of Picasso's late paintings. As an admirer of the artist's work, Douglas felt entitled to condemn the paintings in question as "incoherent doodles done by a frenetic dotard in the anteroom of death." Jacqueline never forgave Douglas's treachery, and never acknowledged him if ever their paths crossed. As I took leave of him, Douglas said defiantly, "I gather you still see Jacqueline. Don't on any account remember me to her." It was his way of sending love.

Douglas may have started his career as a rebel in the cause of cubism, but he ended up as a rebel without any cause at all except a loathing for all forms of progressive art and the American pundits—"the flying rabbis," he called them, "heads on upside down, like a Chagall"—who promoted them. In line with his fogeyism, he adopted an apoplectic manner and took to dressing like his horsy forebears, in ever bigger and brighter checks. Like Evelyn Waugh in old age, he played the role of curmudgeon to the hilt and cherished the belief that everyone but him was out of step. If he no longer inveighed against the British, it was because the French were now the targets of his wrath. However, he went on savaging anyone who dared write about "his" artists, but his tirades were all bark and no bite and no longer to be found in the pages of the *Times Literary Supplement* or the *Burlington Magazine*.

A year or so before he died, a combination of hormonal and glandular problems obliged Douglas once again to become a patient in Nîmes hospital. He sent for his son Billy, as well as an intelligent and attractive young man whom I will call Robin, to rally round what was likely to prove his deathbed. Douglas's condition was so worrying that Robin decided to call his stepfather, a leading endocrinologist, for help. Over the telephone, the endocrinologist dictated a course of treatment that would keep Douglas alive for another year. He was often in considerable pain, but his childish sense of fun and fiendishness continued to

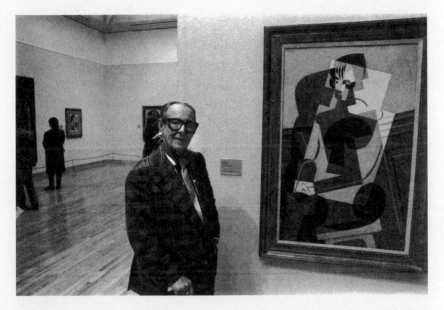

DC at the Tate Gallery in 1983 with Juan Gris's Portrait of Josette *(1916), which he gave to the Prado*

percolate. Douglas's end was in character. "I propose to die on April Fool's Day," he announced in 1984 as he went into hospital for the last time. And after three days in a coma, that is exactly what this hugely gifted, hugely flawed old buffo did.

The pride of Douglas's last years had been his appointment to the Patronato of that great museum, the Prado in Madrid. He was the first foreigner to be thus honored. In gratitude, he gave the Prado his finest Juan Gris, the 1916 portrait of the artist's wife, Josette, because this Spanish master was virtually unrepresented in his own country. He also left the museum Picasso's cubist *Still Life with Pigeons,* an ingenious replay of a subject that he had painted at the age of thirteen at his father's behest and done so skillfully that he had supposedly been rewarded with the parental palette and brushes. Although Douglas had had a reconciliation with the Tate (he had organized an impressive cubist exhibition for the gallery and let it have two of his greatest paintings on extended loan), he left the institution nothing at all. "The English will have Rothenstein to thank for that, my dear." Apart from the Prado, the Kunstmuseum in Basel would be the only other institutional legatee.

Years earlier, Douglas had told me in a moment of pique that he hoped to end like Sardanapalus, the legendary last king of Assyria, whose death inspired one of Delacroix's greatest paintings. Douglas envisioned a funeral pyre in the courtyard of Castille, piled with "all my worldly goods, not to speak of some of my lovers, my dear," and topped off with his corpse. "My pictures and I shall go up in smoke," he decreed. "There'll be nothing left for any of you." As things turned out, there would be a great deal left for his adopted son. The last time we met, Douglas told me that he had asked his son and heir to compensate me for the things I had been unable to recoup from Castille. Billy behaved impeccably. He returned the Prud'hon, the Braque *Firebird*, a Picasso drawing, and one or two other items of personal significance; he also gave me a sum of money, in exchange for a promise that I would make no claim on the estate. The sum was generous, but it did not approximate the value of the property I was obliged to relinquish. I am grateful to Billy, but it was distressing to watch family silver and drawings inscribed to me coming up for sale at Christie's.

Billy proceeded to live in far greater style than Douglas ever did. He bought a beautifully situated house in the Birdland section of Los Angeles—what his neighbor, the actress Coral Browne, used to call the "Swish Alps"—which was home to such stars as Dolly Parton and Madonna. The house's two wings were connected by a long, narrow swimming pool with steps at either end so that when Billy awoke he could swim from his bedroom at one end to the kitchen at the other. There was also a second pool for guests, an orchid house, and a dramatic view through a screen of ancient olive trees and dove-colored smog down to the vast spread of Los Angeles way below.

Billy liked to refer to Douglas as "El Benefactor," and before long, he too saw himself as a collector and employed a curator, David Crownover, to procure important examples of tribal art. He employed another curator, Dorothy Kosinski, to organize exhibitions of the rapidly dwindling Cooper collection in London, Basel, and Dallas. To celebrate the openings of these shows, Billy would lay on elaborate parties. In honor of the Basel opening he put a number of us up in Basel's best hotel and treated us to three days of lavish festivities. For his London gala Billy re-created the colonnades of Castille on the parade ground of the Chelsea Barracks. As the evening was cool, he provided cashmere shawls for women guests. The party was said to have cost a vast sum. Douglas's old friends felt that these extravaganzas did not commemorate his collection so much as highlight its dispersal, for Billy turned out to have sold the cream of El Benefactor's crop to the cosmetics heir Leonard Lauder. True, he also embarked on a plan to chronicle Douglas's life and catalogue what had once been the world's finest private collection of cubist art, but he died before anything came of these efforts.

When Billy invited me to visit his spectacular new house in March 1989, I was appalled to discover that he had contracted AIDS. The courage and humor with which he faced up to his illness impressed those who knew him. When a melanoma developed in his brain, Billy did not hesitate to undergo a horrendously painful and intricate operation. He flaunted his scarred forehead like the badge of bravery it was by tying his head in piratical bandannas and behaving as if nothing were the matter. (A dislike of passing unperceived was yet another legacy from his adoptive father.) Trust Billy to plan a dazzling send-off for himself: a funeral fit for a head of state, with a live performance of Mozart's *Requiem* in a large Los Angeles church, followed by a Hollywood-style reception beside the pool. After Billy's death the masterpieces remaining from Douglas's collection and the tribal artifacts and deco furniture that Billy had bought for himself came up in a series of sales at Christie's early in 1992. They fetched around $30 million. During his lifetime Billy had been a very generous donor to AIDS-related charities, to which he also left a large part of his estate. He told me he intended this bequest to be his memorial.

SELECT BIBLIOGRAPHY

Berberova, Nina. *Histoire de la Baronne Boudberg*. Paris: Actes Sud, 1988.

Berthoud, Roger. *Graham Sutherland: A Biography*. Geneva: Faber & Faber, 1982.

Beyeler, Ernst. *Fondation Beyeler*. Munich: Prestel, 1997.

Briolle, Cécile, Agnès Fuzibet, and Gérard Monnier. *Rob Mallet-Stevens: La Villa Noailles*. Marseille: Editions Parenthèses, 1990.

Clark, Thekla. *Wystan and Chester: A Personal Memoir of W. H. Auden and Chester Kallman*. New York: Columbia University Press, 1996.

Drabble, Margaret. *Angus Wilson: A Biography*. London: Secker & Warburg, 1995.

Feliciano, Hector. *Le Musée Disparu: Enquête sur le pillage des oeuvres d'art en France par les Nazis*. Paris: Austral, 1995.

Freeman, C. Denis, and Douglas Cooper. *The Road to Bordeaux*. London: Cresset Press, 1940.

Gilot, Françoise, and Carlton Lake. *Life with Picasso*. New York: McGraw-Hill, 1964.

Gold, Arthur, and Robert Fizdale. *Misia: The Life of Misia Sert*. New York: Alfred A. Knopf, 1980.

Greilsamer, Laurent. *Le Prince Foudroyé: La Vie de Nicolas de Staël*. Paris: Fayard, 1998.

Guggenheim, Peggy. *Out of This Century: Confessions of an Art Addict*. New York: Universe Books, 1979.

Hugo, Jean. *Le Regard de la Mémoire*. Paris: Actes Sud, 1983.

Kernan, Nathan, ed. *The Diary of James Schuyler*. Santa Rosa: Black Sparrow Press, 1997.

Late Picasso: Paintings, Sculpture, Drawings, Prints, 1953–1972. London: Tate Gallery, 1988.

Lord, James. *Picasso and Dora: A Personal Memoir*. New York: Farrar, Straus & Giroux, 1993.

———. *Six Exceptional Women*. New York: Farrar, Straus & Giroux, 1994.

Malaparte, Curzio. *The Skin*. Translated by David Moore. Evanston, Ill.: Northwestern University Press, 1997.

O'Brian, Patrick. *Picasso*. New York: G. P. Putnam's Sons, 1976.

Pope-Hennessy, John. *Learning to Look: My Life in Art*. New York: Doubleday, 1991.

Rorem, Ned. *The Paris Diary of Ned Rorem*. New York, G. Braziller, 1966.

———. *The Final Diary: 1961–1972*. New York: Holt, Rinehart and Winston, 1974.

Rothenstein, John. *Brave Day, Hideous Night*. London: Hamish Hamilton, 1966.

Spender, Stephen. *Journals, 1939–1983*. Edited by John Goldsmith. New York: Random House, 1986.

Weidenfeld, George. *Remembering My Good Friends*. London: HarperCollins, 1994.

Weisweiller, Carole. *Je l'Appelais Monsieur Cocteau*. Monaco: Editions du Rocher, 1996.

INDEX

ILLUSTRATION CREDITS

All works by Pablo Picasso © 1999 Estate of Pablo Picasso / Artists Rights Society (ARS), New York

All works by Francis Bacon © 1999 Estate of Francis Bacon / Artists Rights Society (ARS), New York / Courtesy of The Tate Gallery, London / Art Resource, New York

All works by Georges Braque © 1999 Artists Rights Society (ARS), New York / ADAGP, Paris

All works by César © 1999 Artists Rights Society (ARS), New York / ADAGP, Paris

All works by Paul Klee © 1999 Artists Rights Society (ARS), New York / VG Bild-Kunst, Bonn / Courtesy of The Kunstsammlung Nordrhein-Westfalan Düsseldorf

All works by Graham Sutherland © 1999 Artists Rights Society (ARS), New York / Pro Litteris, Zürich

Grateful acknowledgment is made to the following people and organizations for providing artwork included in this volume:

Tania Alexander, *A Little of All These* (London: Jonathan Cape, 1987): page 51

Cecil Beaton, courtesy of Sotheby's, London: page 47

Peter C. Brandt: pages 13, 199

Thekla Clark: pages 62, 63

Lucien Clergue: pages 239, 265

Photograph by Denise Colomb, courtesy of Musée Picasso, Antibes: page 193

Robert Doisneau / Liaison Agency: pages 86, 129, 209, 250

David Douglas Duncan: pages 92, 210–211, 270–271

© Gloria Etting / Condé Nast Publications: page 104

Hulton Getty / Liaison Agency: page 159

R. Guillemot-Connaissance des Arts-Edimedia: page 88

© Horst P. Horst / Condé Nast Publications: pages 89, 95, 103, 106, 186, 189

Jean Howard: page 257

© 1989 by David Levine, courtesy of *The New York Review of Books:* page 222

ILLUSTRATION CREDITS

James Lord: pages 85, 206, 208, 213

© 1999 Artists Rights Society (ARS), New York / ADAGP, Paris / Collection of Jean Nicolas, courtesy of Jean-Louis Cohen: page 120

Courtesy of the National Portrait Gallery, London: pages 29, 56, 65

© Edward Quinn / The Edward Quinn Archive, courtesy of Scalo Publishers Zürich: pages 18, 70, 80, 124, 126, 232, 248

Courtesy of Michael Raeburn: page 170

Wendy and Emery Reves Archival Collection, courtesy of Dallas Museum of Art: page 230

Fredric and Hilde Ridenour: page 64

Roger-Viollet: pages 83, 108, 148

© David Seymour / Magnum Photos: page 110

All other photographs are from the collection of the author.

A NOTE ABOUT THE AUTHOR

John Richardson is the author of A Life of Picasso, *Volumes I and II (the first volume won the 1991 Whitbread Book of the Year Award). He lives in New York City and Connecticut.*

A NOTE ON THE TYPE

This book was set in Caledonia, a Linotype face designed by
W. A. Dwiggins (1880–1956). It belongs to the family of
printing types called "modern face" by printers—a term used
to mark the change in style of the type letters that occurred
around 1800. Caledonia borders on the general design of
Scotch Roman but is more freely drawn than that letter.

Composed by North Market Street Graphics,
Lancaster, Pennsylvania

Printed and bound by Quebecor Printing,
Martinsburg, West Virginia

Designed by Iris Weinstein

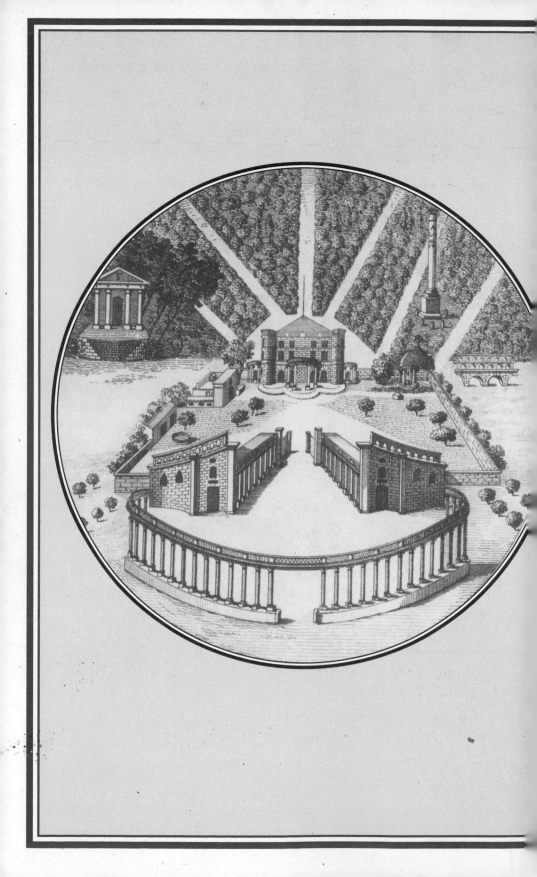